The Cubs
the Whit

The Cubs and the White Sox

A Baseball Rivalry, 1900 to the Present

DAN HELPINGSTINE

McFarland & Company, Inc., Publishers

Jefferson, North Carolina, and London

All photographs are provided through the courtesy of Leo Bauby.

LIBRARY OF CONGRESS CATALOGUING-IN-PUBLICATION DATA

Helpingstine, Dan.
    The Cubs and the White Sox : a baseball rivalry, 1900 to the
present / Dan Helpingstine.
        p.   cm.
    Includes bibliographical references and index.

    ISBN 978-0-7864-4669-8
    softcover : 50# alkaline paper ∞

    1. Chicago Cubs (Baseball team)—History.   2. Chicago
White Sox (Baseball team)—History.   3. Baseball—Illinois—
Chicago—History.   4. Sports rivalries—United States.
I. Title.

GV875.C6H45   2010
796.357'640977311—dc22   2010034347

British Library cataloguing data are available

On the cover: Cubs catcher Michael Barrett scuffles with his White
Sox counterpart, A.J. Pierzynski, during a game on May 20, 2006,
at U.S. Cellular Field in Chicago (AP/*Daily Southtown*, David
Banks).

Manufactured in the United States of America

McFarland & Company, Inc., Publishers
    Box 611, Jefferson, North Carolina 28640
        www.mcfarlandpub.com

To anyone who has had any connection to
the Mississippi Valley Writers Conference

Acknowledgments

I first would like to thank my wife, Delia, and daughter, Leah, for their help in preparing this book for publication. Not only did they do a great deal of hard work, they had to put up with me stressing out as I neared a deadline.

Special thanks go to Jeff Wimble. His expertise helped not only in properly citing sources but the formatting of the manuscript that made it more readable and accessible.

I am grateful to everyone who agreed to be interviewed for this book. Personal stories add to any book; in this case, they provided some valuable history.

Special thanks go to Mark Liptak and Tom Shaer for their encouragement and assistance with the project.

Leo Bauby allowed me access to his great sports photo collection and provided technical help. The stories and the book itself have been enriched by his contribution.

And of course, my thanks go to McFarland. I have enjoyed the professional relationship immensely and am happy to be associated with one of the leaders in baseball and other historical research.

Table of Contents

Introduction

So long, Murphy
How we hate to see you lose
So long, Murphy
We know you will have the blues
We'll all feel sorry for you, Murphy
While we cheer
So long, Murphy
Maybe you will win next year.[1]

—*Sox fans serenading Cubs owner Charles Murphy to the tune of "So Long Mary" at the beginning of the 1906 World Series. The last line echoes the famous expression for Cub fans of waiting until next year. Unlike all other seasons, in 1906 there was a next year and a year after that. The Cubs won the World Series in both 1907 and 1908.*

"The New Chauffer."
Title [*sic*] of cartoon in an October 1950 edition of the *Chicago American.*
New White Sox manager Paul Richards is the behind the wheel of a
"Sox Mobile" that utilized a bat for a fender and baseballs for tires.
Richards is shown saying, "I understand you have been havin' trouble
with this car running in reverse." The hood ornament, in the form of a
miniature baseball player, said, "Anyhoo, we went further than the Cubs."[2]

—*This cartoon, while taking a jab at the Cubs, said a great deal about the plight of both teams during that era. Often in Chicago baseball history each set of fans could only take solace in the reality that the other team was as bad or worse.*

The co-existence of the Chicago Cubs and White Sox is unique in major league sports. No single market has experienced a two-team rivalry for such a long period. For more than a century, the two franchises have operated in the Windy City. Although they have played in different ballparks, different leagues, and attracted different fan bases, the teams shared the common thread of not

1

winning championships. The 2005 appearance and win in the World Series for the White Sox ended almost a half-century where neither team made it to the Fall Classic and nearly nine decades since a world championship was won for Chicago. However, this shared disappointment has not bonded baseball fans in the Chicago area. If anything, it continued to cause constant friction between the rival fan groups, each holding onto its tradition amidst the frustration of being also-rans.

The dual baseball history began in 1900 when Charles Comiskey relocated his Western Association team from St. Paul to Chicago. The new American League had yet to be recognized as a major league entity. The senior circuit allowed the move into a key National League city only if the AL team played on the South Side. National League officials thought that playing near the stench of the stockyards would depress attendance.[3] Meanwhile, the infant Chicago franchise took the Cubs' old name, White Stockings, which was eventually shortened to White Sox.

The National League miscalculated American League attendance. National League games had become known for numerous fights, constant profanity and baiting of umps. The new American League decided to clean things up, which included respecting an umpire's authority.[4] Attendance in several American League cities, including Chicago, surpassed that of the National League. With the combination of attendance and the AL raids of NL talent, the National League was forced to recognize the junior circuit as a major league organization.

Baseball hysteria hit Chicago in 1906 with the all–Chicago World Series. The *Tribune* wrote that the "Big town on the lake is baseball dizzy, which is several degrees worse than batty."[5] City hall employees were given the day off for the first game, fans ripped at the fences to try to get a look, and scalpers did a brisk business. City councilman Charles Martin, a White Sox fan, was arrested for brawling with a drunken Cubs fan.[6]

By winning a major league–record 116 games, the Cubs were considered the far superior team — at least on paper. Before the Series started, the North Side club was selling tickets to a post-season celebration and thinking about how to spend its World Series money . Over-confidence could not have helped them.

The 1906 Series win for the White Sox is remembered as a huge upset. Yet, maybe it wasn't as big an upset as some thought. During the last two months of the season, the "Hitless Wonders" averaged four runs a game, matching the production of the Cubs offense that season.[7] White Sox pitchers threw an amazing 18 shutouts and 10 one-run games from August 1 through the remainder of the season.[8] The Cubs were still the better team, but the Sox were playing very well going into the postseason.

Since 1906, the Cubs and White Sox have appeared in the postseason in the same year only once: In 2008, the Cubs were swept by the Dodgers and the Sox were outclassed by Tampa Bay. During these first-round series, the Chicago teams combined for a total of one win. Since 1906, there has never been a time when there was a real chance of another all–Chicago World Series.

With the construction of Comiskey Park in 1910, the White Sox put additional pressure on the Cubs in competing for local baseball interest. During the early twentieth century, major league franchises built all-wooden stadiums because it was thought to be cost effective. However, the Polo Grounds burned to the ground in 1910, and many fans feared going to facilities they thought were fire traps. Comiskey Park was considered a state-of-the-art facility because of its concrete-and-steel structure. The White Sox began outdrawing the Cubs, mostly due to a new, safe and modern stadium.[9]

With new ownership, the Cubs moved into what became known as Wrigley Field in 1916, giving the North Side a modern stadium. Wrigley and its surrounding neighborhood evolved over the decades and are considered now one of the reasons the Cubs outdraw the White Sox every season. The near century-old facility has its own structural problems, and it will be interesting to see how the Ricketts family maintains and rehabs the second-oldest stadium in major league baseball.

The lack of a joint World Series did not stop the teams from trying to achieve Chicago baseball bragging rights. During the many years when neither team appeared in the Series, the Cubs and White Sox played in a post-season City Series. As with the current six games of inter-league play, fans got emotionally involved for these games. From 1903 to 1943, the two teams played in 25 series. In one season, 1927, the Cubs refused to play because White Sox players apparently had been cheering for Cub losses during the key month of September. The White Sox won 18 of these series, with one tie.[10] Interest in the series waned after 1943, and the two teams haven't faced each other in the postseason since. White Sox fans held this ID card as a symbol of their South Side pride:

Whereas the South Side baseball club,
Hereinafter known as the White Sox, has once again demonstrated
Its superiority over the North Side baseball club,
Hereinafter unmentionable,
This certificate entitles the bearer to
Windy City Bragging Rights
By virtue of being a lifelong White Sox fan.
(Valid until Satan needs a space heater)[11]

Richard J. Daley, Chicago mayor from 1955 until his death in December 1976, took his Chicago sports seriously. During the sixties, when the Bears contemplated a move to the suburbs, Daley told the franchise it would forfeit

This was quite a gathering. Bill Veeck, Harry Caray, Chicago mayor Richard J. Daley, and Daley's later successor, Michael Bilandic. Daley was a lifelong White Sox fan who only saw them play in one World Series during his adult life.

the right to use the name "Chicago" if it went through with the move. Living in the Bridgeport neighborhood surrounding Comiskey Park, Daley was the city's premier White Sox fan. According to journalist Mark Liptak, Daley took his family to Sunday doubleheaders on many occasions. No matter what was happening in game two, Daley packed up his family at 6:00 P.M. and headed for home, Liptak said. Dinner was waiting on the table in the Daley household.[12]

The image of the White Sox fan mirrored that family-oriented and working-class ethic. During a great deal of the sixties, White Sox home games didn't begin until 8:00 P.M. Whether by accident or design, this starting time gave the fan the opportunity to go home and have dinner before going to the ballpark. Until 1968 mid-week home night games were rarely if ever televised. Without TV breaks, games generally didn't stretch late into the night unless they were extra-inning affairs. Fans could see a night game and still return home at a reasonable hour to get a good night's sleep in preparation for work the next day.

Many feel the blue-collar label that has been associated with White Sox fans is no longer applicable. The stockyards are gone. U.S. Steel Southworks, a Chicago South Side mill that at one time employed 10,000 workers, is also gone. Wisconsin Steel, another South Side factory, employed slightly over 3,000 before closing its doors permanently in 1980. Across the border in northwest Indiana, tens of thousands of steelworkers saw their jobs eliminated as factories closed or downsized. Were the White Sox fans still the true blue-collar worker now that Chicago's industrial base had been decimated? And how about those hard-hat fans who could sit out in the Wrigley Field bleachers during the late sixties? One dollar got them into the game; they weren't exactly the rich man's set.

The 1970s was the first full decade of divisional play. During that decade, neither Chicago team won a division title. Each set of fans took comfort that the other team was losing. The White Sox had only two winning seasons — 1972 and 1977 — during the decade. From 1973 to 1983, the Cubs had no winning campaigns, with their best showing an 81–81 finish in 1977. The 1970s symbolized a Chicago baseball futility that had been decades in the making.

During the mid- to late eighties Chicago was sometimes referred to as "Beirut by the Lake." Harold Washington sat as the city's first African-American mayor and his four-year tenure brought Chicago's racial and ethnic polarization to the forefront. Emulating 1906 city councilman Charles Martin, Washington warned one political opponent during a stormy city council meeting in the following manner: "You better watch it, or you'll get something in your mouth you don't want."*

Although Cub and White Sox fans were as divided as the Chicago City Council, they shared some of the same experiences during the Washington administration. As this book will reveal each set of fans felt threatened by new owners taking over their teams in 1981. They felt their traditions were being trampled upon as major league baseball became more dependent on season-ticket holders and the corporate customer. While the new managements promised a bright new future for each franchise that was meant to leave the old losing ways behind, each set of fans reacted with suspicion and hostility. Mere good intentions were not going to win over fans that easily, even as both teams finally broke through and won a divisional title.

During the first three-plus decades of divisional play, from 1969 to 2000 inclusive, Chicago baseball teams appeared in the postseason six times via five division titles and one wild card entry. Neither team won a playoff series. Twice they lost due to sweeps and five times they dropped three games in a row. Starting with Game Five of the 1993 American League Championship Series, Chicago went on an eight-game post-season losing streak that was finally

---

Actually this is a paraphrase, but the meaning is clear. Threats like that were probably made during many of the first 66 inter-league Sox-Cubs games. Like some of those old political deadlocks, the Sox-Cubs head-to-head competition stood at 33–33 at the end of the 2008 season. Up to that time, the Sox outscored the Cubs 323–322.

snapped by the Cubs in 2003. Their cumulative record in the postseason during these six series was 6–20. The Bears had their Super Bowl in January 1986; the Bulls had their two three-peats in the '90s; even the Black Hawks went to the Stanley Cup Finals in 1992. But the World Series didn't seem possible for either Chicago baseball team. Yet while the Cubs and Sox fans had this misery and frustration in common, they did not love each other. Each fan base took pride in being what the other was not.

This book centers on the curious and unique divide between two sets of fans whose teams play 8.1 miles from each other. Their differences are both real and imagined. Chicago baseball fans are often categorized into various political, economic and social groups, even though these generalizations aren't always accurate. What is clear, however, is the animosity between the two fan groups. Cub loyalists accuse their White Sox counterparts of indifference, disloyalty and bitterness. Sox backers say that Cub fans consist of baseball-ignorant drunks that care more about the Wrigleyville experience than seeing their team win games and championships. Each says the other is jealous of respective traditions, and each detests watching the other experience success.

The rivalry has intensified over the decades. The tension caused by the 1906 World Series exists in every modern-day inter-league game. Players are amazed by the emotions these games generate. White Sox GM Kenny Williams hates the stress of the mid-season matchups. The local media cover these regular-season games as if they were the World Series. The baseball part of the city is on edge with every series.

Some, primarily in the Chicago sports media, despair over the continued fan rancor, wondering why the fans cannot cheer for both teams. However, more believe the Cubs-Sox competition is what makes Chicago a great baseball city. There are not many World Series pennants flying over Wrigley Field or U.S. Cellular Field. But go to a White Sox–Cubs game and dare to declare aloud a love for one of the teams. You might get a mouthful of something you don't want.

1

A Cubs Fan Resurgence

"The Wilderness." That is how author and Cubs fan David Claerbaut described Chicago Cub history between 1946 and 1966 in his book, *Durocher's Cubs: The Greatest Team That Didn't Win*.[1] Claerbaut's imagery of a team wandering in an expansive, unknown land is perfect. In that forgettable two-decade period, the Cubs had only three seasons with a .500 or better record. Their best year followed the 1945 World Series when they registered an 82–71 mark. In 1952, the Cubs finished even at 77–77, and in 1963 the team crept over the .500 mark at 82–80. Those numbers only partially tell the story of Cub futility in the immediate post–World War II era. The Cubs were not taken seriously; a team that had made ten World Series appearances from 1906 to 1945 had become an object of ridicule.

As a result, Wrigley Field wasn't the place to be. In the early 1960s, the Cubs were out-drawn by the White Sox by the hundreds of thousands. There were few rooftop fans, and Wrigley was still more than two decades away from joining baseball civilization by installing lights to make night games possible. On August 19, 1961, I attended my first Cubs game in a nearly empty Wrigley Field. The day was wet and dark, appearing to be in a wilderness of its own. Ernie Banks, a future Hall of Famer who would hit 512 homers in his career, lifted a deep fly to left in the first inning. It was hit well, but the ball was nearly impossible to see in the dark, foreboding sky. Left fielder Joe Christopher settled in front of the well of the wall, where even the ivy looked dark, and finally fans were able to spot the ball right before it dropped into Christopher's glove. Although Banks went on to get two hits and two walks that day, the Cubs lost in eleven innings and were lucky the game wasn't called on account of darkness. During the 1960s, Cubs fans defended the outdated tradition of no night baseball, arguing that baseball should only be played during the day. The argument has been dropped, and the area around Wrigley is now a hot nightspot, especially when the Cubs are playing.

Except for an entire home schedule played during the day, the only Cubs traditions in the early 1960s involved losing. Their 1945 World Series loss in seven games to Detroit seemed to exist in yet another wilderness. World War II was just ending, and the tragedy of 55 million people dying worldwide easily overshadowed anything the Cubs and Tigers did. In the immediate post-war period, when Americans wanted normalcy and the ability to get in touch with baseball again, the Cubs continued to lose. Their greatest asset was Banks, who became one of the team's most popular players of all time. Banks won back-to-back MVP awards for second-division teams in 1958 and 1959. In those two seasons, Banks hit a combined 92 homers and knocked in 272. Meanwhile, from 1951 through 1967, the White Sox established their "Go-Go" tradition with one winning season after another. Their crowning season was in 1959, the year they won the pennant. Then, from 1963 to 1965, the White Sox had three straight 90-plus winning seasons. In 1964, the White Sox won 98, including their last nine games, but still finished in second place, one game behind the Yankees. In the pre–wild card era, that earned the Sox only the frustration of spending the postseason at home.

In 1965, Ron Santo, Billy Williams, and Ernie Banks finished the year with more than 100 RBIs each, yet the Cubs lost more than ninety games that season. With all this run production, why couldn't the Cubs win? The obvious answer was pitching, a problem the Cubs had tried to address with little success. The team had the bad habit of acquiring pitchers past their prime — including Lew Burdette and Curt Simmons — much like the Sox's habit of acquiring hitters who had seen better days.

Then there was the trade in 1964, which sent outfielder Lou Brock to St. Louis in exchange for pitcher Ernie Broglio. Broglio had won 21 games in 1960 and 18 in 1963. In his Cubs career, the right-hander went 7–19. Every Cubs fan is well aware of Lou Brock's Hall of Fame achievements.

In the mid-sixties, Cubs and White Sox fans thought an easy solution to their teams' problems might be a trade between the two clubs. A White Sox pitcher could be traded for a Cubs hitter. The solution sounded simple, but trades are rarely simple. Additionally, one team may have been afraid of being taken advantage of by the other. No big deals were made between the two Chicago clubs. Consequently, the White Sox were unable to get past the Yankees while the Cubs couldn't get over the .500 hump.

The tough, old-school Leo Durocher came in to manage the Cubs in 1966. Even Durocher wasn't a quick fix as the team lost 103 games. Lack of pitching was the usual cause; the Cub staff gave up more runs that any other team in the National League by a significant margin. The Cubs suffered through another humiliating season. Even the Mets and the Astros, expansion teams not even five years old, fared much better. The Cubs finished 7½ games behind New York and 13 behind Houston. It was the second time in four years the Cubs lost 103 contests.

Billy Williams rounding the bases at Wrigley after hitting a two-run homer off Bob Gibson in May 1974. Williams had the most beautiful swing one could ever see.

Leo Durocher standing in the middle of Wrigley Field in September 1970. Behind him fans are dangling programs or other papers to get player autographs. The Cubs were still riding high from the fun of 1969. The Cubs lost that day despite a high-arching two-run homer hit by Ernie Banks in the ninth. The division went to the Pirates.

Stay-at-home moms were still commonplace during the sixties. The Cubs aired TV ads showing several housewives talking about how great it would be to spend a sunny afternoon at Wrigley on Ladies Days. The women looked gentile and civilized sitting in their neatly arranged living rooms, discussing the free admission into the park to enjoy a major league baseball game on a nice summer day. Even with the freebies, the Cubs still were not drawing fans to the park in the early part of 1967. Was there a reason they should?

On Sunday, June 11, the Mets were at Wrigley for a doubleheader. The Cubs were a respectable 26–24, in fifth place, barely ahead of the Atlanta Braves. There were tornado warnings at the game's start and the wind was blowing out — a perfect day for some long ball at the "Friendly Confines." Yet in the first game the score was only 5–3 in favor of the Cubs, with just one homer for each team. One of the most important factors in the game was the continued emergence of Ferguson Jenkins as the number one starter for the Cubs. Jenkins improved his record to 8–3, going the distance with a five-hitter. Jenkins would throw 20 complete games in 1967 to match his 20 wins. Despite his efforts, two years later Leo Durocher would accuse Jenkins of being a quitter.[2]

The second game was the more typical Wrigley Field wind-blowing-out experience with a combined 28 runs on 32 hits. The Mets clubbed four homers, but the Cubs swept the doubleheader by hitting seven, including three by Adolfo Phillips and two by Randy Hundley. The seven homers set a team record for a single game.* Yet by this point in the season, Cubs fans weren't supporting their team much. Although the attendance for this doubleheader wasn't bad by that era's standards, the draw was still a little less than 20,000. Today, with fans on a waiting list for a chance to buy season tickets, the Cubs would throw away a crowd like that.

One barometer for a team's season is its standing on July 4. After closing a homestand on July 2, the Cubs had made their way to second and were inching toward first. Now their fans noticed. Wrigley Field ticket offices were suddenly besieged with ticket buyers, many of whom were not able to get tickets to the sold-out game. July 2, 1967, was an important turning point in Cubs history. The numbers were not the biggest story, important as they were. The Chicago Cubs fans became something different that day, turning from uninterested to almost rabid and uncontrollable.

"Everybody was going crazy," according to long-time Chicago radio reporter Les Grobstein. "There were several thousand people in the street outside Wrigley who just wanted to be a part of the atmosphere. We weren't used

---

*The record was matched on two occasions, both in Wrigley and both against the San Diego Padres. On August 19, 1970, Chicago pounded San Diego, 12–2. On May 17, 1977, the beating was even more intense: Cubs 23, Padres 6. Using two eight-run innings, the Cubs led at one time 22–2. The Padres saved what little face they had left by scoring a few runs in the late innings.

Ferguson Jenkins pitching in 1968. He was 20–15 that season and lost five 1–0 ball games. Jenkins won 20 or more games six years in a row and also picked up at least 20 complete games six straight seasons. He was one of the greatest of all Cub pitchers.

to seeing Wrigley filled when the Bears weren't playing. We weren't used to seeing them [the Cubs] when they were good."[3]

The Cubs won, 4–1, behind another complete game by Ferguson Jenkins. In addition to throwing a four-hitter, the good-hitting pitcher stroked a double and a triple. It was a good win, but something else happened before the game ended that dwarfed the result.

First-place St. Louis had lost the first game of a doubleheader to the Mets. With this defeat, the Cubs moved into first, something that hadn't happened in four years. National League standings were shown by the order of team flags flying along the side of the scoreboard at Wrigley. The Cubs flag had moved to the top. Jubilance ran through the capacity crowd at the ballpark. Even White Sox fans attending this game or watching WGN-TV would have been swept away by the emotion. For years, Cubs fans had only a few good players and a beautiful park. Now they had a winning team — at least for the moment. The Cardinals would climb back into a first-place tie with a win in the second game that day. St. Louis was also a formidable team that wasn't going to be moved aside just because the Cubs fans were starved for a pennant. But nothing was gong to take the excitement away from a day that the Cubs faithful had dreamed of yet hadn't experienced since Germany and Japan surrendered.

Fans didn't want to leave after the game. Since it was so close to the Fourth of July, many had firecrackers and cherry bombs, some of which were thrown onto the field. The *Chicago Sun-Times* reported that cherry bombs "went off in the outfield."[4] In this post–9/11 world, nothing of the sort would have been allowed to occur. Explosions of unknown origins could cause panic. But in 1967, we were not as afraid. These fireworks resembled the "Monster" going off at Comiskey. There was a new fanaticism beginning at Wrigley. Nothing like this had ever happened.

On this day, both Chicago teams were in first place, an occurrence even more significant in one of the last years of one-divisional play. The *Sun-Times* ran a front-page article the next day entitled "First Place, USA!" describing a hysteria emanating mostly from the North Side. It was written by Ray Brennan.

Thomas Hunt and Gerald Halwick were two Cubs fans featured in the piece. They had waited in the Cubs ticket line since 10:30 A.M. but were unable to get into the ballpark, so they watched the game in a bar. Hunt and Halwick were just as excited as the firecracker and cherry bomb throwers, maybe even more so.

"How can you help but love them?" Hunt said. "This is the biggest thing since the Bobby Thomson home run in 1951; really the biggest thing in baseball. This makes the Yankee surge in the '50s look like nothing."*

"Don't misquote me," Halwick chimed in. "I know it's impossible but even if the Cubs finished last now, my year has been made."

Halwick said he had not been working on his job long enough to get a vacation. If his company didn't give him time to go to the World Series, he would resign. As it turned out, Halwick didn't have to face that dilemma of choosing a World Series or the unemployment line.[5]

Almost immediately after going on a road trip, the Cubs went on a seven-game losing streak. They matched that with another seven-game skein in early August. Those fourteen losses made quite a difference as the Cubs finished in third place, fourteen games behind the Cardinals. July 2 was the high point of a season that once again did not conclude with a first-place finish.

Yet this July day was a huge turning point in the history of the franchise. The Cubs discovered they had fans — rabid fans who now wanted to fill their park. Although the *Sun-Times* Brennan article was supposed to gloat about both Chicago teams residing in first place, the story centered almost entirely on the Cubs, especially the electricity in their ballpark and a pennant fever that could only be cured by a Cubs World Series. The White Sox, that boring team of banjo hitters, were being pushed out of the consciousness of the Chicago baseball fan. No, the Cubs didn't reach the World Series in 1967. But with

---

The Yankees won four straight World Series from 1950 to 1953. The team proceeded to play in four more Fall Classics in the decade, winning two of them.

1969 just around the corner, the franchise began its trek toward becoming the more popular baseball team in the city.

In 1969, the country again wanted things to return to some kind of normalcy. War, political assassination, social upheaval and unrest, and a general feeling that everything had gone awry had American society on edge. The previous year, 1968, people wondered when something else would go terribly wrong. Suddenly it seemed that both the country and the world were changing too quickly, and many hoped that things would at least slow down.

Chicago baseball fans, especially Cubs fans, didn't want 1969 to be normal in any sense. Normal meant losing. Normal meant an occasional winning season but no World Series. If anything, a fast change was desired. Fans wanted the feeling that something incomprehensible was happening.

The 1968 season had been a respectable year for the Cubs. On August 13, they were in second place, trying to catch the runaway Cardinals. The Cubs won the first two of the four-game series in Wrigley against St. Louis. However, Chicago was still twelve games behind, and the likelihood of overtaking the Cards was slim. The Cubs needed to sweep the series if they were going to have any chance of making it a true race.

The Cards, like the defending world champions that they were, rose to the occasion and beat the Cubs in the next two games. St. Louis won its third pennant of the decade and had to be recognized as one of the best National League teams of the 1960s.

Yet the 1968 World Series demonstrated that the St. Louis squad was human. The Cardinals went out to a 3–1 lead, making the American League champion Detroit Tigers look like a Little League team. But in the fifth inning of Game 5, with St. Louis leading 3–2, Lou Brock was thrown out at the plate when he could have been safe had he slid. Then in the seventh inning of a scoreless tie in Game 7, the usually reliable Curt Flood misjudged a routine fly in center and slipped on some wet turf when he tried to make up some ground. What should have been an inning-ending out turned into a two-run triple, and the Tigers became the new world champions.

If Chicago could get off to a good start and keep the Cardinals from building a huge lead as they had in '67 and '68, the Cubs would have a good a chance of winning a playoff spot in the first year of divisional play. There didn't seem to be another logical challenger coming out of the new National League East, which also consisted of the Phillies, Mets, Pirates, and the expansion Montreal Expos.

The Cubs began their season on April 8 against the Phillies. Times were different in the late sixties. Cubs fans didn't wait in long lines in cold and sometimes snowy February to buy regular-season tickets in advance. Owner P.K. Wrigley, as a practice, ensured that more than 20,000 seats were available on the day of the game. That day, 27,000 Cubs fans bought their tickets beginning at 8:00 A.M. when the ticket offices opened,[6] and some 41,000 made their way into Wrigley hoping for a great opener and a great season.

But one cloud hung over the Cubs: a speculation begun by Leo Durocher that Banks was at the end of his career. "Mr. Wrigley is the owner of the club and he's Mr. Cub," Durocher said. "Banks is no more Mr. Cub than I am."[7]

Banks' 40-homer seasons were behind him; he hit a meager 15 in 1966. Yet in 1968, a pitchers' year that included a 30-game winner and a hurler who set a record for a season with a 1.12 ERA, Banks hit 32 home runs. His average was only .246, but there was a scarcity of .300 hitters in the major leagues that year. Maybe Banks wasn't done yet. And even Banks credited Durocher with prodding him to finish his career on a high note.

Banks didn't resemble the modern-day home run hitter in physique or style. The '50s and '60s were long before the steroids era produced hitters with 50, 60 and 70 homers on an annual basis. Banks, who began his career as a shortstop, was thin and wiry with an unimposing physique by today's standards. What was imposing was his ability to use his strong wrists to get the bat through the strike zone. His swing wasn't imposing-looking either, but the ball jumped off his bat. If he were playing in the twenty-first century, he would be revered just for avoiding performance-enhancing drugs.

In this opener, Banks demonstrated to the baseball world that the skeptics would have to wait until another day to declare his career over. He hit two homers — a three-run shot in the first and a two-run round-tripper in the third. His five RBIs staked the Cubs to a 5–1 lead. And with Cub ace Ferguson Jenkins on the mound, it appeared that a win in this 1969 season opener was all but in the bag.

Ferguson Jenkins, who would become known as "Fergie," had back-to-back 20-win seasons in 1967 and 1968. He was the first Cubs pitcher to accomplish that feat since Pat Malone in the 1929 and 1930 seasons. Jenkins was tall with an easy pitching motion. The late movement of his pitches made him extremely hard to hit. Jenkins gave up many home runs, but that was partly because he was around the plate so much. Additionally, those home runs rarely hurt since many came with the bases empty.

Jenkins was durable. If the opposition was going to get to him, it had to be early in the game. Jenkins sometimes struggled in the early innings, but he got stronger as he went deep into the game. If he was still in the game by the late innings, it meant the Cubs had a very good chance of winning. Fergie has to go down as one of the best pitchers ever to put on a Cubs uniform.

When Jenkins entered the ninth inning of the game having given up only two runs on six hits, it appeared the Cubs fans had their dream opener. Yet uncharacteristically, Fergie fell apart. Johnny Callison and Cookie Rojas singled, and Don Money then hit his second homer of the game. Suddenly things were tied at 5. Phil "the Vulture" Regan came in one batter too late to relieve Jenkins.

Ernie Banks (right) is the recognizable one. On the left is future South Side Hitman Oscar Gamble. Photograph was taken on September 6, 1969, when the Cubs were in the middle of an eight-game losing streak. After the season ended, the Cubs traded Gamble to the Phillies for Johnny Callison.

Momentum seemed to shift. The Cubs hadn't scored since Banks clubbed his second homer in the third. Barry Lersch, who was making his major league debut that day, seemed to have the Cubs handcuffed. Was this another example of a Cubs meltdown?

By the top of the eleventh, it seemed so. Don Money came through again with an RBI double to put Philadelphia ahead, 6–5. The hit gave Money five runs batted in for the game in what had to be one of the most memorable days in his career.*

Banks led off the bottom of the eleventh. No doubt Cubs fans fantasized about their long-time favorite tying the game with his third homer. Instead, he flied out to right. Catcher Randy Hundley gave some hope when he followed with a single to left. Then came one of the most thrilling and memorable Cub moments of the sixties. Willie Smith, a left-handed hitter, went to the plate for the right-handed Jim Hickman. The Cubs hoped that the percentages would favor Smith against the right-handed Lersch. Up to that point, Lersch had hurled four and one-third innings of scoreless relief.

Smith then launched a deep drive to right-center. The ball landed in the

Money would pick up 5 RBIs in a game one other time during his 16-year career in the major leagues.

second row of the seats for a two-run homer. A game that appeared to be a sure loser turned into a 7–6 Opening Day win.

As with the emotional day on July 2, 1967, Cubs fans celebrated with sheer intensity. A few waited near home plate for Smith to complete his home run trot. The image from WGN Channel 9 gave the impression that the whole stadium shook from raw emotion and cheering. In reality, the cameraman was shaking his camera to create that effect.[8] If a person, Cubs fan or not, wasn't moved by the moment, he wasn't human.

Fake photography or not, Cubs fanaticism was for real. As their team continued to play well, winning eleven of their first twelve, their fans fell in love with them over and over again. "Cub Nation" called their 1969 team the greatest ever. Players found plenty of off-the-field opportunities to make money and promote themselves. As the season progressed, the *Sun-Times* ran a cartoon of Leo Durocher wearing a turban seated by a crystal ball with a shrinking magic number. It seemed that the fantasy of a World Series appearance was a foregone conclusion.

The Cubs faced a tough test when the Atlanta Braves, the leaders of the Western Division, came to Wrigley for a three-game series at the end of May. The Cubs won the first two games, 2–0 and 3–2, and completed a sweep with a 13–4 pounding. The Cubs appeared to be the better of the first-place teams. If they could repeat this performance when meeting Atlanta in the playoffs, it would be on to the World Series. The Cubs' record stood at 33–16.

All the hoopla was a bit much for the White Sox fans. Since the Cubs hadn't won anything yet, shouldn't the promotional stuff wait until after the World Series? The greatest team of all time? What about the 1927 and 1961 Yankees? How about that year's Baltimore Orioles, who were loaded with talent and would eventually win 109 games? Wasn't everything a little premature? Weren't Cubs fans over-reacting?

Maybe the hero worship of the Cubs fans was a bit much, but could it be held against them? Finally, after seasons of humiliation, their team appeared to be on the right side of something historic. The club had six representatives on the National League All-Star team, which included the Cubs entire infield. Not one of the Cubs had a hit in the game, but the National League stomped all over the American League, 9–3. Once again, the National League seemed to be the stronger league. And who was the best team in the National League at the time? The Chicago Cubs.

Detractors and jealous observers said the Cubs were lucky. Winning teams usually are. Yet the Cubs weren't the team that was throwing the ball away or giving up late-inning homers on a regular basis. Yes, the Cubs got some breaks, but they took advantage of them and rarely beat themselves. These detractors sounded like whiners.

The truth was the Cubs finally seemed to put it all together. They had the usual firepower of Banks, Santo and Williams. In addition, the team had the solid middle infield play of Don Kessinger and Glenn Beckert. A common 1969 image was Kessinger going deep in the hole on the outfield grass, backhanding what had looked like a single to left, and then making a perfect off-balance throw to get the runner. Beckert fielded everything hit his way and was one of the toughest outs in the National League. And finally, to go along with the home runs and the new-found defense was a solid starting staff of Fergie Jenkins, Bill Hands, Ken Holtzman, and Dick Selma. Granted, the Cubs didn't have a great deal of speed, but who needed speed to come trotting to the plate ahead of a three-run homer or to play in the small outfield of Wrigley? Speed, shmeed.

And just who was going to stop them? Suddenly the Cardinals were no threat, and then there were the up-and-coming New York Mets. But who played for the Mets?

On August 19, the Cubs beat the Braves again, this time by a score of 3–0 at Wrigley. From appearances the game was well pitched on both sides and seemed to be an ordinary major league game. In reality, this game was anything but ordinary: It was a contest that symbolized the incredible Cub season up to that point. The Cubs played well, had some luck, and made some history.

Chicago scored three runs on a home run by Santo, his twenty-fifth of the season. They wouldn't threaten for the rest of the game or add to their lead. As it turned out, no more runs were needed.

On the mound for the Cubs was 24-year-old lefty Ken Holtzman. Holtzman got off to a hot start in 1967, winning his first five decisions. He was then called to military reserve duty and missed most of the remainder of the season. The young lefty was still able to pick up four more wins and end the season with a perfect 9–0 record. In '68, he slipped to a more Cub-like 11–14 in a year that was interrupted again by reserve duty. In the beginning of '69, Holtzman was as hot as the rest of the Cubs, winning ten of his first eleven decisions, prior to coming back to earth and losing six out of his next nine.

But August 19, 1969, was Ken Holtzman's day. Inning after inning went by with the Braves unable to break through and get a hit. Two late-inning outs made by Hank Aaron were almost as memorable as a tape-measure home run. These outs, while looking ordinary in the box scores, were another indication of why the Cubs had been doing so much winning up to that point. The two outs also added to the drama of the game.

Aaron led off the seventh with the Braves still trailing, 3–0, and still without a hit. The Braves' right fielder smashed a deep drive to left. Announcer Jack Brickhouse had an unmistakable tone in calling the drive. It looked like the no-hitter and shutout would disappear with one swing of the great Aaron's bat. But left fielder Billy Williams wasn't giving up on the ball while he settled into the well of the ivy-covered wall. A powerful wind seemed to blow the ball

The great Henry Aaron during a July 26, 1970, contest at Wrigley. It was part of a doubleheader in which the Cubs and Braves split. A combined eight homers were hit in the twin-bill.

right to Williams, and Aaron's apparent home run turned out to be nothing more than the first out in the inning.

Some witnesses swear the drive actually cleared the wall at one point and was suspended in mid-air before coming back down in the field of play. Can anything actually be suspended in mid-air? Regardless, Aaron felt cheated by the elements that day, and he glared at Holtzman before returning to the dugout.[9]

Aaron then came up with two out in the ninth and Holtzman's no-hitter still intact. He hit what looked like an extremely routine grounder to second, but the ball took a tricky hop to the left. Second baseman Beckert played it neatly, quickly shifting his glove over to snare a ball that could have easily skipped into right field. The steady Beckert made the routine throw to first and Holtzman had his no-hitter. Strangely, Holtzman struck out no one that day.

One key image from the aftermath was the celebrating Santo leaping on Holtzman. It was another moment of Cubs glee and pandemonium in 1969. With all the excitement, it looked like the Cubs' year. Could 1945 have been this good?

The real turnaround came in 1969. Gone were the days when Cubs pitchers were routinely pummeled. Gone were the days when the Cubs merely stumbled their way through a season when their only hope was to not finish last. They beat and no-hit a good team that included not only Henry Aaron but the hard-hitting Orlando Cepeda and Rico Carty as well. Most important, at the end of the day Chicago sat in first place, the same as they had been since that dramatic Opening Day. Their record stood at 77–45, with the second-place Mets eight games back. No-hitters. Great defense. Dramatic home runs. The Cubs had everything. The Braves were a likely opponent in the playoffs, and the Cubs had won that season series 9–3. The regular season was one thing; the playoffs were another. But were the Braves any real obstacle to a Cubs World Series? Was anyone?

As it turned out, there was still one big obstacle for the Cubs: the New York Mets. On September 8, the Cubs went to Shea Stadium to play a two-game series against their closest rival. By this time the eight-game lead had dwindled to 2½, which was not a big deal. Seasons ebb and flow. Seeing this lead shrink was not a major event, no matter how nervous it made the fans feel. A split was all the Cubs needed. Knock two games off the schedule and then hold your own. Instead, things went all wrong for Chicago. In the first game, the Cubs got a bad break and then failed to capitalize on a late-inning opportunity. They were never in the second game.

In the first game, the score was tied at two in the bottom of the sixth. Tommy Agee was on second base after he had doubled for the Mets. Wayne Garrett singled to right and Cub outfielder Jim Hickman came up throwing as Agee headed for home. Catcher Randy Hundley applied the tag and thought his team had cut off a run at the plate. But home plate umpire Satch Davidson saw things differently and called Agee safe.

Hundley nearly had a seizure. Even with all his catching gear, he leapt high. "Safe?" Hundley told author Doug Feldmann. "I tagged him so hard, I almost dropped the ball."[10] Years later, Agee told Beckert, "You guys had me."[11] Suddenly the Cubs weren't getting the breaks. Then they shot themselves in the foot when Santo hit into a double play after Beckert and Williams had singled to start the eighth. The Mets won, 3–2.

The second game was all Mets. Jenkins started with two days' rest, which was probably asking too much even with his durability. Tom Seaver dominated the Cubs and the Mets won, 7–1. Now the margin was down to a half-game.

Late in the game, Mets fans serenaded Leo Durocher to the tune of "Good Night, Ladies." They sang, "Good-bye, Leo, good-bye, Leo, good-bye, Leo, we love to see you go." The singing was loud, in unison, taunting, and arrogant. Yes, the Mets seemed to have all the momentum, but momentum is a funny thing and Chicago was still in first place despite the losses. Yet the fans sang as if it was all over. In reality, it was. By the end of play the next night, the Cubs fell out of first place for the first time in 1969. They had held the top spot for 155 days.

Catcher Randy Hundley hitting against the San Diego Padres in 1969. Hundley, one of the most popular Cub players, hit 18 homers in '69, one below his career high. The catcher nearly had a heart attack when Tommie Agee was called safe on a play at the plate in the sixth inning of a fateful September game at Shea Stadium. The win pulled the Mets within one-and-a-half games of the Cubs.

The "black cat incident" occurred in the top of the first inning of the second Mets game. The feline, appearing to be no more than 10 or 11 pounds, slinked past the Cubs dugout. Cats are proud animals that usually walk with their tail high in the air, their butt exposed to the world. This cat's tail lay parallel to its body, indicating at least some fear or anxiety. Standing in the on-deck circle was Ron Santo with a bat in his hands. Who should have been more scared? Doug Feldmann wrote in *Miracle Collapse* that it was hard to know who was spooked by whom.[12]

Rational people will say there is no significance in crossing paths with a black cat, that curses don't exist. Besides, what if an orange tabby had walked by? Would that also have been some kind of omen? If the Cubs were truly psyched out by a stray animal walking past them, then they let their superstitions play with their minds. Their psyche, therefore, was already in a fragile state and the division race was truly over. Maybe the Mets fans had every right to sing, even if it was to rip a man who once had been a large part of New York baseball.

The Cubs had only one losing month in 1969: September. They would have had to completely turn around an 8–17 mark to stave off the Mets. Maybe

Tom Seaver showing great form on July 14, 1969, at Wrigley. Although he only gave up one run in eight innings, he and the Mets lost, 1–0, to Bill Hands and the Cubs. Seaver and the Mets got their revenge later in the season.

if the club had picked up four or five more wins, fans wouldn't still be searching for answers to the '69 Cubs. They would say the Mets just got hot and it was the Cubs' bad luck that the team was in the same division. But that last month of embarrassing losses and some improbable plays branded the team as chokers. While there can be many theories and explanations for the failure in 1969, there was one consequence for Chicago sports fans, even those with no allegiance to the Cubs. Any time a Chicago team went through a season without a championship, fans had to wonder if they choked. Did a superior team let some weak sister beat them up? Would a whole sports town never build a lasting winning tradition? Were there curses after all?

After the Cubs were eliminated, a local radio station wanted to keep the dream alive through a fantasy. Using computer simulations, the 1969 Cubs were pitted against the greatest teams in baseball history. The program was awful. The broadcasts had fans cheering home runs hit by both sides. If any fantasy is to feel like the real thing, the illusion must be masterful. Fans don't cheer homers hit by the opposition. The program, meant to soothe the collective disappointment of devastated Cubs fans, only made things worse. The World Series remained a fantasy. No one knew when the fantasy would become a reality.

Carlos May in the early stages of his comeback after losing half of his thumb in August 1969. This at-bat was in a doubleheader on May 17, 1970. The White Sox had begun playing well after an awful start. The team lost this doubleheader and was never heard from again. The Sox ownership was actually thrilled with an attendance of a little more than 18,000 for these two games.

Meanwhile, on the South Side, the White Sox had been overshadowed by the Cubs. The Sox had another miserable season. In mid–June, Baltimore came to town for a four-game series, and the Orioles swept the inept Sox. The only competitive game was the first, when Baltimore won by a harmless score of 5–2. In the last three games the White Sox were outscored by a combined 34–5. Sox fan Gerry Bilek went to his first Sox games that weekend. He thought it was a men-against-boys situation.[13]

Compete with the eventual American League pennant-winning Orioles? The Sox could barely compete with the expansion Kansas City Royals. Kansas City won the season 10–8 over the Sox and finished one game ahead of them in the standings. Attendance at Comiskey plummeted. The biggest crowd at Comiskey occurred when the Cubs played the Sox in an exhibition game in late August, a few days after the Holtzman no-hitter.

One thing the White Sox had going for them was hard-hitting rookie Carlos May. Unfortunately, May had an accident while serving in army reserves in early August. An unloaded mortar went off and May lost half of his thumb on his throwing hand. At the time he was contending for Rookie of the Year honors. Suddenly his whole career was in jeopardy. Receiving the award would have been a good thing for the White Sox considering the obsession with the Cubs all summer. Instead, the award went to Lou Piniella of Kansas City, and the White Sox wondered if they had lost their left fielder for good.

Yes, the Cubs squandered a chance at history, but they had won over a city. Perhaps their losing had an even more powerful impact in re-creating their fan base. Some Cubs fans are even more hooked on the team because of the losing. In 1969, the Cubs set a Chicago baseball attendance record by drawing a little over 1.6 million. Since 1984, they have passed that mark routinely. In 2008, they established a Chicago baseball record by attracting more than 3.3 million. The century mark has passed without a world championship. Yet everything that built the aura around the Cubs seems to have started in 1969, when a team became immortalized for missing a chance to go to the World Series.

2

The Comiskey Experience

The light towers from old Comiskey Park could be seen for several miles. Looking like giant waffle grids, the towers lit up the early summer evening sky an hour or two before night games. As a grade school boy, I marveled at the night lights as my father drove me down the Dan Ryan Expressway toward the ballpark. Seeing the lights beginning to warm up and brighten only heightened my anticipation of the first pitch, the atmosphere of the crowd, and the possibility of the White Sox winning the game somehow, some way.

Wrigley Field has always been known for its beauty, but in the sixties Comiskey Park was truly beautiful at night. The outfield of the huge stadium was vast and green and soaked up the light from the looming light towers. Although the walls had no ivy, they seemed to compliment the vastness of the outfield, and the large-dimension "352" and "375" markers down the lines and power alleys seemed to shine. Arched windows lined the wall behind the last row of the outfield seats. Beyond those stately windows and across the street stood baseball diamonds. The whole area breathed of baseball: major league baseball, Little League baseball, and decades of baseball. From the 1920s to the 1960s players like Ruth, DiMaggio, and Mantle visited Chicago. A multitude of White Sox fans suffered in witnessing numerous defeats at the hands of those hated Yankees, the team that symbolized the World Series.

In the midst of this old baseball stadium was "the Monster," a gargantuan scoreboard that dominated the entire backdrop of center field. In addition to posting line scores of the day's major league action, "the Monster" had its upright and rectangular "Sox-O-Gram" that relayed messages to the fans. At night it was easier to read the line scores because it was difficult to decipher the lit numbers in the sunshine. However, neither the updates from other games nor the Sox-O-Gram messages were the real attractions. Fans wanted to see "the Monster" explode, set off lights, make noises and shoot fireworks into the sky above the upper outfield decks to celebrate White Sox home runs. Owner Bill Veeck got the idea for creating this display when he saw a pinball

The "Monster" going off after a Ken Berry two-run homer on a July 18, 1969, night game. It was one of the few bright spots the White Sox had that year.

machine go off in a similar manner during a stage play. White Sox home games had the potential of having a Fourth of July feeling for a few minutes, appealing to the kid in everyone. Opposing teams hated "the Monster" but White Sox fans loved the fireworks chiming in with their cheering. Once, after one of their own homered, Yankee players mockingly celebrated by holding up sparklers.

Yet the large ballpark and the center-field scoreboard also presented a problem. White Sox players walloping homers were a rare occurrence during the sixties. Because of the deep power alleys and the center-field canvas fence 415 feet from home plate, the Sox built their teams around defense and pitching. Even good-hitting visiting teams had a hard time scoring in Comiskey. Bill Melton, the first White Sox player to hit 30 home runs in a season and to win the American League home run championship, thought the team felt it was taboo to acquire long ball hitters. According to Melton, only after his back-to-back 33-home run seasons in 1970 and 1971 did that philosophy change.[1] But meanwhile, the center-field scoreboard stood silent game after game. It was as if the White Sox had a potent weapon they never used.

During the mid-sixties, Cubs fans taunted Sox fans, saying their team lost high-scoring games while the powerless White Sox won boring 3–2 or 2–1 contests. Although Sox fans told their Cubs counterparts that winning was the key thing, the constant pitching duels were becoming tiresome, at least for some. Even the pitchers, good as they were, were somewhat boring. Like power hitters, power pitchers who pile up strikeouts are big attractions for crowds. But in past interviews, standout '60s pitchers Joe Horlen and Gary Peters said they were never concerned about strikeouts.[2] Pitching to spots and allowing their defense to play behind them was their strategy. Both Horlen and Peters in their prime were effective and professional, and at times, dominating in their own way. But exciting?

Playing in low-scoring games worked well when the White Sox were winning. Good pitching, a solid defense, and manufacturing runs is good fundamental baseball. Yet it would have been desirable to have a little balance with some power and an occasional World Series appearance, if not a championship. This type of success did not happen.

In the final days of the 1967 season, with five games remaining, the second-place White Sox lost a chance to go to the World Series when they scored

Bill Melton facing Milwaukee's Jim Slaton during the 161st game of the 1971 season. He trailed Reggie Jackson and Norm Cash by two homers for the American League home run championship. He hit two that night off Slaton and one more the next day to take the title.

only two runs in three must-win games. (In one of the last years of the one-division league, a first-place finish meant a direct trip to the World Series.) Shut out in 26 of 27 innings, the ineptness of the White Sox offense finally caught up with them. These losses were even more embarrassing and heart-breaking because they came against two of the worst teams in the American League — the Kansas City Athletics and the Washington Senators. In a sense, both teams no longer exist since these franchises have moved to Oakland and Texas, respectively. Regardless, when your two leading hitters sported averages of .241, beating any team was not a given.

Despite being contenders in the pennant race for the entire year, the team failed to break the million mark in attendance for just the second time since 1959, their pennant-winning year. Fans were frustrated by the non-ending "getting close but not winning anything" pattern, season after season. The lack of offense increased that frustration. Arguably one of the best hitters for the team during the sixties was pitcher Gary Peters. In one 1968 game, Peters threw a complete game and hit a grand slam in a 5–1 win against the Yankees. A few years earlier, Peters knocked a homer over the right-field wall in Kansas City, almost picking off a cow in an adjoining pasture.[3]

Then came the years 1968 through 1970. These awful and downright embarrassing seasons drove fans away by the tens of thousands and nearly led to the destruction of the franchise. "It was hard to get humiliated in front of 5,000 people," Sox third baseman Bill Melton said, remembering those meager years.[4]

Actually, it was frequently less than 5,000. Huge Comiskey was almost empty during the late-sixties and in 1970. The infrequent eruptions of the center-field scoreboard provided more noise than the empty, quiet stands. Sometimes an individual could be heard screaming or cheering in an otherwise-silent stadium. The fan apathy had to be discouraging for the players and the franchise as a whole. On September 18, 1970, when Melton finally became the first White Sox player to hit 30 homers in a season, barely 600 attended. His 30th homer that season knocked off the second row of the entirely empty left-center field upper deck and dropped to the turf. His accomplishment, celebrated by the exploding scoreboard, was met with barely audible cheering.

It was extremely difficult to be a White Sox fan from 1968 to 1970. After the abysmal 1968 season when the Sox lost 95 and hit only 71 home runs (Barry Bonds hit 73 during his record-setting season), the team offered questionable solutions to their offensive problems. They shortened Comiskey's dimensions from 352 to 335 feet down the lines, and from 415 to 400 in dead center. The power alleys dropped from 375 to 370. The team also installed artificial turf in the infield to increase the chance of a ground ball sneaking its way into the outfield for a hit. The franchise hoped a smaller Comiskey Park would increase run production and fan interest. These hopes, much like earlier fantasies about beating the Yankees, were misguided.

The most immediate consequence of this strategy was that Comiskey was beautiful no longer. Instead of moving the plate out, the team erected a short fence in front of the old wall. Any homer that fell in between the new fence and the old wall seemed tainted. Although the Sox hit more home runs during the next two years, the impact of the shortened dimensions didn't help significantly. Additionally, the artificial turf in the infield made the park look like a pool table. The losing continued, and attendance in 1970 didn't crack the half-million mark.

Contrast the look, feel, and experience of Wrigley to Comiskey back then. There was a regal feeling generated by the vines and stately brick walls at Wrigley, and every seat felt close to the field. During a game I attended there in June 1968, Curt Flood of the St. Louis Cardinals dropped a bunt in between the mound and third base. The full white of the ball could be seen as clearly as if it sat in the middle of my own lawn. Additionally, with no upper deck in the outfield, fans could see how far home runs were hit. The upper decks down the lines didn't protrude as much as Comiskey, allowing sun to cover the field. The Cubs also offered a lineup that could hit the ball out of the park. If the Cubs played in Comiskey, would they need shortened dimensions? It is doubtful the team's ownership would have ever considered it.

The White Sox then did two things that greatly improved the atmosphere at Comiskey. First, in 1971, they tore down the inadequate and short Little League-like fence, and restored the dimensions down the lines and in the alleys. The center-field distance remained at 400 feet.

Secondly, in 1972, they acquired one of the most talented players ever to wear a White Sox uniform. Richie Allen had won National League Rookie of the Year honors in 1964 while playing for the Phillies. During his first eight years in major league baseball, Allen hit 234 home runs. Despite this output and obvious talent, teams couldn't get rid of him fast enough. Why? The answer to the Allen mystery is as complicated as the man himself.

Allen broke into major league baseball at a time when African American players were still uncommon and some teams stubbornly refused to integrate. He was the first African American to play for the Phillies farm system in Little Rock, Arkansas, where he played in 1963. Little Rock was no liberal bastion. In the late fifties, President Eisenhower sent in federal troops to allow for school integration there. Allen suffered racial intimidation and humiliation that would have left any normal person scarred. His 33 homers while playing for Little Rock didn't seem to impress the locals, and Allen continued to be harassed and threatened. From his first game in Little Rock, Allen lived in fear.

His experience with the big league club in Philadelphia was not much different. Allen took to wearing a helmet in the field to protect himself from various objects thrown by fans. At first base, Allen scribbled messages in the infield dirt, which included "BOO" and "Oct. 2." The October 2 date referred

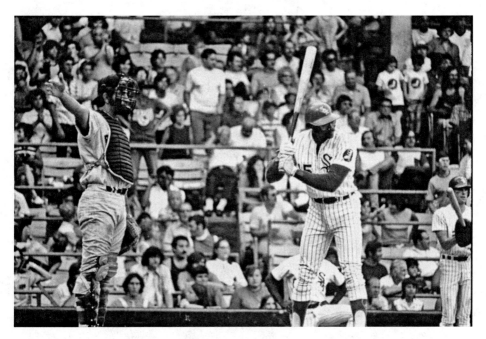

The opposition doing the smart thing: Walking Dick Allen. Allen looks intimidating just standing there.

to the last day of the season in 1969, marking what he hoped to be the end of his career in Philadelphia. Fans responded by booing Allen and hanging banners in the upper decks that also counted off his days playing for the Phillies. One fan banner read "IT WON'T BE LONG NOW, RICHIE!!!!"[5]

Allen was then sent to St. Louis. Despite hitting 34 homers in spacious Busch Stadium, Allen was traded by the Cardinals to the Los Angeles Dodgers just days after the 1970 campaign. After one respectable year in Los Angeles where he hit 23 homers and drove in 95 runs, Allen was dealt to the White Sox in exchange for pitcher Tommy John and infielder Steve Huntz in December 1971.

Leaving Philadelphia was supposed to solve some of Allen's problems, but why was he now with his fourth team in four years? Was he really the bad boy of baseball? It is safe to say that he was the cause of some of his own problems. However, it is also accurate to add that his whole story was not told, or at the very least, not understood. Regardless, the acquisition of Allen was met with both excitement and worry in Chicago.

As for Allen, he apparently was skeptical about joining the White Sox. The Sox won only 79 games in 1971, but the club had improved considerably from the disastrous previous year and it appeared ready to take some steps towards respectability. Melton had won the home run championship on the last day of the season, and Wilbur Wood won 22 while completing 20 of his starts. Some observers thought the acquisition of Allen would make the team a contender.

Allen, however, didn't report for spring training. One unconfirmed report placed Allen at spring training hiding behind the center-field fence in disguise.[6] He supposedly wanted to watch his new team work out and see if they showed any promise. By the time he reported and signed a new contract with the Sox, spring training was over.

Now it was the fans' turn to be skeptical. Did this guy think he was so good he didn't have to report for spring training? Would he be considered a divisive force, the way he was in Philadelphia? Why did the White Sox trade a front-line pitcher for this guy? Was this another Chicago trade gone sour?

At the same time, the owners locked out the players in a labor dispute. This work stoppage pushed the season back ten days and the Sox lost the gate from their home opener that had some great advance ticket sales. Instead, the South Siders had to begin their season in Kansas City, and Sox fans had their first look at Allen in a White Sox uniform on TV.

Both Wood and Royals starter Dick Drago pitched shutouts into the ninth, before Allen showed Sox fans the kind of impact player he would be in 1972. Allen, 0-for-3 up to that point, launched a Drago offering to left-center. Since it was a dark and dreary day in Kansas City, picking up the ball on the TV screen wasn't easy. But from Allen's swing, the apparent contact, and the movement of the Royal outfielders, it was obvious where this ball went.

KC outfielders Lou Piniella and Steve Hovely stopped well short of the wall and got a good view of the massive home run. A common cliché states that a home run is "gone." This hit was really gone. When it cleared the wall, it seemed to disappear in an abyss or black hole and was never seen again. Pirate Willie Stargell said after an Allen shot cleared the roof in Philadelphia's Connie Mack Stadium, "Now I know why they boo Richie all the time. When he hits a home run, there's no souvenir."[7]

The Kansas City shot was the prototype Allen home run. He didn't hit lazy-looking fly balls that barely dropped into the front row. Large parks, even the spacious Comiskey, didn't pose problems for him. Every homer was a demonstration of his sheer power. Either he laced a line shot that cut through the air and ripped into the seats, or he sent some high deep drive that went so far it seemed to dwarf even the largest of major league venues. In the end, Allen thought the American League pitchers were a bunch of wimps who didn't even bother trying to knock him off the plate, though in his book he put it in more graphic terms.[8] They didn't intimidate him; he spent all of 1972 intimidating them. "Allen was scary at the plate," Tiger left-handed pitcher Mickey Lolich said. "When he came up there, he had your attention. I want to forget a couple of line drives he hit off me, but I can't because they almost killed me."[9]

The White Sox lost that season-opening game in extra innings, but that fact wasn't important at the moment. Allen demonstrated his considerable talent, and showed that his spring training absence no longer seemed to matter. If he could hit like that without spring training, who cared about his failure to show?

Richie Allen wanted to be called Dick Allen, a request that had not been granted elsewhere. When the local media and fans easily complied with this simple demand, the first baseman was flattered and wanted to repay Chicago with a great season. Maybe the days of the bad Richie were gone. Maybe he found that Chicago truly wanted him and he would embrace Chicago and White Sox fans. Would the stormy baseball life of Dick Allen become a happily-ever-after fairy tale?

The Sox won their home opener over the Texas Rangers, 14–0, several days later, with Allen picking up two doubles. Even after he made an out in the seventh inning, he demonstrated what kind of hitter he was.

Using his massive down-cutting swing, Allen sent a drive to the deepest part of vast Comiskey. It was caught exactly where the center- and right-field walls met. Though he was out, Allen had again demonstrated how quickly he could get his 40-inch, 40-ounce bat through the strike zone. White Sox fans were accustomed to seeing singles hitters, bunters, and base stealers; they had never seen a player with this kind of offensive ability.

During a Bat Day doubleheader against the Yankees on June 4, the ugly side of Richie Allen seemed to appear again. The White Sox won the first game, 6–1, in front of a crowd of 51,904. Yet when the second game lineups were announced, there was no mention of Dick Allen. Instead, Mike Andrews was playing first. Almost 52,000 people were in attendance, and the team's best player doesn't play in the second game? Against the Yankees no less?

The White Sox could have used their new slugger, at least in the first eight innings. They trailed, 4–2, and picked up only three hits. Not giving up, in the ninth they put two runners on with a single and a walk. Who stepped out of the dugout to pinch-hit? It was the now-familiar number 15 worn by Dick Allen.

There were still many fans left from one of the largest crowds at Comiskey in years. They cheered wildly when Allen made his appearance. Allen strolled to the plate, showing no indication that he was moved by the fan excitement. I've seen people walking their dogs show more emotion. That was the way Allen handled himself on the field. In Philadelphia, he was chastised for it; in Chicago, fans admired him for it.

The Yankees countered with lefty Sparky Lyle, one of the best relievers in baseball at the time. But this was one game Lyle couldn't save. When Allen tore into Lyle's 1–0 pitch, the left-hander wasted no time walking off the mound. He knew Allen had done it. This homer won't be remembered for its

Bat Day, Comiskey Park, 1973. Fans were everywhere. They stood, sat in aisles and dangled their feet off the scoreboard. More than 2,000 had to be given ticket refunds because there was no place to sit or stand.

long distance, but for its power. It was a line drive that never really got far off the ground and barely cleared the shortstop's head. At first it appeared to be one of those hard-hit drives caught by the outfielder, like a ball hit too hard and right into an out. But the drive kept rising and was still climbing when it zipped into the left-field seats. The scoreboard erupted into the early summer-like night. The White Sox had a new hero — a hero with awesome power and the ability to change a game with one swing.

Yet Dick Allen could do more than hit. Although he was no gold glove on defense, he was a good first baseman for the Sox who could steal a base and run the bases well. Watching Allen take a sharp turn around third without missing a step was something to see. He hit for average, and to all fields. Even when striking out, the power and beauty of his swing was evident, and the pitcher had to be relieved when he came up empty. It could be argued, at least in 1972, that Dick Allen was the best player in the major leagues.

It was not just a matter of a standout player having a career year. The White Sox, for all their winning years from 1951 to 1967, never had a player of Allen's caliber. Yes, they had many talented players, even Hall of Fame-caliber players, but no one could impact a game or carry a team like Dick Allen. Several weeks after his game-winning homer against the Yankees, third baseman Melton went down with a back injury and was out for the season. General manager Roland Hemond acquired Ed Spezio from the San Diego Padres to play third. Spezio did a great job in the field but was not an offensive threat. The first-place Oakland A's had the likes of Reggie Jackson, Sal Bando, Bert Campaneris, Joe Rudi, Mike Epstein, Catfish Hunter, Ken Holtzman, and Rollie Fingers. Did the White Sox have a chance competing with a team with that type of talent after losing a key player like Melton? Not really. But they came close, mostly because of Dick Allen. Though they didn't win their division, the 1972 White Sox had the second-best overall record in the American League.

When the Sox tried to challenge the Yankees in the mid–sixties, there was an unmistakable excitement and tension in the air as the first pitch of the game was thrown. That crowd buzz continued to permeate vast Comiskey Park every time Dick Allen came to the plate in 1972. After he lashed the ball to the deepest caverns of Comiskey, there was a different, almost quiet buzz. Fans were awed that someone could swing the bat so hard, hit the ball so far, and do it with an apparent ease. One mammoth Allen homer in 1973 landed where the upper deck ended in left-center field. The ball nearly zipped past the huge deck and left the park completely. Again White Sox fans had tried to remember when their team had a player of this caliber. The answer was obvious: Never.

The White Sox management accommodated Allen, and affection was lavished on him. He was given a TV show. His brother Hank was put on the Sox roster to help ensure him a major league pension. Allen was paid well. Fans adored him. The team made trades in an effort to turn the club into a World Series contender. But the Dick Allen story in Chicago did not end happily.

In 1973, the division hopes for the White Sox ended with a series of injuries, including one to Allen. Many fans didn't believe Allen's injury was bad enough to sideline him for almost half the season. Allen vehemently denied these allegations. Then, in 1974, as the team faded again, Allen "retired" and left the White Sox in mid–September. Though Allen cited a chronic shoulder problem, fans felt he had deserted them and thought Allen was ungrateful after all the affection they had given him. Allen never actually retired in the formal and legal baseball sense, and was traded to Atlanta. He finally ended up in Philadelphia, the place that had so bitterly scorned him. Ironically, he played his last major league game against the White Sox in an Oakland A's uniform, in June 1977.

Losing Dick Allen was crippling to the White Sox. In 1975, the team lacked depth. Once-promising young hitters like Melton and Carlos May were at the end of their careers and had never truly fulfilled their promise. Attendance sank as the team won a meager 75 games. The team's power production dropped to late 1960s proportions. Center-field scoreboard celebrations were few. When the scoreboard did go off, it was a disappointment. The financially depleted team now had little money for fireworks and the shortened scoreboard eruptions were an anti-climax to unfulfilled expectations. By the end of the season the team's financial infrastructure was crumbling, and it appeared that the White Sox were on their way to Seattle, which would end a 75-year tenure on the South Side of Chicago.

Despite his mixed legacy and a missed opportunity at true greatness, Dick Allen impacted the White Sox like no player has before or since. He confirmed that a long ball hitter could thrive in the vastness of Comiskey. He also showed what one player could do to lift a team and re-ignite a dormant fan base. His departure also created a void that no other Sox player could fill. The Sox faithful turned on their own, even booing the annual father-son game on Father's Day. Yes, the White Sox were in awful shape at the end of 1975 because there had been no Dick Allen with his awesome homers, and his calm, confident swagger. And what would have happened to the team if the controversial Allen had never played a game at Comiskey? The team would have run out of money sooner, and the shortened scoreboard celebrations would have occurred earlier. Fans would not have wanted to see more 2–1 contests, win or lose. Seattle and many other cities would have welcomed a new team to their metropolis, even a poorly performing club like the White Sox. Comiskey Park would no longer be home to endless pitching duels, and the large but empty ballpark may not have hosted a major league baseball game again.

3

Bleacher Bums

"The Cubs no longer have fans. They have a cult."
—*Jack Griffin, Chicago Sun-Times columnist in April, 1970*[1]

A picture of the Wrigley Field bleachers taken by Steven Green during the mid–1980s captures some of the old-fashioned aura of that stadium's outfield seating. The photo, which covered Lonnie Wheeler's 1988 book, *Bleachers—A Summer in Wrigley Field*, shows the stadium at 4:35 in the afternoon on a sunny, blue-skied summer day.[2] The bleachers look worn and weather-beaten. In one particular section, the wood on the edge of the seats looks like someone has taken a chisel to it. The paint was chipped and missing, leaving the wood naked in spots. The beloved hand-operated scoreboard listed that day's schedule, and as usual for that time in history, the Cubs played the lone day game in the major leagues. "Nite Game" is placed over the rest of the schedule. As for the Cubs that day, they lost 5–0 to the Phillies.

The bleachers normally wouldn't be mistaken for seating in a major league arena. In addition to needing a paint job, the bleachers appeared to be nothing but boards nailed in place. Foot room and legroom hardly existed. If you were a person who feared intimacy, the Wrigley Field bleachers weren't for you.

Yet the photo captured so much more. Wrigley was shown in a pre-lights, almost innocent era. The Tribune Company wasn't brokering tickets and the roof-top controversies were still a couple decades away. Even the Cubs' loss that day heightened the romanticism. For some Cubs fans the constant losing adds to the team's legacy. At one time, the losing only caused apathy and lack of interest. But then came the late '60s and the hope that a World Series might finally be won. Suddenly a new fanaticism was born in the group of fans who proudly called themselves "Bleacher Bums."

Eventually a play was written about the bums. The White Sox, with their stadium in the same general area of steel mills and factories, were known as Chicago's blue-collar baseball team. But now the Bleacher Bums were characterized

A sign of the times during the early seventies. Packed bleachers on a beautiful day at Wrigley with a peace sign.

as everyday working class fans who were unapologetic hero-worshippers. They wore yellow construction helmets and were cheered on by Cubs pitcher Dick Selma in 1969. Author Saul Wisnia wrote that the original bums were construction workers who came in and out of games before or after their shifts. Their main purpose, according to Wisnia, was to heckle opposing outfielders. Wisnia explained that the bums had evolved into a group of "hippies and hard hats, side by side."[3] It is said that politics makes strange bedfellows and that may be true in sports as well. This was the case in the Wrigley Field bleachers during the turbulent sixties. Dick Selma led the cheers from the bullpen in a season when noise and frenzy were an every-game occurrence during the summer of the championship that never was.

One of those self-identified Bleacher Bums was Chicago radio personality Mike Murphy, who is commonly known as "Murph." He has been a part of Chicago sports talk since the late '80s, when he aired a program on WLS-AM. Murphy left WLS to join a new station, WSCR-AM, when that outlet went on the air in 1991. He has had varying time slots since then and has promoted his show as "fans talking to fans." With his show as a platform, Murphy is one of the most well-known Cubs fans in the city and epitomizes the loyalty of a fan frustrated by a team that has done everything it can to not win a World Series.

"In the late '60s," Murphy wrote, "fans could attend a game by themselves, and choose in a certain section to sit with people they may have sat with in a previous game. This era created fan friendships that last until this day."[4]

Murphy lamented the passing of the old days. He feels there are no real bleacher bums now, and in a sense, that includes him.

"The change at Wrigley," Murphy wrote, "was when the Cubs started the entire ball park on a reserved seat basis in the early '80s. This was except for the bleachers, which were included into 'seat numbered tickets' somewhere in the early '90s. This was exactly the last time I went to the bleachers."[5]

With the concept of advance ticket sales an entrenched reality, Murphy is correct in believing the era of the bleacher bum is over. But he takes solace in the continued practice of fans throwing back home runs hit by the opposition. Murphy remembered the tradition starting shortly after the landmark 1969 season. He credits Cubs fan Ron Grousl for getting the ball rolling. Murphy identified Grousl as "the president of the Left Field Bleacher Bums."[6]

> It was totally unplanned. I was standing next to Ron when it first occurred. Hank Aaron hit a home run into the left field bleachers, which Ron caught on the fly. He looked at the ball and said, "We don't want this stinking ball ... it's an enemy homer!" With that he wound up and flipped it on the fly behind second base. There was a stunned silence for a moment — no one had ever seen anything like this before. Then the crowd went nuts. Cheering, laughing, jeering of the great Hank Aaron. Yes, the fans had just illustrated love for their favorite team. Fanaticism was personified in the act and in the discarded ball. From then on, enemy home runs hit into the Wrigley Field bleachers were expected to be thrown back. And if the recipient of the enemy ball did not immediately jettison the ball back onto the field, the entire bleacher crowd would simply start chanting in unison, "Throw it back, throw it back, throw it back." And it happened EVERY TIME.[7]

One has to wonder if Grousl regretted throwing the Aaron home run ball back after the Braves slugger hit number 715 off Al Downing in April 1974. Regrets or not, there is an inconsistency in Murphy's account, at least regarding the timeline. Grousl told author Rick Talley that he had caught Aaron's 521st career homer, which tied the Braves great with Ted Williams on the all-time home run list.[8] This historic event happened when Aaron homered off Ken Holtzman on June 1, 1969. In his 1989 book, *The Cubs of '69 — Recollections of the Team That Should Have Been*, Talley wrote that Grousl had offered the souvenir back to Aaron as a keepsake of the event.[9] Reportedly, an angry Aaron tossed or threw the ball back because he didn't appreciate the treatment he was getting from Cubs bleacher fans. In the box score for that day, Aaron was slotted in his normal right-field position. Murphy said that Grousl caught the homer in the left-field seats, a logical place for an Aaron homer.[10] Did Grousl circle the stadium to right field to talk to Aaron? Did this tradition start with a different Aaron homer or one hit by a different player? In the end, it really doesn't matter who has the clearer memory. Cubs fans still throw back opposition home runs, at least the ones that are not bouncing down Waveland or Sheffield Avenue. (Sometimes even a few of those are heaved back.) Many White Sox fans who deride this now 40-year-old tradition claim that Cubs fans throw back a ball they bring with them and keep the actual souvenir. Regardless, sometimes opposition homers are thrown back at U.S. Cellular Field, and the tradition has caught on at other ballparks. Throwing back opposition homers is an engrained source of Cub fan pride.

This pride is illustrated by Murphy's use of capital letters. Yet just a few years prior to the bums, there were no big crowds or passion. Cubs fan Jim Weir grew up during the sixties and visited his uncle who lived in the Wrigley neighborhood a good twenty years before night baseball. Weir described the neighborhood as being pretty rough with drunks roaming around at night. "Even though it was only one dollar for a bleacher seat, my uncle didn't want to pay it," Weir recalled. "So he'd approach the man guarding the gate around the sixth inning and ask if we could just go in and watch the game. He'd go to a different gate every time. When we got in, we usually didn't have a hard time finding a good seat. One game went into the 16th or 17th inning, so we actually got to see nine innings for free."[11]

In 2008, with tickets hard to come by, Weir found it easier to see the Cubs on the road rather than trying to catch them at Wrigley. He traveled to St. Louis and Pittsburgh to see his favorite team play their way to the National League Central Division title.

Getting a ticket to a game in the late sixties wasn't quite that difficult, but it's doubtful whether any fan could have walked in free during the late innings as the team improved. Meanwhile, the fanaticism of the Bleacher Bums drew attention, sometimes the wrong kind of attention. Opposing players accused the bums of throwing all kinds of things at them. The bums denied this, saying they helped police the bleachers to ensure that things didn't get out of hand. Cardinal and ex–Cub left fielder Lou Brock was not impressed. "Somebody's going to get hurt out there," he said.[12] Brock claimed various things were hurled at him, including a dry cell battery that just missed his head. Fruit, especially apples and oranges, seemed to be favorite projectiles. Brock was convinced that the Bleacher Bums were going to ruin any chances of Cub success in 1969.[13] (Not that he really cared about any newfound success of the Cubs.)

It was a strange problem for the Cubs. For years, fans restricted themselves to watching the team on WGN. Suddenly, they were everywhere and their passion made some of them uncontrollable. The team released a letter from Ernie Banks to the fans published in the *Chicago Tribune* during the early part of the '69 season. The sappy letter asked for compassion for opposing outfielders and reminded fans that these players actually could end up being a Cub someday.[14] It is difficult to determine if the letter had any impact. Most likely it had none.

Regardless of these problems, the baseball side of Chicago now belonged to the Cubs. In late August 1969, the Cubs played the Sox in their then-annual exhibition game. Bill Gleason, a *Chicago Sun-Times* columnist, wrote of a strange thing happening on the way to Comiskey Park. Car after car seemed to be zooming past him on the expressway. Where were they going? From the turnout of 33,333, they had been heading to watch a game that meant nothing. The White Sox had not and would not crack the 30,000 mark for any other home game that season. Gleason had one suggestion for the now-sagging White Sox: Get some players — if not winning players, at least some interesting players. According to Gleason, Sox owner Arthur Allyn doubted that anyone would bring their families to the dangerous area around Comiskey. But Gleason wrote that all those cars passing him on the Dan Ryan were full of kids. "Many more came on buses and elevated trains," Gleason wrote.[15] "They came, as they used to come, to see ballplayers."[16] Gleason further suggested that the Cubs play the Sox in games that actually counted, in one of the early calls for inter-league play. He continued:

> The lesson for baseball is that the Cubs and Sox should meet in at least four official league games a year, not for what those games would do at the box office, but for what they would do to stimulate interest in baseball in this vast metropolitan area.[17]

The home openers in 1970 markedly demonstrated how the entire complexion of Chicago baseball had changed and how it may have helped if Gleason's advice was taken.

A paltry crowd of a little more than 11,000 showed for the White Sox opener against the Minnesota Twins. The Sox lost, 12–0, and the game wasn't as close as the score. In the next three home games, the White Sox couldn't break the 3,000 mark. As in most Chicago Aprils, it was cold, feeling more like early winter. Although the sun was bright, the vast emptiness of Comiskey made the weather seem even colder. Only a few of the die-hards were willing to brave the cold to watch a team on its way to one of its worst seasons ever. The franchise was on the verge of a total collapse.

There couldn't have been a bigger contrast to the Cubs' first home game a week later. As usual, well over 20,000 tickets were sold on the day of the game. Thousands of Cubs fans descended on the box offices in the early morning, hoping that the team could re-capture the magic of 1969 without the September burnout. More than three times the Sox's Opening Day crowd watched the Cubs beat the Phillies by one run for the second straight year to open their home season. Yet this opener lacked the excitement and fun that had symbolized most of the games in 1969.

This time there was no come-from-behind win. In fact, starter Ken Holtzman almost blew a 5–0 lead when he gave up four in the ninth. In the end, he picked up the complete game to preserve the win, but the fan celebration that followed did not make people feel good about the upcoming season. In fact, the Cubs felt they had to take some action to secure their own ballpark.

According to press reports, this was one mess that couldn't be blamed on the Bleacher Bums. Fans in the bleachers were cursing and throwing things at the Andy Frain ushers who had stepped out to protect the field at game's end. One seventeen-year-old either fell or jumped from the bleachers down to the field. A group of ushers surrounded the teenager and started kicking him. Fans rushed onto the field from other directions and fights ensued. Another fan tried to rip off the cap off Glenn Beckert's head and scratched his forehead. Beckert felt fortunate that no damage had been done to his eye. Reportedly, the Bleacher Bums were in the bar across the street and were disgusted when they saw how things had gone out of control at the ballpark. "These kids are animals," one bum said. "They dress like us and try to look like us. But they're bums, not Bums."[18]

It is one thing for a few objects to be thrown at opposition outfielders. It is another when one of your own players feels threatened, the ushers you employ to keep order beat someone senseless, and the ushers themselves are attacked. The Cubs brass responded quickly. The unrest of the sixties had to be on their mind and they were undoubtedly determined that Wrigley Field was not going to be a miniature version of the 1968 Democratic Convention. Ushers, most of whom were in their late teens, had even been called "pigs."[19] The 1970 opener spurred the construction of the basket that still juts out from the outfield walls today. In 1970, Cubs fans were relieved that the purpose of the basket was to prevent fans from going onto the field while not obstructing anyone's view. Today many Cubs fans may not even know why it is there.

Fan controversies aside, the Cubs actually got off to a great start in 1970, jumping out to a 12–3 record on the strength of an eleven-game winning streak. They won all of their games at Wrigley in the month of April, going 10–0. But a 1969-style collapse started early, and by the All-Star break the Cubs' record stood at 43–42. Unlike 1969, no one was trying to calculate magic numbers.

Back in 1970, Sunday doubleheaders were common. On July 26 the Cubs played a twin bill against the Atlanta Braves. The temperature stood near 90, the sun shined on Wrigley like it shined on nowhere else, and a crowd of more than 39,000 enjoyed it all. The Cubs were only two games over .500 but only 4 games out of first. No, it wasn't like 1969, but the team was again hitting well and most of the other ingredients were still there. They were still in the race.

Braves first baseman Orlando Cepeda put a damper on things by hitting solo home runs off starter Bill Hands in the second and fourth innings. After one of the homers cleared the left-field wall, the ball came flying out of the bleachers and back onto the field. As the ball bounced toward the infield, Wrigley Field roared. For some reason, second base umpire Chris Pelekoudas took exception to this new practice and tried to throw the ball back into the left-field seats. The crowd derisively laughed when his throw hit in the middle of the summer green vines.

With one out in the bottom of the fourth and the Cubs down, 2–1, Jim Hickman stepped up to the plate. Hickman, one of the original Mets, had some so-so years before coming to the Cubs in 1968, but 1970 was going to be his career year. He already had 21 homers coming into the game, as well as the winning hit in the All-Star game two weeks earlier, when he picked on a Clyde Wright breaking ball.* Hickman showed off that perfect swing in the fourth inning. It had a slight upper cut, which golfed a knee-high pitch some, and seemed effortless. Yet the ball jumped off his bat. The center fielder sent a high and beautifully arching shot into the bright sky and to deep left. The drive shot its way deep onto Waveland Avenue and the game was tied at two. You could almost hear Jack Brickhouse yell, "Hey, hey." And Hickman wasn't done hitting homers for that doubleheader.

The roof caved in on the Cubs in the top of the fifth. Manager Leo Durocher ordered a two-out intentional walk to Hank Aaron to load the bases. Normally no one would argue about walking Aaron with runners in scoring position, but Orlando Cepeda was due up, and he had already hit two out of the park. One wonders what Bill Hands must have been thinking as he readied himself to face Cepeda again.

There was no opposition souvenir for the Bleacher Bums to heave back this time. Cepeda rocketed an ineffective Hands offering halfway up the center-field hitting background for a grand slam. You could hear the second guessing throughout the crowd after the ball banged against the green background and then rolled to a stop at the wall's edge. The Braves, behind seven Cepeda RBIs, won, 8–3.

In the second game, the Cubs salvaged a split with a 7–6 win when they scored five in the first. Billy Williams hit an opposite-field homer for his 29th and Hickman nailed his second dinger of the doubleheader. Hickman would finish his career year with 32 homers, 115 RBIs and a .315 average.

This was entertaining Cubs baseball. The ball flew out of Wrigley. Hickman, Williams, and Santo combined for 100 homers and 358 RBIs in 1970. Williams completed the campaign with 205 hits, and the Cubs finished second in the National League in scoring, with 806 runs. There was plenty of talent on the team. Why were they struggling just to stay over .500? Was 1969 or the first five months of 1970 just a fluke?

On September 5, the Cubs played the hated Mets at Wrigley. Chicago

---

With a picture-perfect swing, Hickman drilled a single to center with two outs. Pete Rose scored the winning run for the National League with his famous collision with catcher Roy Fosse, which injured Fosse and ruined his career

Cubs radio play-by-play man Vince Lloyd with manager Leo Durocher at a press
luncheon in 1971. The two men weren't always this friendly. On one occasion, Durocher
threw Lloyd's pipe into a toilet.

was in second place, one-half game behind the first-place Pirates. New York
stood in third, two games back. Cubs fans had to be thinking of the previous
September when their team lost that two-game series at Shea. The Cubs could
vindicate themselves for that failure by pounding the Mets and finding some
way to get past the Pirates.

Going to a game in 1970 was very different than it is now. Ticket brokering
wasn't sanctioned by a major league franchise. Game day general admission
seating was not sold in advance and was a great value for the fan. If you arrived
early enough, you could get a seat close to the field with a great view. On September 5, 1970, Cubs fans showed up at Wrigley before 7:00 A.M. They camped
out at the park to get in line for the general admission seating. Wrigley opened
at about 9:30 A.M. Fans didn't walk to their seats; they ran to get as close to
the field as possible. Then they had a four-hour wait until game time.

"I only went to doubleheaders," recalls Cubs fan Greg Redlarczyk. "The
second game would end about six or seven, so it was a 12-hour day for me.
We'd always get seats down the right-field line so we could see into the Cubs
dugout. Usually we got right behind the box seats."[20]

The fans who settled in for batting practice were not bored awaiting that

September 5 game against the Mets. The Cubs went first and put on quite a show. Home run after home run shot out of Wrigley, making the early arrival worthwhile. The hitter who made the biggest splash was Willie Smith, the 1969 Opening Day hero. Smith launched numerous shots onto Sheffield Avenue. Going to Wrigley was already an experience and the start of the game was hours away.

By the time the first pitch was thrown by Ken Holtzman, the park was packed with a little more than 39,000 worked-up fans. No, it wasn't 1969, but the atmosphere was intense. The beer flowed, the fans yelled, and Wrigley was a wall of noise. There was still hope for big things ... the same hope that had been dashed the previous year.

There was another significant difference about baseball in 1970: Starting pitchers went deep into the game. In the ninth, Holtzman was still on the mound for the Cubs, and Mets starter Jerry Koosman was slated to come out for the Chicago ninth. The Mets even chose to let Koosman bat in the eighth with two runners on with two out. Koosman struck out as the Mets passed up an opportunity to put the game out of reach.

Holtzman had pitched well except for giving up three runs in the fourth. The lefty then faltered in the ninth, giving up a two-out, two-run double to catcher Jerry Grote. The Cubs trailed, 5–1.

But the Cubs weren't done. After Joe Pepitone singled to right, Ernie Banks stepped up to the plate. Using his strong wrists, Banks sent a deep and towering drive to left. The ball landed over the left-field wall for a two-run homer. Suddenly, it was a game again, as Chicago inched back to within two at 5–3.

Catcher Randy Hundley singled to left and Wrigley was alive for the first time since the first pitch of the game. Could it be like early 1969 again? Could this be another great comeback, and would the Cubs make a giant step toward the playoffs?

The answer was "no" to all three questions. Tug McGraw was summoned and he retired the next three batters in order. The Cubs had lost a winnable game, 5–3.

A little less than two weeks later, the Cubs played their final home game of 1970. Facing the Cardinals, they were still very much in the race, but they looked lifeless that day. In front of a middle-of-the-week crowd of less than 17,000, the Cubs gave up 22 hits to St. Louis and lost, 9–2. It was just another dreary, cloudy, and damp September day, and the no-lights Wrigley was dark and quiet. No one in the listless crowd acted like the Cubs could prevail in the Eastern Division even though they were only two games out.

Then Ernie Banks led off the ninth. Banks was no longer the regular first baseman for the Cubs. His 12 homers in 1970 were the lowest single-season total of his career since he had broken into the big leagues on September 17,

1953, exactly 17 years earlier. Chicago fans, thinking that Banks would be retiring and that this would be their last live look at "Mr. Cub," gave their longtime favorite a standing ovation. Banks brought the fans to their feet again with a line shot single to center.

In remembering the late '60s, Banks listed a litany of events that he felt affected not only major league baseball, but the country as well. "Haight Ashbury, Woodstock, Kent State, Chicago Democratic Convention," Banks recalled as he referred to these important events.[21] He thought the stormy times of the sixties prompted parents to send their teenagers to Wrigley to get away from the trauma and turbulence of a scary and changing society.

Banks said he also thought of those who weren't at the games. "I always thought of the shut-ins, the ones who couldn't come to the games," Banks recalled. "They inspired me to play the game."[22] ("Shut-ins" was a term Jack Brickhouse used many times on the air.)

As for the Cubs, they remained only two games out after the final home loss to the Cardinals. They also had the misfortune, however, of playing their last fourteen games on the road. One observer, *Sun-Times* columnist Bill Gleason, thought it might help the Cubs to go on the road and escape their own fans. He wrote of Ron Santo: "No longer will he hear such home town chants as 'Santo, you bum! Go and sell another pizza.' Or 'Santo you fat slob, next year Young'll be back and you'll be gone,' and 'Hey, pizza belly. Whycha lose 30 pounds?'"[23]

The season had come full circle. A basket had been built to control some fans and now those fans were perceived as a barrier to winning a division title. Santo had said of the fans only one year before, "They were rabid and loud. They actually became our 10th man on the field. I truly believe they were a catalyst for success from opening day."[24] But a year later the fans yelled insults at the guy as if he were a visiting outfielder.

The Cubs went 7–7 during the season-ending road trip. Although that was not bad, they needed more to overcome the Pirates. Pittsburgh took the East, one of six division titles they won from 1970 to 1979.

Although Banks did not retire after the 1970 season, he had fewer than 100 official at-bats in '71 and was becoming part of Cubs history, at least as a player. He never played in a World Series during his entire career with the Cubs, which spanned over three decades.

While 1970 was another disappointment for the Cubs, they still excelled in comparison to the White Sox. The White Sox lost 106 that year, the highest single-season total in franchise history. Attendance at Comiskey was the lowest since 1943, when there was a World War going on. The White Sox were so laughable it seemed as if Chicago was now a one-team town. In a long-overdue move, ownership purged the team by firing the field and front office management.

The Cubs had respectable years in 1971 and 1972 but didn't come close to winning the division. Their opportunity to get to the postseason had come and gone with the disappointment of 1969. I am convinced that if they had won the division in 1969, they would have gone on to the World Series that year and would have repeated the feat in 1970. Instead, they had two second-place finishes, which frustrated their fans as much as the White Sox bridesmaids appearances during the early '60s.

They should have won in 1969 and 1970, but they didn't. Yet they had pushed the White Sox to the number two position in Chicago baseball. Cubs fans were not only optimistic and loyal, but fanatical and cult-like.

4

There's Nothing Like an Opening Day

"Things are a little short."
—1970 White Sox team owner John Allyn, explaining to his
players that the team was supposed to order six dozen bats
— but purchased only half that many.[1]

The year 1970 provides a number of dubious images to those White Sox fans who care to remember it. A third baseman camps under a pop-up in foul territory, loses it in the lights and has it hit him in the face. A center fielder runs down a fly ball on the warning track only to have it go off his glove and over the fence for a three-run homer. Visiting teams tire themselves out running around the bases after constantly pelting White Sox pitchers. Empty seats stretch out as far as a fan could see.

Then there were the auxiliary scoreboards positioned on the façade in the upper deck. The linescore was simple. On top, in large, capital, white letters was the word VISITORS. Directly below were the words WHITE SOX. The final score next to VISITORS was almost always larger than the final score next to WHITE SOX. Many times the final score next to VISITORS was embarrassingly higher than the one next to WHITE SOX. And it didn't matter who the VISITORS were.

In August the team actually played fairly well. The White Sox began calling themselves "The Big White Machine." In a fun way, they were comparing themselves to the Cincinnati Reds, who had been dubbed the "The Big Red Machine." The Reds had Johnny Bench, Tony Perez, and Lee May. The White Sox had Carlos May, Bill Melton, and Gail Hopkins. The Reds won 102 and went to the World Series. The White Sox lost 106 and finished last for the first time in 22 years.

Financially strapped or not, by September John Allyn saw he had to do something. From 1968 to 1970, his ball club would lose 295 games. So Allyn

46

fired Ed Short, the only general manager the team had in the post–Veeckian sixties. Also dispatched was solid baseball man, long-term White Sox employee, and manager Don Gutteridge. An era that boasted winning seasons, near pennants, and solid baseball now ended with a team that had bottomed out like some addict who had finally lost everything.

The new brain trust was general manager Roland Hemond and field manager Chuck Tanner. Both came from the Angels organization. Tanner managed the Angels' AAA minor league team in Hawaii, which outdrew the White Sox by 2,000 in 1970. Both were confident they could turn around a franchise that had lost its fans and position in Chicago.

"It was drawn as a dismal picture to me," Hemond recalled of the White Sox situation almost 30 years later. "I was told by numerous people, 'Roland, that's a hopeless situation. They're not drawing, financially they're not in a good position at all, and you're going into a difficult task.' There were others who were saying there were no prospects in the organization. But I was young and excited about undertaking the job so it didn't disturb me to hear those things."[2]

Between October 13, 1970, and March 30, 1971, Hemond moved 27 players. In addition to Jay Johnstone and Mike Andrews, the Sox picked up outfielder Rick Reichardt and pitching prospect Tom Bradley. None of these players could be considered superstars, but they had some talent and they gave the team a new look. Some Sox fans called into radio talk shows during spring training of 1971 and actually said the team might not be that bad. Yet enthusiasm for the revamped team was tepid.

The Cubs had their great Opening Day in 1969, a portent to a season that made a second-place team immortal to Cubs fans of that generation. Amazingly, the White Sox actually had two great Opening Days in 1971, and the sports city of Chicago was caught flat-footed. These season openers — the first one on the road in Oakland, and the second one at Comiskey Park two days later — briefly but dramatically re-ignited a sports hope that had abandoned the city, especially on Chicago's South Side.

Charles Finley was one of the last "family owners" in major league baseball. Though not as well loved, Finley was as controversial as the charismatic Bill Veeck. Finley, for all his fighting with fans, players, and the baseball establishment, continually looked for ways to create new interest in the sport. He introduced the orange baseball in spring training, used a player only as a pinch-runner, and dressed his team in colorful uniforms to contrast the drab traditional baseball cloth. The uniforms caught on, but the orange baseball didn't. The specialized pinch-runner disappeared after he was picked off in the ninth inning of a World Series game against the Dodgers. In 1971, Finley's Oakland A's, after almost two decades of mediocrity in Kansas City and Oakland, were ready to contend in the American League West. Charlatan or not, Finley finally had amassed some young talent and molded it into a balanced team.

Finley decided a great way to start the season was with an event that had never happened in baseball history — an Opening Day doubleheader. Facing the White Sox, a team with 106 losses the year before, seemed to ensure an Opening Day sweep. Finley's up-and-coming A's would have a fast start. In the end, it was another one of Finley's bright ideas that didn't work.

Yet who could blame the man for trying? The White Sox had dropped 16 of 18 in the season series against the A's in the disastrous 1970 campaign. Oakland outscored Chicago 160–95, and won all nine games in Chicago. On May 24, A's first baseman Don Mincher homered over the Comiskey right-field roof. The entire experience was humiliating for the White Sox. Mincher's home run, bounding toward the Dan Ryan Expressway, only made it worse.

The Opening Day doubleheader only drew mild interest in the Bay Area, with little more than 23,000 showing up. Even more disappointing for Finley and the A's was that the White Sox swept the doubleheader — something Chicago did only once in 1970. The White Sox lost 13 twin bills that year.

The White Sox erased a four-run deficit to win, 6–5, in game one. They then trounced the A's, 12–4, in game two with the help of four home runs. Well, actually three home runs. Left fielder Carlos May had homered but amazingly missed home plate because he was too busy high-fiving a teammate. The A's noticed, tagged home plate and turned the round-tripper into a triple. Yet it was no matter that the White Sox had committed another Chicago-style baseball blunder. This team was not going to lose 106 games.

In the A's doubleheader, one of the 1970 holdovers helped add to the new optimism. Bill Melton demonstrated that his 33-homer season from the year before was no fluke. Melton homered in each game; his second was a two-out grand slam that iced a five-run sixth inning. In recalling his feat to me, Melton asked, "Did I do this?"[3] Yes, he did.

Bart Johnson, a young, hard-throwing right-hander, had been the victim of Don Mincher's Comiskey Park roof shot the year before. In game two, he went the distance and picked up nine strikeouts. Pitching was something the Sox had little of during the previous two seasons. The young, high-kicking Johnson had a live arm and some real moxie. Considering hitters' late reactions, it looked like Johnson had a real major league fastball. Was the team really good?

The White Sox then headed back to Chicago to face two-time defending division champion Minnesota. In capturing the first two Western Division crowns in 1969 and 1970, the Twins had manhandled the Sox by winning 25 of 36. Many of these losses came at home in front of small crowds of dwindling White Sox diehards, who probably had better things to do than watch their favorite team get pummeled.

Roland Hemond was cautiously optimistic about the turnout for the home opener. He hoped 25,000 would show for the 2–0 White Sox. He was off by almost 20,000.

The weather for the April 9 contest was not particularly good. It was a typical Chicago early spring day with overcast skies and a cold bite in the air even when the sun came out. Yet as time drew closer to the first pitch, Comiskey Park uncharacteristically swelled with White Sox fans the team probably didn't know existed. In the picnic area under the left-field seats, concession workers frantically tried to keep up with food orders. A bright red fire shot up through a grill as a cook worked searing hamburgers and steaks. He was literally and figuratively sweating. The area, almost totally abandoned during the past few years, was packed with hungry fans looking forward to the beginning of the White Sox home season. The 1971 home opener drew more than the last three home openers combined and represented 8.4 percent of the total 1970 gate. Up to that point, the paid crowd of more than 43,000 was the largest ever for a home opener. With guests, the total attendance was 44,250. The turnout included some 31,000 walk-ups. As for the concessions, they were all gone by the fourth inning.

In addition to the encouraging numbers, the emotion and excitement in the park matched those early-sixties games against the Yankees. These intense emotions had been absent from the old ballpark for too long and could be felt and heard in the bottom of the first inning.

Hitting with two out and none on, Mike Andrews laced a line drive into the left-field corner for a double. After the Sox had scored 18 runs in the doubleheader against the A's, many fans probably thought this was the start of another offensive onslaught. Regardless, the park sounded so different, so emotional, and so loud.

Bill Melton followed, and the crack of his bat had the crowd ready to roar again, only his hard-hit line drive was snared by Twins third baseman Harmon Killebrew. For a moment the atmosphere was deflated, although that letdown wouldn't last. The fans responded again, and again it involved Killebrew.

Young right-hander Tom Bradley was on the mound for the White Sox. Bradley, with his big-rimmed glasses, looked more like a physics professor than a pitcher. (He actually had a degree in Latin.) But Bradley didn't pitch like a geek and was ready to challenge Killebrew when the Sox were ahead, 1–0, with one out in the sixth. The short but powerful third baseman hit 41 homers in 1970, the eighth time he reached the 40-homer mark in a season. With a full count, Bradley wound up and unleashed a fastball. Killebrew's swing showed why he eventually hit 573 homers in his career. His bat not only ripped through the strike zone with speed, but his cut was perfectly level, and he was able to fully extend his arms. But all his power and mechanics didn't help the Twins' slugger this time. The future Hall of Famer struck out.

The game was far from over, yet as Killebrew slowly returned to the dugout, Comiskey Park erupted as if the mighty Casey had made the last out. The year before, Killebrew's beautiful swing probably would have launched a drive capable of knocking down the upper deck. On this occasion, he came up empty because Bradley had thrown one of the best fastballs delivered by a White Sox pitcher during the last three years.

In the bottom of the ninth, the game was tied at two. Utility infielder Rich Morales stood on third base with two out. Jay Johnstone, a left-handed hitter, was scheduled to face lefty reliever Ron Perranowski. Playing the percentages, manager Chuck Tanner sent up right-hander Rich McKinney to pinch hit.

Just who was Rich McKinney? He was a 24-year-old infielder who had a total of 120 career at-bats. He was a near-rookie but looked formidable in the batter's box. He didn't choke up, and held the bat high in the air, giving the appearance that he could hit the ball as far Killebrew had done so many times. And, on this occasion, he hit the ball as hard as Killebrew could have.

McKinney's line drive down the left-field line slammed into the turf and bounced up to left fielder Cesar Tovar on two hard hops. Fans sitting in the lower boxes down the line could hear the ball cutting through the early spring grass. It would have been interesting to see how far the ball may have gone if McKinney had gotten under it. Regardless, his clutch hit gave the White Sox their most exciting win in recent memory.

The season, of course, was still very young. The White Sox were 3–0. However, the fans reacted as if the Sox had taken a 3–0 lead in the World Series. Several hundred fans ran onto the field, and the White Sox had no way of controlling them. At least the fans were not destructive. Many ran around the infield, sliding into bases. Others tore around the outfield in no general direction while running in shear delight. Fans that remained in the stands were in no hurry to leave. This was in total contrast to 1970 when the Sox had been beaten and humbled time and time again. The scene looked like something out of 1969 Wrigley. Although Sox fans refused to admit it, they wanted a team that matched the excitement generated by the North Side club.

Underneath the stands the excitement continued as fans screamed, yelled, and exchanged high fives. The noise was deafening; the excitement was barely containable. Many still didn't want to leave, and they weren't.

A logical question would be: Why was there so much excitement and emotion about one game, even if it was the home opener? Because by 1971, Chicago fans felt like they lived in a sports second city, where disappointment reigned and championships were nonexistent.

The Bulls were becoming an excellent team but their championships were still twenty years away. Sox fans didn't cry when the 1969 Cubs faded, but that burnout seemed to taint the whole sports town. After their 1963 NFL championship, the Bears steadily declined over the rest of the decade. On their way to a 1–13 season in 1969, the Bears lost a game to the then–St. Louis Cardinals, 20–17. On one play, quarterback Jack Concannon decided to call a timeout. He pulled his hands out from the center to signal the timeout but the center snapped the ball. The ball bounced off Concannon and into the air. St. Louis linebacker Larry Stallings caught the ball and began running. Thinking there was a timeout, the Bears stood around and watched as Stallings returned the "fumble" 62 yards for a touchdown. The Bears had a chance to tie the game in the last second but place kicker Mac Percival's 26-yard field goal attempt went wide.

That wasn't the worst for the Bears. Their 1–13 record, the worst in the NFL, usually meant they would get the first draft pick. The Bears had every intention of picking quarterback Terry Bradshaw out of LSU. The problem was the Pittsburgh Steelers were also 1–13, which meant there had to be a coin toss for the first pick. The Steelers won the coin toss, took Bradshaw and went on to win four Super Bowls with their number-one pick. The Bears didn't win their lone Super Bowl until 16 seasons later.

Sox fans that day didn't know yet but could have sensed that more disappointment in Chicago sports was coming. Six weeks later the Black Hawks led the Montreal Canadiens in the Stanley Cup Finals three games to two. They were on the verge of a championship when they led, 3–2, in the last period at Montreal. The game was a CBS national telecast, and the network camera occasionally focused on the Stanley Cup trophy. Black Hawks fans had

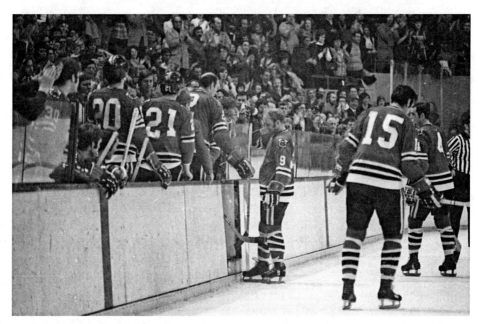

Black Hawks great Bobby Hull (#9) returning to the bench after scoring a goal. In 1971, the Black Hawks, like the other Chicago franchises, had lost a championship in a mind-boggling way. A now-revived franchise extinguished that memory with the 2010 Stanley Cup.

to be fantasizing about a trophy presentation and their team celebrating in the locker room. The trophy would erase the memories of the White Sox *el foldo* act in the last week of 1967 and the Cubs nightmare of 1969. Fans would forget about the Bears' fumbling ways and not even think about the Bulls, still one dominant player short of winning something meaningful.

Needing less than twenty minutes of hockey to hang on and win the cup, the Hawks let it slip away. Usually reliable defenseman Bill White tried to clear the puck out of the Hawks' zone but missed. Canadien Pete Maholovich stole it, moved in on Tony Esposito, and beat the Hawk goalie on his glove side. The game was tied. Montreal added another goal to win and force a deciding seventh game.

In Game Seven back at the old Chicago Stadium, the Hawks led, 2–0, in the second period. Then Jacques Lemaire of the Canadiens took a shot from beyond the blue line. It was a shot most NHL goalies handled with ease. But the Hawks' great goalie Tony Esposito lost sight of it and the puck banged into the net behind him. The Stadium went silent, and the championship seemed to be slipping away.

Momentum shifted and Montreal took a 3–2 lead. For the rest of the game, the Hawks pounded away at Canadien goalie Ken Dryden. Jim Pappin, who had scored two goals in Game Six, including a beautiful break-away score, was denied from close in by Dryden on a play that looked like a sure goal for the Hawks. Montreal held on to win and afterward skated around the Stadium ice, holding up the Stanley Cup trophy. The Stadium fell silent again.*

Additionally, the Black Hawks were one of the six original teams playing in a one-division league that formed the NHL until expansion exploded in the late sixties. In the 1926–27 season, the team fired coach Pete Muldoon. According to *Toronto Globe and Mail* sportswriter Jim Coleman, Muldoon told team owner Frederic McLaughlin, "Fire me, Major, and you'll never finish first. I'll put a curse on this team that will hoodoo it until the end of time."[4] This became known as the "Curse of Muldoon." Although Coleman later recanted the story, saying he needed something creative to meet a column deadline, the Black Hawks didn't finish first until the 1966–67 season.

As for the White Sox contributions to Chicago sports angst? During the late '60s their two best pitchers developed sore arms and were never effective again. Another young promising pitcher died in an automobile accident. A talented rookie outfielder who could hit the hell out of the ball blew off half his right thumb in a military accident and was never the same again. Another young outfielder with star potential showed awesome power by slugging a

---

*Back in the politically incorrect days of 1971, fans were allowed to smoke in their seats. There was also a haze from the Stadium ice caused by the 85-degree temperature. Did the smoke and haze hamper Esposito on Lemaire's goal? He later said there was no excuse for not making that save. Regardless, an excellent chance for a championship was lost.

homer over the Comiskey Park roof but never became a consistent major league power hitter and made some strange-looking plays in center field. Other young prospects fell well short of expectations, causing fans to have no expectations whatsoever.

So on April 9, 1971, fans wanted to believe in something, and hope for anything. Rich McKinney's bullet of a line drive gave them that hope. The White Sox looked like a real team that day, winning a close game against tough opposition. Maybe, just maybe, a Chicago team could actually do something — could actually win something.

Did the Sox deliver in 1971? Well, no. The 3–0 start turned into a seven-game losing streak and the Sox ended up four games under .500 for the season. And what of Rich McKinney? He had his career year in 1971, picking up 100 hits and eight homers. The Sox traded him to the Yankees after the '71 season. After that he picked up eight homers over seven seasons and never hit above .246. It was a minor miracle that his career lasted as long as it did.

Yet the White Sox needed that Opening Day to revive hope and bring back fans discouraged by all the failures of the Sox and every other Chicago team. The simple fact was the White Sox were the worst-performing Chicago franchise, similar to an out-of-control space ship plummeting to the earth to disintegrate before everyone's eyes. The opening days of 1971 helped right that ship, but more bad luck and losing was on the way.

5

Media Strategies I

"They lost a generation of fans."

*—This was the assessment of longtime Chicago radio and television
reporter Chet Coppock and Chicago-born sports journalist Mark Liptak.
Each used the exact same words. Others agreed when describing the decision
by the Chicago White Sox to move from WGN Channel 9 to WFLD
Channel 32 in 1968.*[1]

"He told them he wasn't giving anything away;
he told them he was creating fans."

*— Ernie Banks in late 2008 when talking about P.K. Wrigley
explaining his decision to continue with free broadcasting of Cub
home games to fellow owners.*[2]

"Arthur Allyn thought he was going to make a lot of money."

*— Lorn Brown, White Sox radio and television game broadcaster during the
late seventies and early eighties, discussing the short-term strategy of the
White Sox ownership in the late 1960s. The White Sox did make some
money but the decision had long-term disastrous effects.*

"Ahhhhhhh."

*—A woman fan, screaming in delight, was caught on a TV mike in
an otherwise quiet Channel 32 broadcast of a Sunday game in the
spring of 1968. She could be heard distinctly by the small TV audience
and sounded like she was the only fan attending the game. White Sox
second baseman Tim Cullen had been caught in a rundown between first
and second and somehow found his way safely back to first. The White Sox
had picked Cullen up in a trade earlier in the year when they sent shortstop
Ron Hansen to the Washington Senators. Later in the year Chicago traded
Cullen back to Washington. Who did they get in return? Ron Hansen.
Too bad the TV decision couldn't have been reversed so easily.*

"I have difficulty recalling the descriptive phrases."
— *Jack Drees, when talking about his new challenge as Sox play-by-play TV man beginning with the 1968 season. Drees was known more for his football and horse-racing broadcasts and was considered a consummate professional in those areas. But he spent most of the 1968 spring training catching up since he had been away from baseball broadcasting for some time.*[3]

Another turning point in Chicago baseball history came in 1968. No, neither the Cubs nor the White Sox played in a World Series; no player crashed the 60-homer barrier; and though a pitcher won 31 games that year, he didn't wear a Chicago uniform. The importance of 1968 was the impact of a media strategy that benefited the Cubs greatly in the short and long run. As for the White Sox, a seemingly lucrative but short-sighted media plan nearly destroyed its franchise and still impacts the team today.

A team's fan base is built over generations. No one single exciting season or championship will help a team set attendance records for any long period of time. The White Sox finally broke the nearly nine-decade Chicago baseball championship drought by winning the World Series in 2005. From 2005 to 2008, the team enjoyed its best four-year attendance period, drawing almost 10.5 million fans. Yet even today, the team's attendance problems are not totally over. Many fans are still leery of an ownership that some consider to be more concerned about budgets than winning. Although no one on the White Sox will publicly say it, 2009, in a large sense, was a rebuilding year. What happens if the rebuilding fails? Will the team need to rebuild its fan base again?

A different type of rebuilding for the White Sox occurred in 1968. The team severed its 20-year association with WGN-TV Channel 9. Almost the entire Sox schedule would be aired on WFLD Channel 32. Jack Drees replaced Jack Brickhouse as the TV voice of the team.

"I remember Channel 32 in its early days," baseball fan Katherine Jacobs recalled in a fond tone. "Channel 32 was owned by Marshall Field, who also owned the *Chicago Sun-Times*. *Sun-Times* reporters would appear on Channel 32 to talk about stories they were working on. That was when the *Sun-Times* was a great newspaper."[4]

So WFLD, at least in part, was used to promote another media outlet. How well would it succeed in promoting the White Sox? Would it help the White Sox in a direct financial way? With the White Sox on their own station, would they have an identity totally separate from the Cubs? The first goal for major league baseball franchises during the sixties was to draw one million fans. Reaching that figure alone didn't make a team profitable. But back then, attendance from everyday fans was the major funding stream for a ball club. Anything less than a million fans meant bad things for any major league baseball

Radio man Lou Boudreau with Cubs pitcher Rick Reuschel in 1976. By the end of 1970 no major radio outlet was interested in airing the White Sox.

organization. And for the White Sox, despite some success in the sixties, attendance was dropping as the decade progressed. In 1966 and 1967, the team failed to break the one million mark. Attendance had been falling every year since the Sox set a record in 1960, when the club basked in the glow of the 1959 World Series. Although the White Sox still hoped to improve attendance, the Sox now sought a new revenue source: Television.

"The White Sox were tired of splitting time with the Cubs," says sports journalist Mark Liptak. "Arthur Allyn [White Sox owner at the time] thought he should be getting a bigger piece of the pie. And WFLD made a good offer."[5]

"The White Sox were almost broke," Chicago sports radio talk show host Chet Coppock recalls. "They got a million dollars a year. But here was the error. WFLD was an UHF station that had only 9 percent penetration of the market. Ninety-one percent of Chicago couldn't see the White Sox. Meanwhile, the Cubs had Banks, Santo, Williams and Jenkins. All of these players were box office attractions. The kids became enamored with the 1969 Cubs. The White Sox were falling off the map."[6]

Chet Coppock was just starting out in his Chicago broadcasting career in 1968, working as an off-the-air employee for WFLD. Coppock remembers WFLD as a fledgling station with a microscopic sports department. He mentioned a time when retired Bears great Red Grange had come into town and the station had no on-air people to interview him. Coppock volunteered to do the interview so he could demonstrate his journalistic talent. But he compared the decision by the White Sox to move from WGN to WFLD to the wreck of the *Edmund Fitzgerald,* an ore ship that sank in Lake Superior in late 1975, killing all 29 crew members. The tragedy was immortalized in a song by Gordon Lightfoot in 1976.

"The stab wounds were fatal," Coppock said, describing the decision to move the White Sox to WFLD.[7] Coppock's tone grew more intense as he looked back at what he perceived as one of the worst things the franchise has ever done.

Jack Brickhouse agreed that the move to Channel 32 was the wrong thing to do. He is quoted in the biography *Jack Brickhouse — A Voice for All Seasons* by Janice Petterchak as saying:

> On paper it looked great, a five-year deal with a five-year option, for a lot more money than WGN had offered. Allyn thought, I'll have my own station; I won't have to share time with the Cubs.
> But it turned out to be a bad idea. WFLD was a UHF station; above Channel 12 was UHF. It was not as reliable as VHF, especially in the summertime, because its low-carrying sound waves could not penetrate the foliage on trees and bushes. Also, in those days, a lot of sets couldn't get UHF without a good adapter. One of the reasons WFLD wanted the White Sox was that viewers who wanted to see the games had to buy adaptors.
> But the White Sox did not play good ball those years, and the Cubs were somewhat better. We killed them in the ratings. They were getting asterisks; we were getting fifteens, twenties, twenty-twos. Today, my gosh, that's unbelievable. After the first five years, WFLD was taking such a beating that they didn't take the second five-year option.[8]

Mark Liptak has said that it would have made more sense to see if local network affiliates would have taken on the White Sox.[9] Technical problems would have been nonexistent in comparison and the team would have had more exposure. But Liptak said these network affiliates were not going to preempt their prime-time programming to accommodate the White Sox.[10] So WFLD it was.

According to Coppock, "Jack Brickhouse implored Arthur Allyn not to go WFLD. Jack negotiated TV contracts. He was a very good negotiator and he had power."[11]

"Jack Brickhouse has been associated with the Cubs for so long," Mark Liptak said. "But he loved the Sox. Brickhouse was shocked that the Sox were leaving WGN. He met with Arthur Allyn after the 1967 season to get the Sox owner to change his mind."[12]

But Allyn remained undeterred and the White Sox had a new flagship TV station, debuting on April 10. The baseball season had been postponed due to the assassination of Martin Luther King. It was the traumatic year of 1968 and American cities burned. The neighborhood around Comiskey was not considered safe. Even though the White Sox came so close to going to the World Series in 1967, the Opening Day crowd in 1968 was a minuscule 7,756. As bad as the turnout was, the game was worse.

Cleveland pounded Chicago, 9–0. Pete Ward was in right field, and he played fly balls into triples. The White Sox picked up two hits, both singles. The opener was memorable for all the wrong reasons. Then things worsened. Chicago lost its next nine.

Starting the season with a 10-game losing streak and scoring 13 runs in the process was not good for TV ratings. It also didn't help that the team's new TV voice was not catching on with the fans. Jack Drees was a seasoned announcer in other sports. As the quote at the beginning of the chapter indicates, he was a little rusty when it came to baseball. He also didn't have the charisma and the Chicago feeling of a Jack Brickhouse.

"There wasn't a more decent guy than Jack Drees," Chet Coppock said of the 6'6" announcer. "But he was vanilla and had no connection to Chicago. Brickhouse also had the ability to sell the neighborhood."[13] The White Sox–Bridgeview neighborhood had a bad reputation before the turmoil of 1968, even though the reputation wasn't always earned. The Wrigleyville area was considered by some as not much better or even worse.

Meanwhile, the chemistry in the Channel 32 booth wasn't working. Drees did play-by-play for five years and had four different color men. Billy Pierce was the most popular of the color men, even though he had no TV voice. It helped that he had been a great pitcher with the Sox. In 2007 a statue of him would be put up in U.S. Cellular Field. But Coppock said this of the once-dominating left-hander: "Even Billy would tell you he wasn't a color man."[14]

No, hardly anyone said a bad word about the likable Jack Drees. But for the most part, White Sox fans of that generation remember Cubs-White Sox announcer Jack Brickhouse. It was Brickhouse who called the 1959 pennant-clinching game and suffered along with White Sox fans during the mid-sixties as the club just couldn't match up with the prowess of the Yankees.

By today's standards Jack Brickhouse would be known as an unrepentant homer, a play-by-play man who would never say a negative thing about the home team. Fly balls just short of the warning track were described as well-hit drives even when they became routine outs, and losing teams were valiant in their effort no matter how lackluster their performance appeared to be. Somehow, he thought a critical comment took something away from his broadcast.

In portraying himself, Brickhouse was self-mocking, once describing himself as "all-thumbs" in a beer commercial. He also had an "aw-shucks" attitude, somehow never getting over the fact that he was paid to watch baseball. Jack Brickhouse portrayed himself as the common man who had the good fortune of being behind the microphone.

Until 1988, all Cubs home games were day contests. During his broadcasts,

Brickhouse aimed at three audiences: The stressed-out adult who needed to "forget his problems," the "shut-ins" that had health issues serious enough that they couldn't leave their homes, and starry-eyed kids that dreamed they could some-day be baseball heroes even if it was only in Little League.

The kids seemed to be his main au-dience whether he realized it or not. During one of his "Lead-off Man" seg-ments, when he interviewed players right before game time, he had Ernie Banks demonstrate his swing. In a July 29, 1967, "Tenth Inning" show, which aired his post-game interview, Brickhouse asked White Sox third baseman Ken Boyer about a two-run homer he had hit in the first inning that day. "How many is that for you?" Brickhouse asked. Boyer sheepishly said it was only his fourth.[15] Brickhouse was not trying to embarrass Boyer; he was attempting to give a sim-ple piece of information to his audi-ence. In 1967, there was no Internet, no

Jack Brickhouse in 1979. He was one of the most influential play-by-play men in Chicago broadcast history. A statue of him stands by the Tribune Tower.

ESPN, no instant information for anyone who wanted it. If a fan missed the daily sports page, it was easy to forget how many home runs Ken Boyer had.

Brickhouse had a little kid type of approach to his broadcasting at times. When Ernie Banks hit his 500th career home run, Brickhouse was thrilled that the ball had bounced out of the bleachers so it could it be saved for the Cubs star. In describing the last out of Joe Horlen's September 10, 1967, no-hitter at Comiskey Park, Brickhouse got a little nervous. Shortstop Ron Hansen seemed to be taking a long time to dig the ball out of his glove before throwing over to first. "Throw it, Ronnie, throw it," he yelled into the microphone. Ron did. Horlen had his no-hitter and Brickhouse celebrated.

"He always seemed to be a nice man," said long-time White Sox fan Eliz-abeth Harvey. "He was kind of like your grandpa but I don't think he ever talked down to people. He explained a lot of what was happening on the field and I think he helped create a whole generation of Cubs fans."[16]

Hal Vickery traces his origins as a White Sox fan to watching a WGN broadcast in the late fifties at a relative's home. Brickhouse enthusiastically called a double by Sox shortstop Chico Carrasquel. Later when he went home, he told his family about the double, and reveled in Brickhouse's emotion. From that point on, Vickery was hooked as a Sox fan, but also remembered Brickhouse as the type of announcer who seemed to be speaking directly to kids. "Brickhouse described a play and then said, 'If you're scoring,'" Vickery recalls. "That's how I learned to keep score."[17]

It seemed that WGN-TV, as a broadcast rule, chose to educate the viewership. In the mid-sixties, the station began broadcasting the Black Hawks' away games. Hockey was not known to the average fan like other sports. So Hawk announcer Lloyd Pettit (who was the radio voice as well) would patiently go over the rules of the game. Again and again he slowly and methodically informed his viewers what constituted icing and offside. Before long, his "shot and a goal" became as familiar and exciting as Brickhouse's "hey-hey." In the late sixties a song was composed for the team and its last line has Pettit's signature call. The song is still used today, although some younger fans may not know the origin of "shot and a goal."

During one Hawks home playoff game in the early seventies, several fans sat in Comiskey Park huddled around hand-sized radio. They weren't getting play-by-play description of the Sox game. They were listening to Pettit as he frantically described the Black Hawks being outplayed by an opponent. The only thing that kept them in the game was their standout goalie, Tony Esposito.

On the left is Lloyd Pettit in 1970. Pettit was one of the greatest hockey announcers of all time. He was instrumental in helping create a rabid Black Hawk fan base during the sixties. "A shot and a goal" was his signature call.

As the opponent pounded away at Esposito, Pettit's voice turned raspy as he called the non-stop action. Finally he said, "I'm getting hoarse, ladies and gentlemen, I'm getting hoarse." During another opponent foray into the Hawks' zone, Pettit yelled or actually gasped into the microphone, "There's a shot and save, another shot and save, and Esposito holds on." The Hawks' goalie squeezed the puck in his glove to stop the action and force a face-off. Pettit got to rest his tired throat as the Black Hawk faithful cheered their goalie. Back then, in the old and small Chicago Stadium, the announced and legal capacity was a little more than 16,600. But the team sold standing-room tickets by the scores and fans stood two and three deep in the upper balconies. Crowds sometimes exceeded 20,000. In the old-fashioned and cozy stadium, the noise generated by 20,000 rabid fans had nowhere to escape. As a result, it multiplied and fed on itself, and the energy and emotion overcame anyone attending or even listening to the radio. That game was even louder and more intense than usual, with Esposito turning in another one of his great performances. The fan cheering pounded over the airwaves. Back at Comiskey, the listening fans silently gazed at each other in amazement at the pulsating sound, the mental image of Tony Esposito sliding all over the crease and somehow keeping the puck out of the net, but mostly at the performance of Lloyd Pettit. Yes, it was the crowds and players like Esposito that made the Black Hawks such a great attraction at the time. But it was Lloyd Pettit who made people listen. It was Pettit who helped build and educate a fan base. And it was largely because of Lloyd Pettit that several people sat in an almost-hypnotic state and listened to a hockey broadcast while attending a major league baseball game.

"I remember coming home from school and watching the last part of the Cubs game on TV," Cubs fan Greg Redlarczyk remembers.[18] And it was even easier for Redlarczyk because his parents' home was directly across the street from his grade school. Redlarczyk had no use for Brickhouse whom he felt sugar-coated the Cubs' failures and kissed up to P.K. Wrigley. But he didn't miss those television games.

Redlarczyk's pleasant memory is familiar but also significant. Before 1967, Wrigley was empty and the games lacked excitement as the Cubs routinely lost. But when the team finally improved, Wrigley became crowded and noisy. Meanwhile, White Sox viewership dwindled, and the Cubs began converting more and more fans. According to Mark Liptak, Brickhouse was prophetic in more ways than one. Liptak maintains that Brickhouse knew technology was changing and advancing, which meant WGN-TV would eventually become more than a local station.[19] In the end, not only did the Cubs expand their local base, the club attracted fans from across the nation on the WGN superstation. One-time Sox announcer Lorn Brown also worked for the Mets when that team had its TV schedule on cable. Brown said that fans came up and greeted him in many major league cities due to the nationwide exposure of the Mets.[20]

In the book *Center Field Shot—A History of Baseball on Television*, James Walker and Robert Bellamy, Jr., traced the Cubs' media strategy back to the 1930s and 1940s. According to Walker and Bellamy, even back then the strategy was to constantly market the Cubs and Wrigley Field by opening up their team to just about every radio outlet. The authors quote new Giants broadcaster Russ Hodges:

> Chicago was wide open in all other respects so it shouldn't have been a surprise to me that there were almost no radio restrictions either. But I must admit I found it something of a shock to find the press boxes of Wrigley Field and Comiskey Park crawling with play-by-play announcers.[21]

So in effect, appearances in the sixties were grossly deceiving. While the White Sox outdrew the Cubs and piled up winning seasons until the last part of the decade, it was the Cubs who were on the verge of creating a solid fan base with decades of radio and television exposure. In the meantime, the White Sox lost viewers because of the move to WFLD. In 1971, the team could not find a major Chicago radio station to carry its schedule after the 106-loss 1970 season. The White Sox were slowly being pushed out of the minds of Chicago baseball fans because of these media mishaps. Their situation was worsened by their dismal on-the-field performance that rivaled the Cubs' darkest days in their lightless stadium it marketed as "the Friendly Confines."

Much has been said in Chapter 3 about the rivalry between the Yankees and the White Sox. An invasion by the Yankees into Chicago brought large crowds and great excitement when New York was winning pennants and Chicago was trying to upset them. But as the Yankees faded and the White Sox collapsed, the rivalry lost its intensity. In 1964, when New York edged out Chicago by one game to win another pennant, the Yankees' eight dates at Comiskey Park drew 259,807 fans, for an average of 32,475. In 1967, when the White Sox contended and the Yankees did not, New York had seven dates in Chicago and drew only 120,229, for an average of 17,175. In 1969, when both teams were going nowhere, the total for six Chicago dates was 55,614, for an average of 9,269. It can be argued the White Sox lost more fans as their rivalry with the Yankees fizzled and died.

Secondly, over their objections, the White Sox were placed into the newly formed Western Division in 1969. Owner Arthur Allyn complained about harm done to traditional rivalries and lost radio and TV money due to West Coast games. The team lost three home games against such traditional rivals as the Yankees, Tigers, Orioles and Red Sox. At the same time, they gained nine games against the expansion Kansas City Royals and Seattle Pilots. With the Oakland A's recent move to the Bay Area and the creation of the Seattle franchise, the White Sox now had 27 games on the West Coast. In addition to lost revenues, these games were either not televised or rarely seen directly due to the time change. On June 24, 1969, third baseman Bill Melton hit three homers against Seattle and barely missed a fourth when he doubled to left in the ninth. The game wasn't televised, and even if it had been, hardly anyone would have seen it on WFLD. Because of its late start, the game was barely reported on or covered by any media outlet, even locally. The White Sox could have used the exposure for their young hitter during a time when the franchise was completely eclipsed by the surging Cubs.

After the 1971 season, the Washington Senators moved to Arlington, Texas, to become the Texas Rangers. The White Sox again wanted to get into the East as the Rangers were transferred to the West. Instead, the Milwaukee Brewers (formerly the Seattle Pilots) were moved into the East. The Brewers were in their third season in Milwaukee.

"The White Sox made a good case," according to longtime Chicago radio and television reporter and current media consultant Tom Shaer. "But somebody had to be screwed and they [the American League] wanted to shore up the Milwaukee franchise more than the White Sox."[22]

All that can be said about the politics of American League baseball in the early seventies is that the White Sox and Rangers have never had much of a rivalry.

The Chicago Black Hawks and the TV Model for Increasing Attendance

The decline of the Black Hawks began back in 1972 when Bobby Hull left the Hawks for the newly formed World Hockey Association. Hull was the third player in NHL history to score 50 goals in a season. Known as the "Golden Jet," Hull had a slap shot timed at close to 120 mph. He once broke the glass at the Chicago Stadium. On another occasion the force of his shot knocked a goalie flat on his back. The goalie had made the save initially, but the puck hit the ice on its side and rolled in. Hull was known for his rink-wide dashes in which he skated past and through the opposition before terrorizing another goalie with a shot that could hardly be seen. Chicago went to the Stanley Cup finals in its first year without Hull, but would not win the cup until 2010. At the height of the Hawks' popularity in the sixties, fans would have to go to the Stadium at noon the day of the game to buy standing-room tickets. The alternative was getting fleeced by a scalper. As time went on, tickets — even playoff tickets — were easier to come by.

The years 2003 to 2008 were good ones for Chicago sports. The White Sox won their World Series in 2005 and came up with another division crown in dramatic fashion in 2008. The Cubs won three division crowns and came within one game of the Series in 2003. The Bears made their second trip to the Super Bowl. Even the Bulls, who had languished at the bottom of the NBA in a post–Michael Jordan era, won a playoff series. But the Hawks couldn't make it to the playoffs even though half of the NHL qualifies for post-season play. According to a *Chicago Tribune* fan poll in 2007, only 8 percent of Chicago sports fans identified themselves as Black Hawk fans.

For years, Black Hawks fans called for home games to be televised. William Wirtz, who began running the team in 1966, refused to allow it. Less than two months after his death, and with interest in the team tail-spinning, the Black Hawks announced that all their games would be televised for the first time in team history. The deal was worked out with Comcast Sports Net and WGN-TV.

According to information provided on the Black Hawks' website, the move brought immediate results. The 2007-08 team had 12 sellouts and overall attendance increased 47 percent over the previous year. The team site further stated that Hawk merchandise revenue rose by 175 percent and season ticket sales for 2008-09 increased by 300 percent.

In an article by Teddy Greenstein in the February 3, 2009, edition of the *Chicago Tribune*, a new fan poll now showed that 16 percent of Chicago fans identified themselves with the Hawks. At the time the article ran, all twenty-three Black Hawks home games had been sold out. The sellouts would continue with the Hawks' first trip to the playoffs since 2002. The team advanced to its conference finals for the first time since 1996.

Greenstein's article named Black Hawks president John McDonough as one of the architects of the new-found success. McDonough, a former president of the Cubs, has been credited with creating the Cubs' fan convention and as the man behind the marketing strategy that helped build Chicago baseball attendance records. Greenstein wrote that McDonough still felt the Hawks had a long way to go before the franchise achieved real success. "The car is just backing out of the garage," Greenstein quoted McDonough as saying. "We haven't even hit the street yet."[23]

How much of the Hawks' resurgence was due to its new television policy? Of all the major sports, hockey can be the toughest to follow on TV. The game is incredibly fast, the puck can be hard to pick up, and many goals happen due to tip-ins that are hard for even the most savvy hockey fan to see. Yet it was clear in the 2008-09 season that televised games didn't detract from home attendance, and team interest was only increasing. It remains to be seen if television and other marketing strategies will provide the hockey team with a larger fan base.

Would a different TV strategy in the late sixties have been a help to the White Sox? One thing can be said: More fans saw Cubs games than Sox games on TV and now more fans go to Wrigley than to U.S. Cellular Field. It is a long-time trend that shows no signs of changing.

6

A New Cult Figure

"I'm not Veeck. I don't sit around and say
'What's the craziest thing we can do?'"[1]

— *Chicago White Sox vice president and chief
marketing officer Brooks Boyer*

"Typical low-rent stuff ... their fans are so consumed with
jealousy that they'd rather see the Cubs lose than their team win.
My simple response is: The Cubs don't NEED any advertising
to get fans to come out to their ballpark."

— *Cub fan post on chicagoist.com in response to a 2004 advertisement
depicting the differences between Cub and Sox fans*[2]

The actual ad, entitled "Sox Pride," ran like this:

THEY: Are lovable when they lose
WE: Hate losing
THEY: Champions in 1908
WE: Champions as recently as 1917
THEY: Believe they are cursed
WE: Agree
THEY: Got Wood
WE: Got lumber
THEY: Have a fan who says, "Woo."
WE: Don't
THEY: Need tickets? See a broker
WE: Call 966-SOX-GAME[3]

Oh, and the mayor likes *us* better. [The team can now proudly add that the president likes us better, too.]

At first glance, the commercial seemed a little childish. It came across as "my team is better than your team" in the same way as saying "my dog is better than yours." The commercial was aired in the middle of June, about 10 days before the 2004 Crosstown Classic that started in U.S. Cellular Field. And it described White Sox fans as smarter and more sophisticated than a bunch of Cubs fans who believed in curses and a grown male mascot. It also cleverly took a shot at a potent asset of the Cubs: their attendance.

It was galling and funny, but there was a risk to running the advertisement. What if the Cubs came into the South Side and made mincemeat of the White Sox? Who would be the rube now? Yet the audacity of the advertisement was one of its true assets. White Sox fans wanted nothing to do with a loudmouth shouting "Woo-woo." Curses have nothing to do with losing, and White Sox fans hate losing. Now come down to our ballpark and make something of it, if you dare.

Cubs fans were appalled and some of the media echoed those feelings. What was this sniping at Cubs tradition? Is it the same old White Sox fan pettiness? Why do the White Sox and their fans worry about the Cubs so much? Cubs fans could not care less about what happens on the South Side.

In a sense, it was a little surprising that the organization let marketing man Brooks Boyer run the ad. Six years earlier, the then-flagship station of the White Sox, WMVP-AM 1000, put an advertisement on a billboard in the Wrigley area that read, "Major League Baseball 8.1 Miles South." The Sox had signed Albert Belle to a five-year contract and the Cubs seemed to be headed for another putrid season. Cubs fans even proclaimed the signing of Belle as "unfair." Jerry Reinsdorf was not crazy about the billboard, and the White Sox as an organization denied any involvement with the advertisement. He requested that the board come down, and his request was granted. "I know they meant it in good fun, but I didn't like it," Reinsdorf told the *Sun-Times* in 1997. "I know how I'd feel if they did it to us. We have nothing against the Chicago Cubs."[4]

"That was stabbing, taking a real shot," Brooks Boyer told Teddy Greenstein of the *Tribune*, in reference to the 1997 billboard. He was quoted in a Greenstein article on the commercial that ran in the June 15, 2004, edition of the *Tribune*. "That's not what this ad is about. We are who we are. We can poke fun at ourselves."[5]

In 1997, Cubs president John McDonough said he was flattered by the attention. And as things turned out, the Sox would have no reason to gloat. That year turned out to be both a public relations and on-the-field disaster.

Actually, laughter was needed on the South Side to provide comic relief to the manic-depressive state of the franchise. A rift had opened between the White Sox organization and its fans, beginning with the players union strike, which ended the 1994 season. The White Sox were in first place at the time, and it was widely believed the team had a real chance of going to the World Series. Having only a one-game lead over second-place Cleveland, the White Sox were not guaranteed to win its division. Yet many thought 1994 was the year. When baseball resumed in 1995, anger was heaped on Jerry Reinsdorf, the other owners, and the players. The new Comiskey Park, which drew more than 8.1 million in its first three full years, was now half-empty as the White Sox failed to regain their pre-strike form.

The White Sox were hurt by the 1994 work stoppage more than any other team. The club appeared ready to take Chicago back from the Cubs, who were in last place at the time of the strike. The strike put the Cubs fans out of their misery. For Sox fans, the misery was just beginning. Going into the last weekend of 1995, the Cubs had an outside shot at the wild card; the White Sox had been out of the pennant race from the beginning of the season.

With time, things only worsened. In an August 10, 1996, game, the White Sox led the Baltimore Orioles, 4–3, going into the top of the eighth. Sox starting pitcher Wilson Alvarez gave up two doubles, and the game was tied. Alvarez then allowed a third double that shot into the gap and knocked against the wall. Terry Bevington, who had never been a popular manager, came out to a bevy of boos to pull his pitcher one batter too late. The frustration and anger, brewing since the 1994 strike, resonated throughout the ballpark.

Then came July 31, 1997. Declaring the White Sox out of playoff contention, Jerry Reinsdorf shipped three veterans to San Francisco for six unknowns. Reinsdorf engineered this deal despite the fact that an injured Robin Ventura was returning to the lineup with the White Sox only 3½ games behind the first-place Indians. The San Francisco deal became known as the "White Flag Trade." Many White Sox fans fumed. The trade represented another rebuilding effort, as it appeared that the 1990s would mark the fourth consecutive decade with no World Series appearance. The year 1959 represented the only time the team made it to the Fall Classic since the 1919 Black Sox scandal. How long was this rebuilding going to take?

The year 1998 came and went with no healing between team and fans. On a Sunday afternoon on July 19, the White Sox played the division-leading Cleveland Indians. In one of its best performances of the year, Chicago won easily, 8–1. Starting pitcher Mike Sirotka threw a complete game four-hitter. Frank Thomas hit a towering home run to center. The Indians, who committed three errors, were never in the game. It was a beautiful summer day with a sunny, cloudless sky, and everything seemed right on the South Side of Chicago.

Yet everything wasn't right. Many of the more than 23,000 in attendance were Indians fans who made the trip down the toll road for the contest. The left-center-field bleachers were packed with Indians faithful who screamed insults at Sox left fielder Albert Belle, who had left Cleveland to sign his five-year deal with the Sox. The Sox were still rebuilding and their fans weren't warming up to the concept. Without the Indians fans, new Comiskey Park in 1998 would have looked like old Comiskey Park in 1970. Despite seeing their team get pasted that day, Indians fans arrogantly sneered that "the Jake" (the

Danny Darwin in 1997. He was part of the infamous "White Flag Trade." The trade created a more widening rift between the White Sox and their fans.

nickname for Cleveland's Jacobs Field, now known as Progressive Field) was always selling out and never would look like this.

Meanwhile, rebuilding continued into the 1999 season and fans still weren't warming to the concept. Opening Day at Comiskey in 1999 was an awful experience for team and fans. Wintry conditions and a fierce wind made it feel like January. Worse yet, the White Sox played a terrible game, committing five errors and losing, 10–5, to the powerhouse Kansas City Royals. Greg Norton had been inserted at third to replace the departed Robin Ventura, who as a free agent had moved over to the Mets. Norton looked totally out of his element, and even had a hard time making a throw to second on a force play. Norton, who was not a third baseman by trade, should not have been put in this position. The crowd of 26,243 was the lowest home Opening Day turnout in nearly a quarter of a century. It appeared that attendance would remain a problem.

White Sox players couldn't help but notice the fan apathy and wanted to prove something when they went to play the Cubs in Wrigley Field on the weekend of June 11–13. When leadoff man Ray Durham went to the plate to start the opening game, he didn't walk. Instead, he almost ran, he was so anxious. Durham and the rest of the team responded by sweeping the Cubs. Shortstop Mike Caruso, one of the cornerstones of the White Flag Trade, hit the game-winning homer into the Wrigley right-field basket to complete the sweep. It was one of only two homers Caruso hit that year in 529 official at-bats.

White Sox fans celebrated. A sweep at Wrigley? Who would have thought it? This was the year after Sammy Sosa's 66-home run barrage and the Cubs' wild-card championship. Weren't the Cubs the superior team with a chance to go the playoffs? Sox fans loved to point out that year that the Cubs disintegrated after the White Sox sweep. Going into the series they were in second place with a 32–24 record and just two games behind first-place Houston. After the series, they won one and then went on a five-game losing streak. At the beginning of July, the Cubs lost four straight, giving up 60 runs in the process. The North Siders' 1999 season had started with such hope, but the Cubs ended up in last with a 67–95 record. The White Sox, a team with far less expectations, finished 21 games behind first-place Cleveland but still won eight more games than the Cubs. Sammy Sosa hit another 63 home runs, but did it matter? It was just another decade without a World Series.

The White Sox hoped the three-game Cub sweep would win back their estranged fan base. It didn't. Immediately following the Cub dismantling, only 15,457 showed for the next home game, a 9–7 win over Tampa Bay. White Sox radio broadcasters were beside themselves with disappointment. Where was everybody? What did the team have to do to draw again?

At the SoxFest fan convention in January 2000, manager Jerry Manuel told fans he expected a great deal from his team that season. Having such expectations seemed a little unrealistic since the club had suffered three straight losing seasons and was still a young team. But Manuel insisted that he wasn't going to accept youth as any excuse for failure. It was time to step up and perform. The rebuilding was now supposed to produce some winning.

After losing to the Cubs on June 10 but winning that three-game series, the White Sox stood at 37–24. Surprisingly, the South Siders stood on top of the AL Central, two games ahead of the defending champion Indians. Maybe Manuel was right in making his demands. This team looked ready to contend.

But this was Chicago baseball. Fans had been let down in a variety of ways, including a strike that made a season and a declared Central Division title meaningless. The Sox were heading out on a seven-game road trip with three in Cleveland and four at Yankee Stadium. If this team were really as good as advertised, a 4–3 or even 3–4 trip against two of the top teams in the American League would go a long way in demonstrating the club was for real.

The White Sox lived up to Jerry Manuel's expectations and then some. Chicago actually went 7–0 while winning in just about every conceivable way. The trip was topped off by a 17–4 shellacking of the Yankees that had the 52,000 fans in the Bronx booing their defending world champions. During the seven games, the Sox scored 70 runs. They came home 20 games over .500, increased their lead by 5½ games on the second-place Indians, and sported the best record in all of baseball.

Matt Cianchetti was one fan who wanted to go out to Comiskey to cheer on the triumphant Sox when they began a homestand against the Indians. He was surprised to find that he could only get a couple of seats in the top regions of the dreaded upper deck. On the way to the ballpark, he found himself in a huge traffic jam, and couldn't get off the expressway until the game reached the fourth inning. Then he couldn't find a lot to park his car, and he saw many fans still roaming the streets looking for tickets. With no place for his car, Cianchetti left his tickets at the will call window and went to a bar to watch the game.

"We later heard on the radio that the game was a complete sellout and the reason the parking lots were all sold out was that an estimated 56,000 people had descended on the ballpark," Cianchetti said. "Maybe they thought they could park and just go up to the ticket window, only to find the game was sold out. Not to mention they blocked those who had tickets from getting in."[6]

Having too many fans come to their ballpark was a nice problem for the Sox to have. But it was not all peaches and cream. Some fans, who felt they had supported the team in bad times, held signs that read, "WHERE WERE YOU?" There was some bitterness in the midst of success as part of the crowd was looked upon as bandwagon jumpers. And the next night only a little over 20,000 showed to watch a first-place team on an eight-game winning streak.

Playing well in June is one thing, but one of the true tests of a team is its standing on the first day of September. The White Sox returned to Chicago after another successful road trip in which they took two out of three from both Seattle and Oakland, the two top teams in the American League West. More importantly, the club was still safely perched in first place in the Central. Cleveland was still within striking distance, but no collapse from the White Sox seemed imminent. The team seemed to be heading to the playoffs.

However, unlike in June, there were no traffic jams created by throngs of fans. Only a little more than 16,000 bothered to come see a first-place baseball team in a two-team city that hadn't experienced a meaningful division championship in seven years. The White Sox played a dramatic game, scoring six in the eighth inning to erase an 8–3 deficit to win, 9–8. Though relatively small in number, the fans who attended screamed with delight.

As September wore on and the White Sox drew closer to a division title that few other than Jerry Manuel had expected them to win, attendance wasn't great and enthusiasm didn't run high. Playoff tickets were relatively easy to get. The team finished the season drawing over 1.9 million, a nice increase from the listless 1999 season. But the 2000 season still remains as the lowest attendance mark of any franchise division winner.*

The media and sports pundits were stumped by the apparent fan apathy. But it appeared that the bitterness of the middle and late '90s had remained. The White Sox had the best record in the American League, but the happiness seemed restrained. Would fans ever return? Regardless, the White Sox were swept from the playoffs by Seattle.

By the beginning of 2004, the rebuilding effort that began with the White Flag Trade in 1997 was officially over. Jerry Manuel was fired after the 2003 season and replaced by Ozzie Guillen. None of the players acquired in the unpopular trade remained on the White Sox major league roster. The rebuilding did produce some success with a division championship and the development of such players as Paul Konerko, Magglio Ordonez and Carlos Lee. But the World Series appearance remained elusive, and after the end of 2004, the Sox waved good-bye to Ordonez and Lee in different but decisive manners.

Thus, by the middle of 2004, the franchise still needed to rebuild its fan base after all the bitterness. The hiring of Ozzie Guillen was a signal that the team was heading in a new direction. Yet it was a commercial that helped start to reverse the ten-year trend of drooping attendance and fan alienation.

To put it simply, White Sox fans were enthralled by the ad noting the difference between Sox and Cubs fans. Okay, so Sox fans can be grouchy, can bitch a lot, and don't care to understand what is so great about Cubs tradition. But they are what they are and they don't want to be identified with an obnoxious cheerleader or think losing can be associated with fun in some way.

"It had a specific theme," Greenstein said, referring to the ad. "It gave the fan base a surge of pride because it celebrated the difference between them and Cub fans."[7]

Also, the White Sox faithful don't want to be a fan of both teams. Finally someone in the city understood who they were and embraced them.

Brooks Boyer was that man. Some thought the ad had too much attitude and jealousy, but Boyer seemed to take the criticism in stride. The marketing

---

*This excludes the strike-shortened 1994 season where the division title had no value and attendance comparisons are not valid.

man was acting like a campaign manager advising his candidate to solidify his base to win his party's nomination. Consensus building and reaching out to the other side could happen later. For now it is needed to win over the faithful, the activists, and the lifelong partisans. The candidate can be a statesman later. And for the White Sox, offending Cubs fans was the last thing the team needed to worry about. For too long, their political base had strayed and it was time to bring that base back home.

The White Sox team website biography on Boyer stated, "In 2005 and 2006 the team's 'take the field' audio and video montage were well received by Sox fans."[8] That is an understatement. Fans are mesmerized by the video that runs through Sox history in a few minutes. They are hypnotized by the images of old newspaper headlines, the different uniforms during the ongoing decades, and the action highlights of dramatic home runs, championship celebrations (few that there are), and other moments that bring memories — memories of baseball, personal memories that range from childhood to adulthood, and history, lots and lots of history. What is sometimes missed is that every game is history and one thing that will bring fans to the park is the idea of being a participating observer of that history. Each fan experiences his or her memories watching that video. They will watch it time and again, making damn sure that they are in their seats when the video runs, even though the images never change. Yet in a sense, those images do change and they provoke that feeling part of the team history that enable fans to identify with the team again and again.* "It [the White Sox montage] gives me chills even when it is 80 degrees," Greenstein said.[9]

Boyer, like any marketing person, will admit that a winning team will make the selling effort so much easier. The White Sox needed that 2005 world championship. But as Chicago baseball fans know more than anyone else, a World Series doesn't happen every year. The selling has to continue, especially when it comes to cynical White Sox fans. And at the end of 2008, Boyer had a simple but effective idea.

It was a black towel event when the White Sox faced the Minnesota Twins in a one-game playoff to decide which team was going to be the American League Central Division champion. Rally towels were nothing new. However, doing something like this was new for a White Sox game. Boyer wanted every one of the 40,000 fans to wave a towel. The promotion was referred to as a "black out." The image of rabid fans waving towels over their heads was a sharp contrast to the images of dark and empty stadiums that dominated Chicago White Sox history for the better part of four decades.

Boyer also had something that was missing from the Sox marketing depart-

---

*Boyer had worked for the Bulls' marketing department for ten years before coming to the Sox. The Bulls routine of player introduction was a production that could give goose bumps even to a casual fan.

ment for years: An attitude. On the morning of the September 30 showdown with the Twins, Boyer appeared on WSCR-AM 670 The Score with morning hosts Mike Mulligan and Brian Hanley. Boyer hyped the game that had sold out in about an hour and then threw out a challenge to the Twins. "They look at themselves as piranhas," Boyer said of Minnesota. "They're coming into 40,000 sharks tonight."[10]

Forget that the Sox won only one of nine contests in the Minnesota Metrodome. Forget that the Sox had lost the season series to the Twins and that many were whining that it wasn't fair that the Sox got to play at home because of a coin flip. Not only were the Twins going to face a determined team, they would have to deal with a hostile crowd. That was the continued brilliance of Boyer's marketing. The team was making the fans part of the action and hopefully part of the winning.

The White Sox clinched the division title with a 1–0 win, and many White Sox fans will always remember center fielder Brian Anderson's diving catch to end the game. Later, during the playoffs, Tampa Bay manager Joe Maddon remarked about how well the White Sox play in their own building after Chicago's lone playoff win.[11] Was that because U.S. Cellular Field is designed for Sox home run hitters? Or does it also help to play in front of an enthusiastic crowd that had not been there even during the division-winning year of 2000? How much does marketing help create this environment?

Contrast this to what front office man Stu Holcomb told team organist Nancy Faust to do in 1970. Holcomb gave the Sox organist a list of Sox players and their home states. He instructed her to play the state song when the player came to the plate. The White Sox had several players from Oklahoma. How likely would it be for fans to recognize the Oklahoma state song? Not likely at all. Would they even care if someone told them it was the Oklahoma state song? How is that for getting fans involved?

The season before, the team ran a weekly highlight show on seldom-watched WFLD. One show ran a so-called highlight of White Sox infielder Sandy Alomar getting picked off first. Yeah, that is what a fan wants to see: One of his own getting caught leaning the other way. Why don't they just say how lousy they are?

The successes from the 2005 through the 2008 seasons, with two 90-win teams, two division crowns and a world championship, did wonders to recharge the White Sox fan base. Yet fans also have responded to Brooks Boyer's marketing. He has put a cheerful face on the organization, which has helped erase some of the fan alienation of the nineties.

Brooks Boyer may consider himself as being far different than Bill Veeck, a man who felt slighted by the current White Sox ownership. But their main philosophies are at least similar. Fans want to feel a part of their team and that will not happen if that team only worries about numbers.

Organist Nancy Faust shown during her first year with the White Sox in 1970 at her center-field station. She has been a fan favorite ever since.

I attended the July 10, 2004, White Sox game against Seattle. The Sox led, 3–2, and closer Shingo Takatsu came in to finish off the ninth inning. As he exited the bullpen, a gong went off and echoed through the stadium, an obvious reference to Takatsu's Japanese ancestry. The 37,405 in attendance loved it and loved it more when Takatsu got the side out in order. Fun was returning to South Side baseball.

A Little Marketing Goes a Long Way

> "We just put it up to get interest in inter-league play
> and to kind of stir things up."

The above quote was from an innocent-acting Mitch Rosen in 2008.[12] In 1997 he was with WMVP-1000, the radio sports talk station that also carried White Sox games. To help increase ratings for those broadcasts, Rosen was behind a marketing campaign that could only be construed as "sticking it to the Cubs." In the middle of Wrigleyville, a billboard that read, "Major League Baseball 8.1 Miles South" was erected.[13]

"It was a little Sox love in Cubs territory," Rosen recalls about his billboard. He is presently the program director at WSCR 670-AM, the Chicago sports talk radio station that now carries the White Sox. Rosen said that he had a station intern drive over to Wrigley, then note his odometer and make the trek back to Comiskey Park. His "a little Sox love" was easily seen from the Wrigley Field bleachers. He said that someone tipped off the *Chicago Sun-Times* and the paper published a photo of the billboard. A copy of the photo sits on Rosen's desk.[14]

"It was all in fun," Rosen maintains, further explaining that was also meant to hype other WMVP programming. A picture of WMVP personality Kevin Matthews was on the board. "No one threw tomatoes at it," he said of the Cubs' fan reaction.

It is Rosen's recollection that the sign remained for the duration of the station's lease. He doesn't remember taking it down early, as Jerry Reinsdorf requested. However, he now understands why Jerry Reinsdorf had a negative reaction to it. "Everyone is a partner," he said in describing the major league baseball community. "I wouldn't do this now. I'm smarter. I was more of a renegade back then."[15]

Rosen also feels that the Cubs-Sox fan tradition is unique. He thinks that any North Sider cheering for the White Sox or a South Sider pulling for the Cubs is rebelling against their parents since he believes there is no in-between in Chicago baseball fandom. "You can't be both," Rosen maintains. "You can't be bi-fanial. Either you are a Cubs or a Sox fan."[16]

A Little Love from the Cubs

To the tune of "Take Me Out to the Ballgame":

Take me out to the skybox
Take me out to the park (As in Comiskey)
Buy me some champagne and brie for a snack
I don't care if I can afford to get back
Cause it's 30 thousand bucks and you're out
At the old ballgame.

This little parody comes from the memory of Tom Shaer. As he recalls, there was a print ad in a magazine founded by sportswriter Bill Gleason in the early 1980s that carried this little piece of poetry. The magazine, which offended Jerry Reinsdorf greatly with something called "100 Questions," had a short life.[17] Before it expired, the ad appeared with the form of a "mascot" from WGN radio. The mascot was a bird with large beaks that usually said, "Hi,

I'm Chicago." The mascot was mainly used to promote WGN is some harmless way. But this satire had some real bite to it.

The intention here was obvious. The Cubs, now owned by the Tribune Company, were not the corporate entity fans feared they might be. The corporate guys were on the other side of town, converting upper-deck seats into skyboxes and catering to the upper-crust fan. As far as it being the old ballgame? Well, it was a new ballgame, which had nothing to do with the average person who made it out to the ballpark three or four times a year. The White Sox couldn't have been amused.

"It's pretty amusing that it cost only $30,000 to rent a sky box back then," Shaer said. "They go for $150–200,000 or probably more now." As for the "100 Questions" [which speculated about many things, including Reinsdorf], the Sox CEO was highly offended by the advertisement. Shaer stated that Reinsdorf filed a protest with the commissioner's office.[18]

By the late 1990s, after the two teams made peace, Reinsdorf wanted the WMVP billboard taken down quickly. The biggest rivalry still exists between the teams' fans, if not the owners and front offices.

Yet the "Sox Pride" ad aimed and made a direct hit, and Brooks Boyer became a White Sox fan cult figure.

7

Back in the Wilderness

"...especially when Mr. Wrigley was alive..."[1]

More than thirty years after Cubs owner Philip K. Wrigley died, Mike Veeck still referred to him as "Mr." From 1946 until 1977, when Wrigley passed away, the Chicago Cubs had few high moments. The team's most successful era during these thirty-plus years covered 1967 to 1972, although this brief period of winning was marred by lost opportunities. Not one championship of any kind was won. The Cubs had a difficult time holding onto talented African American players like Oscar Gamble, Bill North and Bill Madlock. Fans often ridiculed a baseball ownership with a landmark downtown building and a successful gum company but a lousy baseball team. Ironically, present-day Cubs fans cringe at the idea that their ballpark could lose the Wrigley name to corporate sponsoring. But when the Wrigley family finally sold its interests to the mega-corporate Tribune Company in early 1981, very few mourned the end of an historical era that covered sixty years. The Tribune Company boasted of a "new tradition" that was supposed to end the old tradition of competing for last place.

However, the partial Mike Veeck quote came as a response to a question concerning the competition between the Cubs and White Sox during his father's second tenure as owner, which began with the 1976 season. No, back then the Cubs weren't the hot item they are now. But how did his father feel about competing with the North Side club for the attention of the Chicago baseball fan during the seventies?

"You didn't go after the Cubs," said Mike, regarding the White Sox atmosphere that was dictated by his father. "Especially when Mr. Wrigley was alive."[2]

Although the competition between the Cubs and White Sox fans is intense, it is unlikely the owners or men holding top positions in team management will add fire to that competition. Yes, an Ozzie Guillen or José Valentin may stir the pot some with some attitude about the Cubs tradition, but owners are in a select group and generally don't snipe at one another.

Yet the Bill Veeck edict banning Cubs criticism goes beyond any feeling of solidarity one owner would feel toward another. The Veeck family got its start in baseball when William Veeck, Sr., became president of the Cubs in 1919. Although identified primarily as a two-time White Sox owner, Veeck Jr. was responsible for planting the outfield ivy and the construction of the hand-operated scoreboard at Wrigley Field. And the Cubs seventh-inning "celeb fest" that began with Harry Caray leading a sing-along actually originated with Bill Veeck.

"He was still fairly mobile," said Mike, referring to his father and mounting health problems. "He would get around Comiskey and would hear Harry sing along with Nancy. [White Sox organist Nancy Faust played "Take Me Out to the Ballgame" in the middle of the seventh inning.] Harry was trying to help Nancy out because people liked her. Harry didn't understand at first why something sounding so bad was attractive."[3] Actually, Bill Veeck thought bad singing from Harry was what made the concept so appealing.

So the only White Sox owner that had the team compete in the World Series between 1919 and 2005 had a deep and long connection to the Chicago Cubs that extends to the present. And the two teams had something else that connected them during the mid-seventies that, in a sense, gave both sets of fans comfort: Both were extremely bad.

The Cubs were not on the verge of leaving town, to Seattle or anywhere else. Yet by the beginning of 1976, all their big-name players had been traded or had retired. The club had returned to losing. The late sixties and early seventies success seemed to be an aberration as the Cubs were now entering four decades without having appeared in the World Series.

At the beginning of the season, a Cubs fan I knew said that he truly looked forward to seeing many games at Wrigley that summer. He had no delusions about the team contending for anything but the lower half of the Eastern Division. Instead, he fantasized about sitting in the warm summer sun, drinking a cold beer and watching the opposition smack tape-measure home runs. He hoped, in an almost childlike fashion, that one of these long homers would crash through a window in one of the Waveland Avenue apartments.[4] The early Cubs' performance stirred these fantasies.

The Cubs began their home season with a 5–4 win over the Mets in front of a home-opening record crowd of 44,818. The next two games gave more of an indication of the kind of season the team would have.

In the second game of the series against the Mets, Dave Kingman hit a two-run homer off Cubs reliever Tom Dettore. *Tribune* reporter Richard Dozer wrote that some believed the homer traveled 600 feet, making it one of the longest homers of all time. Dozer thought "it was one of the hardest ever hit out of Wrigley Field and was last seen bouncing somewhere off toward Irving Park Road."[5] Irving Park is roughly a half-mile from Wrigley.

Reds catcher Johnny Bench looks a little unnerved as Bobby Murcer scores in a Wrigley Field game in April 1977. The Cubs won this contest, 2–1. The ball club got off to a great start and, for a time, looked like they could truly contend for the Eastern Division title. They ended the year dead even.

The Cubs won the game, extending the winning streak to four. But the bad times were yet to come as they lost their next five, giving up 52 runs in the process.

Kingman hit two more homers the next day, with the second being the most crushing blow. It was a three-run shot in the ninth that erased a one-run Cubs lead. Dozer estimated the distance of this home run was around 450 feet, and wrote that it was the shortest of the three Kingman had hit in the two-day span. Despite the homers, Kingman expressed doubts that he would ever want to be a Cub even with his long home runs soaring out of Wrigley.

"I'm too homer conscious here," he said. "I seem to do better in large parks."[6]

Kingman would join the Cubs in 1978. In three seasons, including 1980 when he played in only 81 games, Kingman belted 94 homers, including 48 in 1979. Cubs fans didn't take to Kingman because they didn't think he was fan friendly. When he was sent back to the Mets, no North Side fans missed him.

Meanwhile, another Cubs killer went to work several days later. Phillies third baseman Mike Schmidt hit four consecutive homers in an 18–16 Philadelphia win. The Cubs led the game at one time, 13–2, only to see the Phillies

pile on 14 runs from the seventh through the tenth innings. Schmidt became only the second National Leaguer to hit four consecutive homers in a game. The other was some fellow named Robert Lowe, who he pulled off the feat in 1894.

Philadelphia also pounded out 24 hits, the second-highest total in franchise history. The team record of 26 was set on August 25, 1922, and that was also against the Cubs. As for the Cubs on that pleasant spring day, it must have been tough to lose a game after scoring 16 runs on 19 hits. As for their fans? Richard Dozer described them as "shell shocked." But the carnage wasn't over yet.

Three weeks later the Dodgers were in town and used seven homers to beat Chicago, 14–12. There was a familiar graphic in the *Tribune* game-day coverage. The line on the hand-operated scoreboard showed nothing but crooked numbers for the visitors. Los Angeles scored in every inning but the ninth. The last team to score a run in every inning was St. Louis on September 13, 1964, also at Wrigley Field.

Cincinnati then came into town and swept a three-game series. The last two scores were 14–4 and 14–2. The Cubs had lost five straight, and gave up 54 runs. They were beginning to look like the Cubs of the fifties and sixties when opposing teams fattened up their offensive stats while flattening the Cubs.

In late June and early July, the Cubs went on a nine-game losing steak. Twice they gave up 10 runs, 13 once, and were also hit with a nine spot. The Cubs fan who visualized sitting in the warm sun watching opposition belt out homer after homer was getting his wish.

If there was anything consistent about the post–Williams-Santo-Banks 1976 Cubs, it was their losing. The North Siders lost games by the bunches, as these streaks indicate:

Four losses: April 15–21
Five losses: May 4–9
Six losses: June 4–9
Nine losses: June 25–July 4 (first game of doubleheader)
Six losses: July 11–July 19 (time period partially interrupted by the All-Star break)
Four losses: July 24–26 (time period included a doubleheader loss to the Montreal Expos, a team on its way to 107 defeats)
Five losses: September 5–9
Five losses: September 23–28

I attended a defeat during the September 23–28 losing streak, an extra-inning loss at the hands of the Pittsburgh Pirates. Fall had begun, the sun had gone away, the vines were beginning to turn brown and the crowd was sparse. The series ended the next-to-last homestand of the year. No one held up signs

Opposite: **Dave Kingman during his days with the Cubs. He hit many long home runs in his career, many against the Cubs.**

reading "Wait Til Next Year." The Cubs were on their way to completing their fourth consecutive losing season. The Opening Day crowd was by far the best the team experienced all year. In fact, no single-day attendance topped the 30,000 mark for the rest of the season as a young and thin pitching staff struggled to keep home runs off of Waveland and Sheffield avenues. The mania that accompanied a trip to Wrigley was still years away.

By the end of the 1975 baseball season, it seemed that no one cared about the White Sox. Attendance barely topped three quarters of a million. Late in the second game of most doubleheaders, the huge Comiskey Park was almost deserted. The baseball sounds from the field could be heard distinctly. What was missing was the sound of fans cheering or even the summoning of the beer man. The White Sox came close to picking up their second last-place finish in five years.

Dick Allen, the savior of the early seventies, was gone. He had "retired" before the end of the 1974 season. In his three years with the club, Allen was never with the team at the season's end. He went home early once the White Sox were eliminated from the division in 1972; he was injured 1973; and in 1974, he gave his team a tearful farewell with three weeks left in the season. The club had lost its biggest star and had no one who could come close to replacing him. Meanwhile, fans felt deserted by a player who couldn't wait until the end of the season to call it quits. And as it turned out, Allen had not quit yet.

Carlos May had started his career with the White Sox in 1969 with great promise. He had homered twice in the home opener that year, with neither homer needing the shortened distance of the Little League fences. Bob Elson said in his understated manner that May "could really hit that ball."[7] But an accident in the army reserves took off half of his right thumb. May would have some decent years, but his potential was never reached. He made an appearance in the World Series, but that was only because the White Sox traded him to the Yankees in the spring of 1976. In 1975 he hit a somewhat-respectable .271, but had only eight homers and 53 RBIs. His career was on the decline.

In 1970, Bill Melton was the first White Sox player to hit 30 homers in a season at a time when it meant something to reach that level. The next year he became the first White Sox player to win the American League home run championship. At the top of his game Melton hit two types of home runs in Comiskey Park: high arching drives into the upper deck or long pokes deep into the center-field bullpen. By the end of 1975, his homers were unimpressive flies barely making it into the front row of the lower deck. White Sox fans had hoped he would be the home run hitter they had longed for and rarely seen. In 1975, Melton's power numbers dropped off and fans booed him. He feuded with Harry Caray, and most fans were ready to side with Caray. When the season ended, he asked general manager Roland Hemond to trade him because he no longer felt that he could play in the hostile atmosphere of Comiskey

Bill Melton being congratulated by Dick Allen while Carlos May waits to do the same. Against Baltimore Allen had singled with the bases loaded and two out. Melton followed with a homer into the upper deck and the Sox had five explosive runs. The Melton-Allen power combo never really lived up to its potential.

Park. Hemond accommodated him by sending him across the country to the California Angels. Like May, Melton had suffered an off-the-field injury that affected his overall performance. Like May, his career died too quickly and that death took the team down with him.

Hemond thought that center fielder Ken Henderson was one of the main components in making the White Sox a real contender. Henderson came over from the Giants and was injured in May 1973 in a freakish play at home plate. He had a good comeback year, hitting 20 homers in 1974. But in '75, he was lumped in with Melton as one of the big reasons the White Sox played fifth-place baseball. Neither Melton nor Henderson was delivering with men in scoring position. In 1976, Henderson played elsewhere.

By the end of 1975, the White Sox resembled the man without a country, only the club was a team without players. Their owner, John Allyn, was a man without money. After years of rumors, it finally looked like the White Sox would leave Chicago. Seattle, which had lost the Pilots after one season, was more than willing to welcome the luckless franchise into its midst. So what if it hadn't won a World Series in 56 years?

Enter Bill Veeck. In what his son Mike called "a crusade," Veeck led a group of investors to buy the team and keep it in Chicago. No one else locally expressed interest in a losing ball club with a dwindling fan base and an outdated stadium. It was Veeck, or the Chicago White Sox would become the Seattle White Sox or the Seattle Something Else.

Controversy surrounded Veeck throughout his career in other markets, and controversy followed him to Chicago. Although the 1959 White Sox finally made it to the World Series after a 40-year absence, many Sox fans never forgave Veeck for some of the trades he made in the early sixties. It was strongly believed that Veeck stripped the team of some young talent that could have bought the Sox more trips to the World Series. Many thought Veeck was a good promoter but a bad baseball man when it came to putting a team together. Son Mike thought his father was judged unfairly. "He made some bum trades," Mike said in 2009. "But he was a pretty good judge of talent."[8]

Even as Mike described his dad as being a better baseball man than most thought, he laughed about the acquisition of free agent Ron Blomberg. Blomberg, with only two at-bats (with no hits) in the 1976 and 1977 seasons was the first player to be slotted in at the designated hitter spot in 1973. Veeck, hoping that the injury-plagued Blomberg could come back like Eric Soderholm had, signed the former Yankee to a guaranteed four-year deal. Blomberg started out the '78 season by hitting a game-tying homer in the ninth inning of the Sox home opener in front of more than 50,000. The come-from-behind win made Sox fans remember the 1977 "South Side Hitmen." But Blomberg hit only four more homers during the rest of the season while playing part-time. He was released by the Sox and collected the remainder of his contract without playing another game. Blomberg tried to catch on with another team but couldn't. The White Sox played sub–.500 ball until the 1981 strike-shortened season.

For the 1976 season, Veeck tried to re-ignite interest in the club by reviving memories of the "Go-Go" era. He began by hiring Paul Richards to manage the club. Richards had been field manager for the Sox during the early part of the fifties when the team began a long streak of winning seasons. Next, he acquired Ralph Garr from the Atlanta Braves. Garr, known as the "Roadrunner" because of his speed, had won the NL batting title in '74 with a .353 average. That average dipped considerably in 1975, but Garr had been a .300 hitter most of his career and it was hoped he would regain that form. It was also announced that the center-field fence would be taken down, leaving a 445-foot poke to the bleacher seats. With Comiskey more cavernous than ever, pitching, defense, and speed were again supposed to be the main ingredients to winning. This was done despite some previous lukewarm responses to a team that had a history of not having big-name impact, everyday players.

Veeck also tried to pump more life into the club in other ways. He had noticed that the scoreboard fireworks had been shortened, and he promised to restore what he had created years before. Also noticing that Comiskey looked ridiculous with its artificial turf infield, Veeck tore the turf out. He then gave the park a face-lift by painting its exterior. Everything was changing.

On Friday April 9, 1976, the reborn White Sox began their season at Comiskey. The spring day was crisp but the sun was out in a cloudless sky. McCuddy's Bar was filled with Sox fans. The "hope springs eternal" feeling normally reserved for the North Side of Chicago radiated around Comiskey. It had been gone for a long time, or at least since the end of Allen's MVP season.

Bill Veeck walked through the lower deck an hour or two before game time. Fans surrounded him to shake his hand and pat his back. It was quite a sight to watch as Veeck had come to a full stop as fans stepped up to greet him. Many were glad the White Sox did not leave Chicago and they showed their gratitude to the man who made that happen.

Wilbur Wood started for the White Sox. From 1972 to 1974, Wood put together some amazing stats that have not been matched by any present-day pitcher. True, he was a knuckleballer, which made it easier for him to achieve these feats. Yet he still has to be given a great deal of credit for going out to the mound time and time again. In this four-year period, Wood started 184 games, won 90, had 85 complete games, and logged in 1,390 innings. His lowest total was in '74 when he piled up 320 innings.

"He made our staff better because of the innings he pitched," Sox general manager Roland Hemond said. "He would go the distance and the bullpen was rested on the day he pitched. And the bullpen could pick up pitchers on other days rather than being used so often."[9] Hemond was putting it mildly. In 1972 and 1973, Wood started almost one-third of the season for the Sox. He pitched on two days' rest on many occasions, and not only helped preserve the bullpen, but also aided in keeping a thin starting staff fresh. And all of this happened after he had appeared in nearly 241 games as a reliever from 1968 to 1970.

On August 12, 1972, in the middle of a heated division race, Wood threw an 11-inning complete game in beating the first-place A's in Oakland, 3–1. Oakland right fielder Brant Alyea singled in seventh and tied the game 1–1 with a two-out homer in the ninth. Alyea was the only Oakland player to get a hit. It was Wood's 20th win of the season.

On May 26, 1973, the White Sox and Cleveland played to a 2–2 tie in 16 innings. The night game was suspended at that point and picked up two days later. Wood came in and threw five innings of two-hit, one-run ball and the Sox won, 6–3. Then, in the regularly scheduled game, Wood started, went the distance, and picked up a four-hit shutout.*

This constant usage caught up with Wood in a July 20, 1973, doubleheader in New York. He couldn't get anyone out in the first, and all six batters he

---

Amazingly, in the sixteen-inning game, Indians starter Gaylord Perry and Sox starter Stan Bahnsen each went 13 innings. The White Sox ended up using only three pitchers in a 21-inning contest.

faced scored. Thinking that Wood really hadn't thrown all that much, manager Chuck Tanner started Wood in game two as well. Wood got through the first three innings fine, but was hit for two in the fourth and five in the fifth. When he was taken out of the game in the fifth, classless Yankee fans booed him.

All this work had to be catching up with him. In 1975, Wood won 16 but lost 20. His ERA rose above four for the first time in his career. He still logged 291 innings, but he gave up 309 hits to go along with 92 walks. It never helps to allow more than 400 men get on base during a season.

On Opening Day 1976, Wood looked like his dominant self. He went the distance with a six-hit shutout. His performance added to the optimism of the day. If the White Sox had any chance of having any success in 1976, Wood was needed to lead the way.

That Opening Day, everything else went right except for a scoreboard dud when newcomer first baseman Jim Spencer homered in the fifth. Fans waited for the new-and-improved scoreboard display but the "Monster" refused to perform, sputtering and then dying out. Other than a fireworks failure, a minor glitch, nothing ruined the perfect start to what many hoped would be a new era manufactured by a second-time owner.

The fun continued during the May 31 home game against the Texas Rangers. It had rained for several days before this game. Comiskey Park was a soggy mess, and a dense fog hung over the stadium. The White Sox trailed, 2–0, in the bottom of the first. With two outs and the bases loaded, Chet Lemon hit what looked like a harmless fly to medium left field. Ranger left fielder Tom Grieve started in and then stopped, his arms spread in frustration. He had lost the ball in the fog. When it finally came down, the ball plopped in the wet grass and just laid there. Many fans saw it but Grieve still didn't know where it was. As the fans screamed in delight, Sox runners circled the bases. By the time Grieve finally located the ball, Lemon was on his way to third with a slide, beating Grieve's throw easily. The inning should have ended; instead, the Sox had a 3–2 lead. And poor Tom Grieve. That night he went 0-for-4 at the plate, including three strikeouts.

Fans down the first-base line thought the fog was just another Veeckian way of getting an edge on the competition. They imagined Veeck on top of Comiskey with huge fans blowing the fog over the field only when the White Sox were up to bat.

The umpiring crew conferred after the end of the inning. A short time later, it was announced that the umpires would stop the game any time the fog got too dense. Boos rained down on Comiskey. Many fans apparently thought the fog was a bigger weapon than anybody in the Sox lineup. The game was stopped on several occasions, and the fans were never happy.

Yet nothing took away from the fun of the evening. The Sox won, 9–4, and actually had a respectable 21–19 record. A division title wasn't likely, but maybe they could at least improve over the dismal '75 season when the team looked lifeless. To some cynics, the season actually ended three weeks earlier.

Wood was on the mound again taking a shutout into the sixth in Detroit. Ron LeFlore hit a line drive back up the middle and it slammed right into Wood's knee. Wood hit the ground in pain, unable to do anything but cry out in agony. The left-hander was done for the season. His career then declined.

Nine days later the White Sox traded the once-heralded Carlos May to the Yankees for left-hander Ken Brett. Brett had a decent season for the Sox, winning 10 games, and ended up leading the staff in wins. But the loss of Wood was immeasurable, and his injury was only a sign of the bad things to come in 1976.

By the All-Star break, the club was eight games under .500 and sinking. The offense was anemic. The outfield defense was non-existent. On one occasion, manager Paul Richards went to the mound to instruct pitcher Bart Johnson to pitch around a hitter. Johnson pointed to the outfield and asked, "How do I pitch around them?" Richards replied, "Young man, you have a point."[10] The team lacked so much that one year was too short a time to turn things around in any significant way.

On August 8, Sox players went to play the first game of a doubleheader against the Kansas City Royals while wearing shorts. Massive Royal first baseman John Mayberry said the White Sox were "the sweetest team he had ever seen."[11] Newspaper photos showed the Sox sitting in the dugout with legs crossed resembling the Rockettes. Bill Veeck laughed that they had been stuck with one of the coolest days in the summer when the team decided to show off their kneecaps. The Sox won the game, 5–2, and the object was to have fun.

As with his other unusual promotions, Veeck had his critics. Some said that he was only embarrassing his players. Veeck was a promoter, people said, but that didn't mean his players were. After all, this was a major league baseball team.

Any embarrassment from the short pants day was eclipsed by a season headed on a downward spiral. Joe Goddard of the *Chicago Sun-Times* wrote an article at the end of August about Paul Richards, depicting the Sox manager as bored with his job. Another charge, made by unnamed players, was that Richards was out of touch with his team. The photo accompanying the story showed Richards bundled up in a Sox warm-up jacket sitting alone at the end of the dugout, isolated from the team. The article could not have instilled confidence in Sox fans that the team was heading in the right direction.

Bill Veeck held a news conference with Richards, demanding that any players who spoke to Goddard come forward and air their gripes. And, as Veeck had to have known, none did. Though the players were called cowardly and Goddard was accused of being unfair to a man who had agreed to be only a caretaker manager for a year, White Sox credibility took a significant hit. Things only worsened.

In the 30 games remaining after the Goddard story, the Sox won seven and lost 23. This included 15 defeats in their last 16 contests. The team barely avoided losing 100 games, as it secured last place in the American League West. If the team hadn't quit, it gave all the appearances of doing so. All the optimism accompanying the hopeful Opening Day vanished. Other than a two-man no-hitter thrown by John "Blue Moon" Odom and Francisco Barrios in July, there were few highlights to the season.

Mike Veeck remembers glumly walking through Comiskey Park after the home season ended, feeling that the organization, including himself, had let his father down. "I was so heartbroken," Veeck recalled. "We failed him in that we didn't do more to increase attendance. I should have sold 20,000 more tickets."[12]

Even if Mike Veeck had sold an additional 20,000 tickets, attendance still would have fallen short of a million. Attendance had improved over the previous year, but creating interest in a last-place team is a challenging task for any front-office person. The White Sox just weren't very entertaining in 1976, especially when their leading home run hitters finished with 14.

For all Chicago sports fans the mid-seventies was a dark period. The Bulls had some great teams in the early part of the decade, but none reached the NBA finals. Even the winning team could be hard to watch since part of their defense was their offense. The Bulls used the 24-second rule to the maximum to set up a shot. The problem arose when they fell behind and they didn't have the time to be throwing the ball around. By the 1975-76 season, the club had fallen from the NBA elite. They were still 16 seasons from their first championship.

The Black Hawks were advertised as the "winningest team in Chicago," and from 1961 to 1973, there was no disputing that claim. The Hawks had gone to the Stanley Cup finals five times in that period and were considered a dangerous team in the playoffs. However, by 1976, the team was in a real decline. I attended a game in late December 1976 where the Hawks trailed, 6–4, in the waning minutes against the St. Louis Blues. No forward came up to fore-check and no defensemen came up to assist in attacking the Blues' zone. The Hawks were more than happy with letting the Blues skate away with a road win. The old Stadium was filled with boos. It is one thing to be out-manned; it is another thing to not care. On Christmas Day, a few days later, long-time coach Billy Reay was fired. The team chose to tell Reay of his demise by slipping a note under his office door. With this cowardly act, a proud era was over. Another Stanley Cup final appearance didn't happen until 1992.

The Bears had the best runner in the NFL in 1976. Walter Payton amassed more than 1,800 yards in his second full season. Yet, the Bears finished at a mere 7-7. The dead-even record was actually the best mark the team had up to that point in the seventies. In 1977, the Bears made their first post-season trip since their 1963 championship and were pounded by the Dallas Cowboys,

37–7. After a lousy season in 1978, the Bears returned to the playoffs in 1979. They were again one and done. The following year mediocrity prevailed again. Signs were held up at Soldier Field imploring Coach Neill Armstrong to return to the moon.

So by the end of the 1976 season, Cubs and White Sox fans had no reason to be jealous of each other. Their best memories centered on opposition tape-measure home runs and a fly ball lost in the fog. Both teams played in a fog and it didn't appear to be clearing any time soon.

8

The Bill Veeck Swan Song

Disco Demolition. Until the 2005 world championship season, those two words hung over the franchise like a smoky, dark cloud. The memory of a summer night in 1979 that went terribly wrong did not have the same effect of the Black Sox scandal or the disappointment of unfinished business in 1994. But the memories of bonfires in the middle of Comiskey Park are impossible to erase and perhaps the most vivid image of the seventies. In a way, Disco Demolition symbolized the frustration of a decade where winning was rare and misfortune ran rampart. As the recollections of 1959 faded and the popularity of the Cubs increased, the franchise was teetering on the edge of destruction, with attendance still an unsolved problem. Once again, it seemed like the team had one foot in another city.

Teams crave excitement at their ballpark. The films of disco night clearly demonstrated emotion ready to burst in the middle of the summer heat and humidity. But it was the wrong kind of emotion. One huge banner hung over an upper-deck façade reading, "DISCO SUCKS." The game didn't matter; the White Sox were not what brought people into the park that night. The only real surprise was that things didn't get worse.

When contacting Mike Veeck for an interview for this book, I wrote that I would not ask him anything about Disco Demolition. That may seem odd, as I was passing up a chance to get one side of the story from the man behind the promotion. Yet in all the stories about Disco Demolition, all I saw was a fascination about an out-of-control situation that caused a rare forfeit of a major league game.* One important and significant thing happened that night: The Veeck era ended. His ownership was marginalized and credibility ruined. Bill remained a true baseball outsider for the rest of his life, and the whole affair almost took son Mike down as well.

Disco Demolition provided some real explosive ammunition for Bill

---

*Although as bad as everything appeared, Lorn Brown said that it was not a riot or the dangerous situation the press reports said it was. Brown witnessed the disaster from the White Sox radio booth.

Veeck's critics. Get some players, they railed. Promotions do not bring loyal fans to the ballpark in the long run. And now look what happened. This promotion literally blew up in your face, and your city and team was embarrassed in front of the entire country. Finally, will you realize that time has passed you by?

Disco Demolition may not have happened if the White Sox had been winning. Maybe if the team had been contending, more thought would have gone into the idea. Perhaps better advanced ticket sales would have limited the number of disco haters into the park and the situation would have been controllable. Or maybe the whole promotion would have been rejected as unnecessary. Disco Demolition happened because the team wasn't all that entertaining. The Hitmen had been dismantled and other free agents traveled everywhere except to the South Side of Chicago. I did ask Mike Veeck this: Didn't the White Sox realize how frustrated fans were with the team's inability to draw the top talent to Chicago's American League team?

"We were frustrated, too," the younger Veeck said. "We really needed another $20 million to run the team right. But Dad just couldn't go back to his investors and ask for the money."[1]

Meanwhile, Mike Veeck said he was inconsolable after the fiasco. His father tried to cheer him up, saying the promotion worked too well. But even when Bill tried to cheer up his son, the elder Veeck was losing support from one of his better friends in the media, Bill Gleason. No one wanted to defend the Sox owner during one of the true low points in his major league career. "This is an indictment of management," *Sun-Times* columnist and Veeck admirer Bill Gleason wrote. "That's where the blame belongs."[2]

This was actually written in a column three days before Disco Demolition. Gleason had written about the sad state of a team that was again playing sub–.500 ball. Veeck would get no support from Gleason after Disco Demolition. The headline to Gleason's column on the promotion read, "The Horror at Comiskey." Politically, Veeck was isolated.

It was around the time of Disco Demolition that Veeck was looking to sell the White Sox. Attendance had dropped and Comiskey was again being described as out-of-date and in terrible shape. Who was Veeck going to sell to? Marvin Davis of Denver. This meant the franchise would be moved to Colorado.

"Bill Veeck has to be held accountable for two things," Tom Shaer said. "His dismantling of the 1959 pennant winners and the planned move to Denver. He was going to be paid $500,000 a year by Davis to be a consultant and back then that was a lot of money."[3]

In addition Shaer said this about Veeck's second reign as Sox owner: "Bill Veeck had run a horrible organization." Shaer also used the word "saint" next to Veeck's name, questioning the working-class image of a man who apparently was ready to abandon Chicago and make some money at the same time.[4]

Eddie Einhorn told author Gerald Eskenazi regarding Veeck and the possible Denver move, "He was always the hero, and we were always the bums. That's the irony of it. But that's life. What can I tell ya?"[5]

The Denver deal didn't jive with the fans' image of Veeck. But what is the final legacy of Bill Veeck? It is as complicated as the man is controversial.

Former Chicago TV journalist Mike Leiderman described Veeck as "running out of steam" during the late '70s, but also said, "I loved being with Veeck. He was unique and very much worth knowing. We spent a lot of time at Comiskey just talking about baseball."[6] "I am a baseball fan because of Bill Veeck," says Katherine Jacobs, a South Side Chicago resident.[7]

Veeck ran the Cleveland Indians in 1948. That was the last year Cleveland won a World Series and one of the last years the city of Cleveland enjoyed a world championship of any kind other than the Browns' NFL championship in 1964. The Indians' paid attendance that year was more than 2.6 million. That Indian attendance record stood until 1995 when the team won a division title in a new stadium.

The only White Sox pennant winner from 1919 to 2005 was Veeck's 1959 squad. Many critics don't give him much credit for that team, saying that most ingredients were in place when Veeck purchased the club that spring.

Then there were the trades Veeck made in an attempt to repeat the pennant in 1960. Bubba Phillips, Norm Cash, and John Romano were traded to the Indians for Minnie Minoso, Dick Brown, Don Ferrese, and Jake Striker. Johnny Callison was sent to the Phillies for Gene Freese. Earl Battey and Don Mincher were traded to the Washington Senators for Roy Sievers. By the end of the 1961 season, Freese, Sievers, and Minoso were gone. Cash, Mincher, and Callison played on until the seventies. Battey or Romano would have provided some right-handed punch to counterbalance Cash and Callison. Who knows what the Sox would have done with these players to complement the solid pitching they had in the mid-sixties?

And, of course, there were the numerous stunts and promotions that some labeled as bush league and harmful to baseball. The little person sent up to the plate to get a walk and spacemen invading Comiskey were ripped by many.

Yet there are the unmistakable contributions made by Bill Veeck that are still in use today. Putting names on uniform backs resulted from an older fan telling him she couldn't recognize the players and because Veeck reasoned that not everyone could afford a program.[8] Even with the mass exposure baseball gets today, it can be difficult for fans to recognize players, especially because of expansion and the fluid movement of free agents.

Dan Dorfman, one the fans I interviewed for this book, grew up living in the Comiskey Park neighborhood. He recalls running outside to hear the scoreboard going off. Many teams now have fireworks-shooting scoreboards, even though Veeck was criticized by the baseball establishment for putting up

Johnny Callison facing knuckleballer Hoyt Wilhelm in May 1970. Callison flied out to center on this at-bat, but the Cubs won the game in extra innings.

the "Monster" at Comiskey Park. The present ownership knew they couldn't put up a new stadium without a monster-type scoreboard. The display brings out the child in everyone and baseball is a kids' game.

Veeck and his family also had their connections to Cubs traditions. The Sox owner was the one responsible for the vines on the outfield walls at Wrigley. It is those vines that add true color to the old park and has made the Wrigley image instantly recognizable all over the country. The beauty of Wrigley is a marketing tool, with the park sometimes marketed more than the team itself. (U.S. Cellular has its version of vines hanging down on the center-field hitting background.)

The hand-operated scoreboard at Wrigley was another Veeck idea. No one would ever dare suggest to a Cubs fan that a mechanical device of any kind should replace the Wrigley scoreboard. It is not only a novelty, but the scoreboard uniquely keeps fans abreast of what is going on in other games.

Veeck had a simple way of informing the fans of how their Cubs did on a particular day. A "W" flag would be hoisted on the scoreboard to signal a win and an "L" would fly for a defeat. Modern Cubs fans now hang "W" banners outside their home to celebrate a day's victory.

The seventh-inning stretch tradition at Wrigley? We all know that started with Harry Caray at Comiskey. Now there have been "guest conductors" and celebrity singers. It is a media and fan event done to promote the experience at Wrigley, which almost has nothing to do with the actual team itself. The tradition shows no sign of fading away more than two decades after Veeck's death and a decade after Caray's death.

What about the charge that some of Veeck's promotions tended to be demeaning to the game? There are bratwurst and sausage races in Milwaukee. In between innings at U.S. Cellular Field sexy women throw rolled up tee shirts into the stands and dance contests are held on top of dugouts. At other major league venues there are all sorts of entertainment beamed on the electronic scoreboards. Yes, the game is still the main attraction, but teams recognize the importance of making the whole experience around that game more enjoyable for the fan.

Promotions and giveaways? Every team has them. For years, the post–Veeckian White Sox have had a day when fans bring their dogs to a game. Doing things that are just different, like having morning baseball game as Veeck did in 1977? How about the White Sox risking cold weather to have an opening night instead of an opening day in 2000? It turned out to be a beautiful night; the White Sox played an inspired game and the crowd increased by more than 12,000 from the previous year's home opener.

Bill Veeck was the first owner to sign an African American player (Larry Doby) in the American League. As discussed later in the book, Jerry Reinsdorf has led the way in the major leagues for minority hirings in high-powered positions that include managers, general managers, coaches, and radio and TV broadcasters.

Was Bill Veeck a bad judge of baseball talent? The trades of the early sixties would seem to back up that assessment. However, the young nucleus of Rich Dotson, Harold Baines, LaMarr Hoyt, and Britt Burns were on the parent club in 1980. Ron Kittle had been signed to a minor league contract. The new owners had to add many others to create the Winning Ugly Western Division champions of 1983. Yet they, thanks to Veeck, at least had some young talent as a foundation.

And who gave Tony La Russa his first managing job? Bill Veeck.

Regardless of Veeck's accomplishments or failures, one fact cannot be disputed: During his last five years as White Sox owner, the team had four losing seasons, with three 90-loss campaigns. The 1980 slate completed a thirteen-season stretch where the ball club had only two real standout years, and even in those years the White Sox didn't come terribly close to winning anything.

In 1980, events came full circle. On July 13, the White Sox played an inspired game against the Yankees. But, similar to the '50s and '60s, the Yankees came out on top. By the bottom of the seventh, Steve Trout of the Sox and Rudy May of the Yankees were throwing a double no-hitter. The top of the seventh ended with a roar from the just under 29,000 at Comiskey. Reggie Jackson took a third strike for his third strikeout of the day. While Jackson fumed at home plate umpire Don Denkinger, Comiskey Park sounded like 1977. The hated Jackson had been struck out again, the no-hitter remained intact, and maybe, just maybe, if the White Sox could break through with a run or two, history could be made.

With one out, Chet Lemon laced a line drive to left-center for the first hit of the game. Center fielder Ruppert Jones cut the ball off, but Lemon kept on toward second. Lemon flew as he turned around first and slid in safely for a double. The noise level skyrocketed again. Ron Pruitt followed with a single to right, scoring Lemon for the first run of the day. Now fans waited to see if Trout could get six more outs without giving up a hit.

Eric Soderholm, a 1977 alumnus, walked to lead off the eighth and New York had Fred Stanley run for him. Then the no-hitter vanished as Lou Piniella singled to right-center. Stanley headed for third, and Piniella made a big turn around first as the throw came in from Chet Lemon toward third. Shortstop Todd Cruz cut the throw off and then threw to first behind Piniella. Lamar Johnson put the tag on for the first out of the inning. Piniella, angry with himself over his baserunning gaffe, slammed his helmet to the ground. The protective cap shot off the skin part of the infield and bounded toward the coach's box. Comiskey Park roared again, but Trout was still in trouble with a man on third and only one out.

Two batters later it was over. Ruppert Jones singled in the tying run. Rick Cerone followed with a two-run homer deep into the lower deck just to the right of the foul pole. The White Sox meekly went three up, three down in the eighth and ninth. New York had won, 3–1.

The Sox loss was reminiscent of the defeats against the Yankee powerhouses of the early sixties. They played their hearts out but didn't have the firepower to outlast a New York team that just knew how to win. In the top of the sixth, with Cerone on first, Bucky Dent attempted to sacrifice. Dent popped the ball up and Trout made a diving catch. Then, from his back, Trout threw to first to double off Cerone. Yet it was to no avail. After the game a boy about 11 years old asked his father one pertinent question: "Why do the White Sox always lose?" The father didn't have an answer. Of course, it wasn't that the White Sox always lost. The team just couldn't get into the postseason and keep a cynical fan base interested.

During this hard-fought game with the Yankees, there was a murmur throughout the stadium every time Reggie Jackson took his turn at the plate. Jackson, like Dick Allen, was a talented and controversial player. A Nobel

Peace Prize was not in Jackson's future, but fans everywhere recognized his raw ability to hit massive home runs and get a big hit when it was needed. That day the fans cheered with absolute delight with his every strikeout.

Unfortunately, the White Sox had no Reggie Jackson or Dick Allen type of player in 1980. There were some promising young players, but they were still learning their profession. Steve Trout pitched and played as well as anyone but couldn't preserve a 1–0 win, at least on that day. Meanwhile, young fans were going to their parents for answers.

During the last homestand of 1980, attendance totaled a mere 51,868 over the last six games. Two of the "crowds" barely topped the 2,200 mark. The White Sox suffered their fifth losing season out of the last six and fans were tuning out. Some said the franchise was in worse shape than when Veeck's group bought it in late 1975. Regardless, Bill Veeck was leaving major league baseball. He would never return.

Moving outfield fences back and forth depending on the home team advantage. Promotions that worked and promotions that embarrassed. Trades that, at the very least, were debatable. World Series teams and last-place duds. Testifying in court in support of Curt Flood and the overturning of the reserve clause. Reading a story about an unemployed man in the *Chicago Tribune* in 1980 and then giving the man a job. Saving the White Sox for Chicago and then almost ensuring that the team moved to Denver. Whatever can be said about Bill Veeck, his legacy will stir the passions of anyone who loves baseball, especially Chicago baseball.

There are the vines and scoreboard at Wrigley to go along with the Cubs' seventh-inning ritual that makes the experience of going to the ballpark unique. At U.S. Cellular there are the exploding scoreboards, fireworks shows, and a song played at certain times that stretches back to a lovable Veeck team of more than 30 years ago. Cubs and White Sox fans take pride in having separate traditions and loves. It makes up their particular sports identity. But they also have one thing in common. His name is Bill Veeck.

9

Sportsvision: Another Failed White Sox Media Strategy

"He was a genius ahead of his time."

—*This is a general consensus of several White Sox observers contacted by the author in describing Eddie Einhorn and his attempts to generate revenue for the team through television during the 1980s.*

"People used to say, 'Don't put your games on TV. You're not drawing well, and if you're not on TV you won't draw at all.' But I thought it was good for us. I thought we'd make fans, and it would help us at the gate, which is what happened."

— *Coach Ray Meyer talking about winning over new followers for the DePaul University basketball team. The quote was used in How March Became Madness by Eddie Einhorn and Ron Rapoport.[1]*

"Popped it up!"

—*A frustrated Harry Caray reacting to another failed attempt by a White Sox hitter to drive in a run.*

"They enjoyed it in the piracy of their own homes."

— *Former Chicago TV sports reporter Mike Leiderman talking about fans trying to enjoy Sportsvision without paying for the service.[2]*

"Somehow I got painted as Fast Eddie, the hustler who was going to take away all the White Sox tradition. People resented me for coming into town and telling people how to do things. Jerry and I worked for positive changes right from the start."

— *Eddie Einhorn as he was quoted in Bob Logan's 1983 book, " Miracle on 35th Street: Winning Ugly with the 1983 White Sox."[3]*

By the end of 1970, the White Sox were in a shambles. The team had one of its worst seasons ever. Attendance was microscopic. The Cubs had failed to redeem themselves for 1969, but they were still a much better team and at least they contended for their division. The White Sox? No one even wanted to admit they were a fan.

The condition of the team was reflected through its media. WFLD was getting clobbered in the ratings. Bob Elson had been behind the radio mike describing Sox games since 1931. He was popular with many long-time fans, but even some of them were not enthralled with a man who was sometimes described "as exciting as running water." Elson was gone from the scene after 1970. What was just as troubling as a long-time announcer leaving was that no major Chicago radio outlet wanted to carry White Sox broadcasts at the start of the 1971 season. Media exposure for the team was at an all-time low.

Now there is a statue of Harry Caray outside of Wrigley Field. To many fans, Caray is remembered mainly for his broadcast work for the Cubs and is a symbol of the team's popularity. Yet his Chicago broadcasting career actually began in 1971 for the White Sox when Caray did the radio play-by-play. His arrival on the scene was a stroke of luck for the sagging franchise. The White Sox needed someone dynamic to sell their product.

Caray developed his game-calling style very early in his career. After winning their first three in the '71 season, the White Sox reverted to their old patterns and began losing again. In an April 13 extra-inning defeat against the Angels, Bill Melton struck out to end the game in the bottom of the tenth. The White Sox were now in the middle of a seven-game losing streak. "Struck out," Caray said in a depressed tone. Caray sounded liked a disheartened fan as the Sox lost, 3–1, on a dark and gloomy spring day when they managed three lonely hits. That trait of showing displeasure with disappointing home-team performances would endear him to White Sox fans. Many didn't want a Jack Brickhouse-type, forever trying to cast a good light poor on performances. White Sox fans would tell anyone that they could see what happens on the field for themselves, and they didn't want an announcer telling them anything different. Even some Cubs fans began to tire of the sunny Brickhouse style as their team missed the World Series year after year.

On August 23, 1972, Caray went out to the center-field bleachers to do his radio broadcast. Caray had a fishing net to help him fend off foul balls hit straight back of home and toward the booth. That day he took his net with him. General manager Roland Hemond laughed because only three players ever hit a home run that cleared the wall behind what used to be the White Sox center-field bullpen. Why would Caray need that net?

Dick Allen came up to the plate in the seventh inning against Yankees reliever Lindy McDaniel. Allen hit a shot toward center, and from the reaction of center fielder Bobby Murcer, it was obvious Allen had another home run.

Yet this was no ordinary home run. Allen became the fourth player to knock a drive into the Comiskey Park center-field bleachers. The drive had to be at least 470 feet.

There was Caray, plainly seen by the television camera, reaching across his makeshift broadcast table trying to snare the Allen homer with his fishing net. He barely missed getting an historic souvenir, and then conducted an impromptu interview with the fan that came up with the ball. It was the type of entertainment the White Sox broadcasts had been missing for years.

Caray's center-field broadcasts solidified his image as a man of the fans. He didn't need a broadcast booth to do a game. Secondly, he demonstrated that the center-field bleachers were a great place for a fan to see a game. Because the bleachers had no backs and were so far away from the action, they were the cheapest seats in the house. Yet, they were still a great place to watch the game, with its over-the-pitcher's-shoulder view. Caray's presence out there sold the bleachers in a similar method to his selling Wrigley Field years later.

The next season, Caray was in the TV booth for innings one through three and seven through nine. He spent the middle three innings doing the radio broadcast. Caray now was the true "voice" of the Chicago White Sox.

Caray's favorite line during the seventies was "You can't beat fun at the old ballpark." Though he still reacted badly to White Sox defeats and team miscues, Caray always presented himself as having a good time at the game, even when the Sox were losing. WSNS Channel 44 cameras often showed Caray dancing in the booth between innings, but mostly during the seventh-inning stretch. Donning some loud shirt and comfortable-looking pants, Caray didn't look like an announcer for a major league franchise. Instead, he resembled a fan going out and having a few while he watched his favorite team on a hot summer night. And unlike some belligerent jerk, Caray projected the image of the happy drinker who bothered no one and only grew happier with each drink. Some of Caray's supporters denied he drank while he was on the air. However, in a photo that showed Caray doing his last broadcast for the Sox in 1981, there is a Budweiser can sitting in front of him as he again sat in the center-field bleachers. During the politically incorrect seventies, many fans didn't care whether Caray drank on the air or not. In fact, many liked the idea. During the late eighties, he did cornball commercials with beautiful young women wearing short shorts singing he was a "Cubs fan and a Bud Man." In the seventies, he hawked Falstaff Beer, a White Sox sponsor. The beer commercials, the broadcasting from the center-field bleachers, and the interviewing a fan who had just caught a home run ball solidified Caray's image as a working-class guy. Mix in some straight talk and the everyday fan felt as if he had a friend in the broadcast booth.

Toward the end of another disappointing season in 1973, Caray walked through the stands interviewing fans. He strolled through a near-empty and dark Comiskey talking anyone who was willing to come on the air. This was before the explosion of talk radio, and Caray gave these fans a platform to air their gripes. As he stood in the lower deck conducting many on-the-spot interviews, Caray appeared to be truly listening. This was no stunt.

But by the end of the 1975 season, Caray's "tell it like it is" style was no longer popular with the White Sox organization — if it ever had been in the purest sense. He had spent most of '75 ripping Bill Melton and Ken Henderson for not driving in runs. Melton felt as if he was being hounded out of the city. He eventually had a shouting match with Caray in a Milwaukee hotel lobby.

"Why should I have to listen to this?" Melton recalled a year after Caray died. "Roland Hemond didn't like Harry Caray. Chuck Tanner didn't like Harry Caray. The players couldn't stand Harry Caray. And this guy is ranting and raving and making himself a celebrity, which is fine. He was great at what he did. He wouldn't get off the young guys and that caused a lot of turmoil."[4]

The month of September was a dismal end to the Arthur-John Allyn era. The White Sox were a miserable 10–17 and home attendance didn't break the 10,000 mark. John Allyn fired Caray on October 1. That was a strange move, because Caray was the most popular person connected with the White Sox organization, and hardly anyone else listened when the other announcers tried to spin the dreadful season. A few months later, Allyn sold his interests in the White Sox to the group headed by Bill Veeck. When the next season began, Caray was still in the broadcast booth. He was the only announcer to survive the purge of the new ownership.

Bill Veeck then came up with the idea of using Caray to lead the singing during the seventh-inning stretch. "All right, Nancy," Caray would yell out to Sox organist Nancy Faust. In the middle of "Take Me Out to the Ballgame," Caray substituted "White Sox" for "home team." He'd wave his arm as if he were a conductor. In the middle of the song, Caray put his hand by his ear, prompting everyone to sing. Everyone did, and sometimes that was as loud as Comiskey got during the late seventies. The announcer went through the ritual every time, not showing that he tired of the routine at all. Fans reacted the same way.

Caray was accused of many things. He was too much of a homer. He was too negative. He drank too much, or he drank on the air. He reached the point where he thought he was bigger than the team. There was room for only two things in the broadcast booth — Harry Caray and his ego. One thing detractors failed to mention in all the controversy: In his prime, Harry Caray was a great play-by-play man.

Imagine a scenario such as this: A man is on first, and the ball is hit in the gap. In rapid-fire fashion, Caray told the fan how the ball was being played, where the runner on first was, and then, finally, what the batter was doing on the base paths. Even though it sounds easy, most people in the business will tell you that announcing is much harder than it appears. Caray had the ability to see the whole field and quickly relay that information to the fan. In his later years, especially after his stroke, Caray had a harder time describing fast or exciting action. The Cubs had to take him off radio because listeners had no idea of what was happening on the field. Caray no longer had the ability to quickly describe action, and his voice was at times unintelligible. The stroke must have affected his sight as well. During one game in Cincinnati, Caray described a drive caught by the center fielder near the wall as a home run. Only when the center fielder ran in because it was three outs did Caray realize that he called a long out as a homer. He embarrassingly apologized to his viewers. But in his day, Caray was one of the best.

By 1980, more attention was paid to the action in the broadcast booth than on the field. The White Sox weren't entertaining enough to keep the fans' attention. On July 2 of that year, Jimmy Piersall, the Sox color man, attacked Rob Gallas, then a sportswriter for a suburban paper. Piersall choked Gallas, and others on the scene had to pull Piersall off the sportswriter. Then Mike Veeck confronted Piersall in the broadcast booth. Piersall had said that Mary Frances Veeck, Mike's mother, was "a colossal bore." Piersall was referring to Mary Frances's performance on a radio program she shared with husband Bill. Mike then got Piersall in a headlock, telling Piersall that he better not insult Mary Frances again. Comiskey Park became a center for grown men choking each other.

The White Sox were being turned into a sideshow. Eddie Einhorn later called it a "freak show."[5] However, fan support for Piersall remained high, and he returned to the booth with Caray a few weeks after the Gallas incident. Fans liked the no-nonsense approach of both Caray and Piersall in pointing out just how bad the White Sox were. The politically correct stuff could be saved for the Cubs. The worse the White Sox performed, the more popular Caray and Piersall became. If Bill Veeck did anything, he was not going to break this team up, even with the occasional embarrassing behavior.

Change. Most people are resistant to it. It's scary and uncertain. One thing is certain. Whoever took control of the White Sox after Bill Veeck was going to be met with plenty of resistance and resentment. It didn't matter who they were, including Jerry Reinsdorf and Eddie Einhorn.

In a large sense, it is ironic that there is a rift between Bill Veeck and the current White Sox administration. That's right, I am using the present tense. In interviews I've conducted for this book, defenders of Einhorn and Reinsdorf go out of their way to criticize Veeck. The team marketing man has gone out of his way to separate himself from the Veeck legacy. Yet in some ways, Einhorn was cut from the same cloth as the man he criticized for running a slip-shod organization.

During the seventies, Einhorn produced the *CBS Sports Spectacular* to

Harry Caray and Jimmy Piersall during their last year as broadcast partners. No other two broadcasters were as controversial or as powerful as these two men. Jerry Reinsdorf and Eddie Einhorn really didn't know what to do with them.

compete with ABC's *Wide World of Sports*. The show aired a variety of sports, but also included offbeat segments like "battle of the NFL cheerleaders" and strongmen racing around with refrigerators strapped to their backs.

"A lot of people criticized us, but audiences ate it up," Einhorn wrote in his book *How March Became Madness*, co-written by Ron Rapoport. "When we finally beat ABC's *Wide World of Sports* one day, I explained to my sportswriter pal Vic Ziegel by saying, 'Our crap was better than their crap.'"[6]

So the program included some lowbrow stuff, but the average viewer enjoyed it. Isn't this some of the same type of criticism Veeck faced?

And there was Einhorn himself. In a September 6, 1982, *Sports Illustrated* article written by William Taaffe, Einhorn was described as "cheeky, flamboyant, a street hustler and proud of it."[7] Doesn't this also sound a little like Bill Veeck? Was Einhorn just as likable? He could have been, for all the fans knew.

But his public image took a beating. In those early years with the White Sox, Einhorn pushed for change that some fans weren't ready for or didn't want.*

As the Einhorn quote at the beginning of the chapter indicates, he was considered the new kid on the block. New kids usually get their noses bloodied in a figurative or literal sense before they are accepted. It was no exception for the new co-owner of the White Sox, and one has to wonder if he ever felt accepted.

"Eddie was fast talking and was a big forward thinker," Mike Leiderman told me. "Chicago is a provincial town. Chicagoans have their own way of doing things." Leiderman added that it didn't sit well with White Sox fans that they considered Einhorn a New York outsider. He said that Chicago has a thing about being a second city and "was always chasing New York." Leiderman said New Yorkers aren't fazed by Chicago's obsession with competing with the East Coast.[8]

Maybe Leiderman is right about Chicagoans and an inferiority complex regarding New York. Yet it didn't help that Einhorn seemed to insult Bill Veeck with his statement about the new ownership running a class operation. Secondly, he didn't seem to understand White Sox fans, and that only further solidified the view of him as an outsider.

In Chicago, the common image of the Sox fan was the working class, blue-collar guy. That is probably an over-simplification of what divides the baseball city. Yet it had been the belief from the start, that Comiskey, which was in the middle of the industrial South Side, drew the lunch-pail crowd. By 1982 that lunch-pail crowd had been bashed with a recession.

Wisconsin Steel, a Chicago South Side steel-making facility that employed more than 3,000 workers, closed one March afternoon in 1980 and never reopened its doors. U.S. Steel South Works, once with thousands of employees on the payroll, had a workforce of about 900 during the early eighties. Eventually it closed for good. In northwest Indiana, thousands of steelworkers were laid off and never returned to their old jobs. Home foreclosures were everyday occurrences. And then outside jobs tied to the mills vanished as well. Manufacturing facilities around the South Side were considered as outdated as Comiskey. Blue-collar work is tough, but it supports a family. Now these same workers didn't have money to do simple things like attend baseball games.

Some of those workers kept their jobs during the recession. Maybe even more would have come out to Comiskey in the early eighties if they had more faith in the economic situation. It would have been advantageous for Einhorn

---

At a recent SoxFest fan convention where I had a booth selling one of my other books, I said hello to Mrs. Einhorn. She and her son had a booth next to me where they were hawking a DVD her son had produced about the Winning Ugly 1983 season. She seemed surprised by my friendliness. No doubt the Einhorn family still felt the sting of a White Sox fan backlash. Being a public figure, especially a public figure connected with a major league franchise, can't be easy.

to acknowledge the bad economic times. The fact that he didn't only helped solidify his image as an outsider who lacked understanding of the fans he wanted to draw to Comiskey. Yet in the middle of an economic crisis, he verbally badgered White Sox fans about buying into a pay-per-view system.

Einhorn was shocked to see the TV deal negotiated by Bill Veeck. The package paled in comparison to even the late 1960s deal that put the White Sox on WFLD. To Einhorn it was simple: Television had to be the new source of revenue for baseball. The White Sox, who had experienced cash flow problems for more than a decade now, could no longer rely on the gate to make the franchise financially solvent or competitive on the field.

"We're not unlimited rich guys," Einhorn was quoted in the *Sports Illustrated* article. "You want to see my statement? Come see it. I lost three million dollars last year. I'm projected to lose three million dollars this year. You want [Steve] Kemp? You want me to sign Kemp? You want [Greg] Luzinski? You want a team to be proud of here, or do you want the Cubs?"[9]

Unpopular as this statement was (except to Sox fans, who must have enjoyed the jab at the Cubs), Einhorn, more than any other owner, understood the power of television, both for creating interest and making money. For years, baseball had poohed-poohed the idea of television as a major force. In the beginning, television screens were small and the baseball establishment thought it couldn't possibly display the whole field. Also in the early post–World War II era, many families couldn't afford to have televisions in their homes. That was why people went to the local tavern to watch the game and stood by department store windows to get a view of one their favorite shows. And most teams, with the exception of the Cubs, didn't think TV was a way to recruit fans. Television was seen as a detriment to attendance.

Einhorn thought pay TV was the answer. He firmly believed that the Cubs weren't competing on the field because of its free TV package. And in the long run, Einhorn projected that the revenue generated by television would surpass the original outlay to purchase the team. Yet by the end of the 1982 season, the White Sox had less than half the subscribers needed to get Sportsvision to the break-even point, much less make it profitable.

"They alienated many fans," sports journalist Mark Liptak says. "People were leery of Sportsvision. The timing was wrong. They may have succeeded in a one-team town."[10] Sox fans weren't happy to pay for TV programming when Cubs games were still free.

Liptak felt the concept might have worked if there was more programming to attract viewers. Specifically, he thought it would have been more attractive if the Sox showed tapes of past games. But he said that in those days it was tough to store and archive tapes of old games. According to Liptak, even if the tapes had been archived, the new ownership looked for this material and couldn't find it. He wondered if the Veecks took it.

Liptak said that major league baseball now mandates that all games be taped and archived. Regardless, he felt that the forward-thinking Einhorn erred in his Sportsvision approach because it needed more than the summertime scheduling of current Sox games. "In '68 and '82, they shot themselves in the foot," Liptak said. "Now those kids are Cubs fans."[11]

While the Sox were shooting themselves in the foot in the late sixties, Eddie Einhorn had one of his largest and far-reaching television successes more than a decade before his involvement with the White Sox. He paid $27,000 for a network called TVS to acquire the broadcast rights for a Saturday night basketball broadcast between UCLA and the University of Houston on January 20, 1968. The two teams played each other in the previous NCAA Tournament; both were undefeated and were ranked one and two in the national polls. The game was scheduled to be played in the Houston Astrodome.

In getting local stations to sign up to air the game, Einhorn had to make two convincing arguments. First, fans would be interested enough in a regular-season college basketball game. Second, stations had to be willing to offend the national networks by pre-empting normal programming.

Einhorn proved that he understood his audience and the power of television sports programming. A crowd of 52,693 showed at the Astrodome to see Houston edge UCLA, 71–69. The game became known as "The Game of the Century."

"Right after the game Guy [Lewis, Houston basketball coach] started pushing to have the NCAA tournament in the Astrodome," Ted Nance, former sports information director at the University of Houston, recalled in *How March Became Madness*. "In 1971, we got the first Final Four ever played in a domed stadium. By then the demand for tickets for the tournament was huge."[12]

Now there are no qualms about any station carrying a regular-season college basketball game, and the NCAA Tournament is a sports obsession for the entire month of March. Even the most casual college basketball fan will predict his own bracket. Einhorn deserves a lot of credit for the popularity and growth explosion of a sports industry.

So if Einhorn was a promotional genius when it came to a college basketball game, and a forward thinker when it came to major league baseball and television, where did he go wrong with the Sportsvision concept?

First, whether Einhorn knew it or not, he had fired one of the first salvos in a battle between the White Sox and their fans that still rages today. Einhorn told fans that he, Jerry Reinsdorf, and the rest of the Sox ownership needed more revenue to put a contending team on the field, so the fans had to ante up. Fans, after experiencing a losing Sox era from 1968 to 1980 and suffering other Chicago sports defeats, wanted to see some results first, so they thought the ownership were the ones who had to ante up. It also had to be discouraging for fans to hear another claim of ownership poverty or at least a limited cash flow. The ownership had to feel frustrated that fans thought they could spend money like the Yankees. Just who was going to win the economic game of chicken? One thing was certain: The new ownership hadn't been around long enough to demonstrate that they were better than the rest of the Chicago sports managers who put together losing teams. Fans had already spent plenty of money on broken dreams.

Second, there was the pay TV price tag. Installation costs were $52.95 and a $21.95 fee per month, a lot of money in the economically strapped times of 1982. Fans were not apt to put up this money in 1982 any more than they wanted to purchase a converter box or new TV to watch UHF in the late sixties.

As it turned out, Einhorn was right in the long run. Paid television would become an important revenue stream for major league baseball. Maybe if Sportsvision had come a few years later as part of a general cable package, it would have been successful. Or maybe if the concept had another spokesman or salesman, more fans would have bought into the idea, even this unpopular one.

"To me, it's un–American," said Harry Caray, the man of the people. "Baseball is a game that belongs to the people. The White Sox were dangling some big figures in front of me, but I got to thinking, 'Where is that guy who made me what I am today, that bartender and that shut-in and that cab driver?' I got to thinking, 'Well, these guys aren't going to be able to afford listening to me.'"[13]

"That's Neanderthal thinking," Einhorn responded. "Nothing is free."[14]

Of course, Einhorn was right. Not about Sportsvision, but about the future of television in baseball. But in 1982 he was losing the political debate to Caray. Caray had built his following over the years and fans didn't even know who Einhorn was yet. And fans, like the baseball establishment had been for decades, were leery of the influence television could have over the game. Who was this television guy telling us we had to fork over money for television? Caray sounded like he was more in touch.

Not buying into the Sportsvision concept for a variety of reasons, Caray left the White Sox. But he didn't just leave. He went to the North Side and took his common man approach with him. Instead of helping the Sox sell a new TV concept, Caray spent the next fifteen years selling Wrigley Field and everything else connected with the Cubs. And for a good portion of that time, he did it on free TV.

10

C.U.B.S. (Chicagoans United for a Baseball Series)

"It was, to steal a famous phrase, 'one small step' for Cubs fans."

— *Opening statement in leaflet produced by a fan group called Chicago United for a Baseball Series describing a meeting the organization's officers had with Bob Kennedy.*[1]

"The only other thing I can say about the meeting is that I hope I can keep my temper under control."

— *Cubs executive vice president Bob Kennedy, not exactly looking forwarding to that meeting with those C.U.B.S. representatives.*[2]

"It's been the same sad refrain every year, for what seemingly has been an eternity. The hope of April always turns into the reality of July and then into the resignation of September."

— *December 1978 C.U.B.S. statement.*

There are several stereotypes associated with Chicago Cubs fans. Just give them a cold beer and some sunshine. Players only need to smile and wave at them. It's Wrigley Field and all the surroundings. Losing is lovable and the continued absence of a World Series title actually has an addicting influence that has fans coming back every season. Go to the ballpark with your cell phone and hope you can see yourself on camera.

If those descriptions fit any Cubs loyalist, it didn't apply to a group that formed a Cubs fan organization during the late seventies. These fans had had enough of the losing seasons and the decades-long inability to get to the World Series. For years, White Sox fans have accused the Chicago-area media of an anti–Sox bias. In the late seventies and early eighties, C.U.B.S. members felt strongly that the media was not sympathetic to their views. They wanted the media to listen. They wanted the Cubs to listen. Losing was not lovable. They even wanted a say in running the team.

Their logo was a backwards "C" with the U.B.S. placed in the middle. Underneath was written 1945–??? The logo was done in a bold black and each end of the "C" looked like a vice coming down on the U.B.S. The entire logo looked menacing, and it was doubtful that these fans could be placated with an Old Style.

The Cubs had played extremely well during the first three months of 1977. On June 28, they were 47–22 and in first place, 8 games ahead of their closest competitors, the Phillies. But they played 25 games under .500 the rest of the way and had to settle for a dead-even 81–81 record. The 1978 season was a forgettable year as they finished four games under .500. C.U.B.S., an organization that described itself as a "permanent, not-for-profit watchdog corporation," was not satisfied with losing records and non-contending seasons.

In their December 1978 newsletter, the organization vowed to take several coordinated actions to get the attention of the Chicago National League Ball Club, Inc. They included:

- Hold monthly meetings to discuss all things concerning the Cubs, which included lack of parking, higher ticket prices, concessions and handling of players.
- Attempt to meet with GM Bob Kennedy to express views as put forward by members of the organization.

Bill Madlock in May 1976. In three seasons for the Cubs, he hit .313, .354, and .339. Yet the team shipped him to San Francisco before the 1977 season.

- C.U.B.S. members to meet as a group at all Wrigley Sunday games to voice disapproval with banners and chants. The organization emphasized that the Sunday outings were still supposed to be fun and things were not to get out of hand.
- Organize a media "blitz" where fans would call into radio shows to get their views out. TV and print media would be contacted as well.
- The possibility of picketing Wrigley Field in April of '79 if the Cubs hadn't taken enough actions to put a contending team on the field. The purpose of the pickets would be to urge fans not to buy box seats or reserved grandstand seating until the club "takes appropriate action."[3]

C.U.B.S. felt only an organized action would have any effect on the Cubs. Without it, these fans thought the ball club would not feel any obligation to put a winning team on the field. It must be pointed out, however, even though the organization had a militant sound to it, its publications never advocated actual boycotts of Cubs home games.

One thing C.U.B.S. did accomplish was a meeting with Bob Kennedy. Three of the office holders of the organization — president Dave Yager, treasurer Ed Ivers, and chairman George Castle — met with the front-office man for more than an hour. Events leading up to the meeting were a bit comical.

C.U.B.S. were more than happy to advertise their meeting to the Chicago media. When *Tribune* reporter Dave Nightingale contacted Kennedy to ask about the impending meeting, Kennedy asked how Nightingale knew about the gathering. Nightingale told Kennedy about a C.U.B.S. media release to that effect.

"They did, huh?" Kennedy said, apparently not sounding too happy. Then Nightingale informed Kennedy that the news release stated this was to be a series of meetings. "It does, huh?" Kennedy replied, and again the tone didn't appear to be a happy one. He then followed with his statement regarding his temper, which, according to Nightingale, was a magnificent one.[4]

The meeting, as described in the next C.U.B.S. newsletter, was cordial enough. The C.U.B.S. representatives expressed their frustrations with the lack of success on the North Side. Kennedy empathized and told the fans he had the same frustration.

"I'm even more frustrated than you fans," Kennedy said. "It's my job, after all. I do want to win worse than anything — after all, I'm a native Chicagoan and I've got family and friends here."[5]

Then Kennedy told C.U.B.S. that their input was welcome. He stated that he was sensitive to other fans' opinions as well, as his office received 30 to 40 letters a day, many of which he answered. He also said he took some calls, since not all the calls were stopped by his secretary. But he finally put the fans' role in running the team in perspective.

"You can make suggestions," he said, "but remember, your job isn't on the line if your suggestion doesn't pan out. If you're a scout or a coach and your job is riding on the success of your input, then you have a right to give me a suggestion and expect me to follow up on it."[6]

The C.U.B.S. newsletter stated that the meeting was a nice opening of communication, although Kennedy didn't make any further commitments regarding future meetings. Meanwhile, the Cubs had another sub–.500 season in 1979. A C.U.B.S. newsletter told Cubs fans that "in many ways the conclusion of the season has to rank as one of the more despicable endings to a Cubs year perhaps in their entire history."[7] The Cubs ended the year with a 9–22 September mark, which can easily be labeled as "despicable." The newsletter stated that the fan organization was needed more than ever.

And it apparently didn't want to hear any more happy talk about waiting until next year. The newsletter ran a cartoon of Jack Brickhouse with headphones and a large number "9" on the left side his sports jacket. He is hanging out of the TV, practically in the face of a Cubs fan sitting in an easy chair with a drink and some snacks. Below the television are the words "The Jack-In-The-Box." With a smile Brickhouse says, "Well, that's the game of baseball, fans. You win some, you lose some." Then the fan is shown sitting across from a blank TV, doing "the slow burn." In an accompanying questionnaire, the newsletter asks fans who they want to succeed Brickhouse in the broadcast booth when the long-time Cubs announcer retired.[8]

By the middle of 1979, the organization's dues-paying members grew to more than 600. But the team kept losing, and some backlash boomeranged on C.U.B.S.

By 1982, the Wrigleys were gone, and C.U.B.S. had very few members. "We're in hiatus now, more or less," Ivers said in August 1982. "We're giving Dallas Green the benefit of the doubt and not taking any stance yet."[9]

Although C.U.B.S. was a fan-advocate organization, it started taking some heat from other Cubs fans. "We were teed off at the Wrigleys in general and Bob Kennedy," Ivers told Paul Sullivan of the *Tribune*. "Lots of people looked up on us as jumping on any negative thing the Cubs did and just didn't like us at all. It's tough to bad rap the Cubs because most fans will come out and see them, win or lose. But there are some people who were frustrated and mad. I believe we were the first organization of fans who really got on the club."[10]

11

Manic Fandom in Chicago

"I just wanted to show the White Sox what it looks like from the other side. It's bush what they do, it's a disgrace to baseball. It makes the game a sideshow, and those fans are just making clowns out of their players with all that jazz."

— *Kansas City Royal Hal McRae on July 31, 1977 as he put down that summer's practice of fan "curtain calls" for Sox players hitting homers.*[1]

"Why should it be any different than any other year?"

— *Former sportswriter Bill Gleason in remembering the pessimism before the 1977 season.*[2]

"Red Sox suck! Red Sox suck!"

— *Simple fan chant during July home game when the White Sox pounded the Red Sox.*

"They stand at the plate when they hit a home run, they run the bases real slow, they tip their hat, they come out of the dugout and tip their hat again. It's bush. It's a joke. I'm surprised it got this far."

— *Hal McRae continuing his rant.*[3]

"A ball in the ear."

—*That is what Hal McRae thought White Sox players would get if they pulled off their curtain calls in the National League.*[4]

"There was something about 1977."

—*White Sox broadcaster Lorn Brown recalling the atmosphere in Comiskey Park that year.*[5]

"I've never heard crowds that loud, not even in 2005."

—Chicago Sun-Times *columnist Richard Roeper in a column that appeared on July 4, 2006*[6]

With all their differences, Cubs and White Sox fans had a few things in common. The obvious thing is that their teams rarely, if ever, go to the World Series. The other thing was when they were having a good time, other teams couldn't stand it.

In 1969, the Wrigley Field Bleacher Bums drew all kinds of fire. True, it is not nice to throw things at opposing players. At Comiskey two years later, Oriole left fielder Don Buford claimed that Sox fans were throwing various things at him, including the backs ripped off of seats. Hard to believe, since the seats at old Comiskey were sturdy. They weren't comfortable, but they were not in the state of disrepair the rest of the stadium was in. Buford had gotten into a fight with Sox pitcher Bart Johnson after Johnson had hit Buford with a pitch. Buford thought Johnson was headhunting because Buford had hit two homers in the game, one of which came off Johnson. The game was the nightcap of a Memorial Day doubleheader on May 31.

It was a different time. Although Buford had charged the mound with a bat in his hand, he was not thrown out of the game. Then, right before his next plate appearance in the ninth, Buford went over to confront a heckling fan in the lower boxes. The atmosphere in Comiskey was already charged. Home plate umpire Nestor Chylak wanted no more of Buford, and ejected him for approaching the fan. Someone threw a soft drink at Buford, but the plastic cup that still had a straw hit Chylak in the neck. Coke splattered his shoulders, but he maintained his attention on Buford and didn't even look back at the stands. The situation worsened when a Sox fan ran onto the field to attack Buford. Oriole players surrounded him and all that could be seen were fists flying as the fan took a beating. The fan was escorted off the field in a bloody mess. The defending world champion Orioles then gave the White Sox a different type of pounding by piling on five more runs in the inning to win the game, 11–3. No one would have ever known that the Sox were ahead, 2–1, on the strength of a two-run homer by Bill Melton at one point.

So, no, fans throwing things at players or running on the field is not a good thing. Running onto the field for any reason cannot be condoned, period. Hero worship should only go so far. But what about some harmless fun?

The Cubs and Ron Santo came under some serious attack after the Cubs third baseman started doing his "heel clicking" in the emotional summer of '69. Santo ran down the line toward the clubhouse after Cubs home victories, clicking his heels in delight. Cubs fans loved it; the opposition thought it was being shown up. White Sox fans and just about any other non–Cubs fan hated it. However, Santo did his routine after the game was over. Presumably the opposition was already making its way into the clubhouse, so many of those players would not have seen the routine. White Sox fans could turn the TV dial. Yet the Cubs were ripped for it. By the end of August, Santo stopped. When their championship dreams ended, it seemed like the whole baseball

Ron Santo during his only season with the White Sox. White Sox fans and Santo never really warmed up to that situation. Santo retired a year later.

world rejoiced. The Cubs and their fans could keep their heel clicking. Santo never did it for the remainder of his career.

Now the 1977 White Sox had their home run curtain calls. And the White Sox were acting like bush leaguers despite having a very improbable season.

What was a curtain call? A White Sox player would hit a home run and then would circle the bases to the tune of the "Monster" shooting fireworks into the sky. Yet the scoreboard celebration wasn't enough. Fans would cheer at such a volume, the home run hitter would feel compelled to step out of the dugout to acknowledge the crowd with a tip of the hat.

One of the most memorable images of 1977 was on July 3 in the first inning of the second game of a doubleheader against the Twins. Jim Spencer had just hit his 12th homer of the season to put the White Sox ahead, 4–0. A *Chicago Sun-Times* photo captured the 6'2" Spencer (though he seemed taller) standing right outside the dugout and saluting the fans in the lower deck. Even in a newsprint photo, it is easy to see the emotion and intensity of the crowd. The Sox would have one of the best months in the history of the franchise, when they went 22–6.

Very few thought the White Sox were supposed to have any success in 1977. No expert ventured a guess that the club could contend for anything. In an April *Sun-Times* column, Bill Gleason pleaded with Sox owner Bill Veeck to do something. Gleason didn't care what it was; he only wanted Veeck to do it.[7] He and many Sox fans had no usual optimism that came with spring. One fan wrote Gleason that he had a fistful of Opening Day tickets but was tempted not to go.

On that Opening Day, the White Sox didn't look like any kind of team. They wore their "softball" uniforms. The pullover shirts were all white except for the black edges around the neck. Their black pants could have been mistaken for pajama bottoms. Why they didn't go back to their traditional pinstripe uniforms with the fancy Sox lettering is a mystery.

But more than the uniforms, it was their overall appearance that was lacking. Lined up for Comiskey Opening Day ceremonies, the players looked like a bunch of average guys preparing for a pick-up game after work. They were probably only recognizable to White Sox fans. Manager Bob Lemon stood at the end with his protruding stomach and a grandfatherly look. He stared off into the distance, appearing to be distracted. One would never think that this team's offense would terrorize American League pitching for most of the summer, especially after they had dropped two of three to the expansion Toronto Blue Jays to start the season.

The White Sox won that Comiskey opener, 5–2, over the hard-hitting Boston Red Sox. Their starter, Ken Brett, pitched deep into the eighth inning and walked no one. The defense committed no errors. From all appearances, the White Sox had played well. But there was nothing memorable about what looked like an average major league game. They hit no home runs and didn't even score after picking up one in the first inning and four in the second. The crowd of a little more than 34,000 was of good size, meaning that pessimistic fans still came out to the park despite threats of being no-shows.

Then they did something that few previous White Sox teams did — they hit. The White Sox had done some hitting in the seventies. They had back-to-back home run champions in Bill Melton and Dick Allen. But those teams didn't have much power other than those two players. In '74 they actually led the American League in homers but one would never have known it, considering their 80–80 record. Additionally, that was in the offensively impaired early seventies when the American League installed the designated hitter to help teams score more runs. Hitting 135 homers to lead the league is not all that impressive, even in the pre-steroid age. How many White Sox look back at 1974 with any fondness?

The 1977 season was just plain different. Everyone was hitting. In reality, they couldn't do much else. Range in the outfield was nonexistent. The only one who covered any ground was center fielder Chet Lemon, and it showed

Opposite: Jim Spencer one year before the South Side Hitmen. The swing looks good here. Twice he picked up eight RBIs in a game in 1977.

with the record number of putouts he made. Third baseman Eric Soderholm missed the 1976 season because of a knee injury and was barely mobile. Shortstop Alan Bannister had a bad shoulder and a hard time making simple throws to first, even when he had momentum toward the bag. First baseman Jim Spencer was the only true defender in the infield, and he showed it by winning the Gold Glove for that position that year.

Maybe that was one reason fans latched onto the team. Maybe they were tired of the no-hit, no-offense wonders of the sixties who couldn't go to the World Series and then flamed out. The hell with defense. How about a team that just could hit the hell out of the ball?

On July 1, the weather was hot. The first-place Minnesota Twins came into Chicago for a four-game series, one game ahead of the second-place White Sox. For the past couple of years, White Sox fans were not used to their team being so close to first at that time of year. As the fans warmed up to their team's hard hitting, they had a recent memory that might lead them to worry about the White Sox failing to show in a crucial series.

On July 21, 1974, the Sox won the first game of a doubleheader against the Milwaukee Brewers, 3–2. Chicago now had a seven-game winning streak, and was only 4 games behind first-place Oakland. With the All-Star break coming up that week, it appeared that the team was catching fire and there was a chance they could contend for the division in a series. In game two, they took a 3–0 lead into the ninth. Taking a doubleheader and extending the winning streak to eight would be a great thing right before the break. But then Chicago baseball happened.

Reliever Terry Forster gave up a two-out grand slam to Deron Johnson and Milwaukee salvaged a game out of the series, winning, 5–3. And it was a loud grand slam. Johnson banged the slam against the exact middle of the upper-deck façade and the ball ricocheted hard back into short left field. It was cruel. The ball didn't end up back on the field because an angry fan threw back an enemy home run souvenir. It seemed as if the home run was shoved in their faces as the winning streak was suddenly ending. The ball appeared to be something dead sitting in the middle of the grass, dead as the White Sox's playoff hopes seemed to be.

Coming back from the break, the White Sox lost five out of their first six, including three to first-place Oakland. Momentum, if there is such a thing in baseball, was gone. Chicago finished in fourth, nine games behind Oakland. The season had been a huge letdown.

So fans in 1977 hoped their team wouldn't be embarrassed in their own park. They didn't want the team swept, or any heart-breaking losses like the

Opposite: **Pat Kelly getting ready to dive back into first. One hopes he didn't skin his knees.**

one against the Brewers in 1974. The White Sox exceeded their expectations and then some.

Scoring thirty-four runs against the Twins, the White Sox swept the series. They even received some good pitching when Wilbur Wood and Chris Knapp picked up complete games. In game two, Jim Spencer posted eight RBIs, the second time he pulled off the feat that season. Spencer homered in the second game of the doubleheader and came out for his curtain call. It was a great moment at Comiskey; it was also something that would be held against the White Sox and their fans in a big way.

At the end of the month, Chicago had another huge four-run game series, this one against the defending division champion Kansas City Royals. The Royals had supplanted the Twins as the second-place team chasing the White Sox. Again the Sox responded. Chicago won the first two games before facing the Royals in a Sunday doubleheader. The first game of that twin-bill turned out to be the high point of the decade.

The White Sox won, 5–4, in 10 innings. Chicago trailed by two in the 10th when Chet Lemon lined a two-homer into the lower left-field seats. It was Lemon's second homer of the game. The winning run came home a short time later on an RBI single by Ralph Garr. According to columnist Roeper, who attended the doubleheader, Comiskey Park almost "crumbled" under the celebration of the dramatic victory.[8] There were slightly more than 50,400 fans at Comiskey that day.

The White Sox had won 22 of their last 27 games in an incredible month. It had been 10 years since their 1967 last-week collapse, and except for 1972, they hadn't contended for anything. The ball club had finally whipped its fans into frenzy, and maybe the faithful felt like taking some credit for the upsurge. What the fans didn't know was that the curtain calls would stop inspiring their team and started inspiring everyone else, especially the Royals.

Kansas City won the second game of the doubleheader, 8–4. Hal McRae homered in the seventh, and then mocked Sox fans with a slow trot and a tip of the cap. After the game he expressed the rant that is highlighted at the start of this chapter. His teammates chimed in, saying the Royals would catch and pass the White Sox. You would never know they had lost three out of four in the series.

The White Sox traveled to Kansas City for a three-game series the next weekend. The inspired Royals socked four homers in the first game, and pounded the Sox, 12–2. They again mocked the White Sox with curtain calls of their own. Up in the Sox broadcast booth, color man Jimmy Piersall said it was over for the Sox not only for that game, but for the season. Broadcast partner Lorn Brown told Piersall if he felt that way, he should leave. Piersall did, and didn't return for the rest of the broadcast. Unfortunately, for the White Sox and their fans, Piersall's forecast was correct.

On August 11, the White Sox fell out of first place for the first time in six weeks. Kansas City still wasn't in first, but the Royals would be. The White Sox were exposed as the one-dimensional team they truly were. Yes, they could hit, but what else could they do?

According to Eric Soderholm, the McRae rant was done for a purpose, and was a crucial turning point in the Sox fading out of the division race. McRae "was making a mockery of what we were doing," Soderholm said years later. "It was psychological and it was smart on their part. We became self-conscious of what we were doing."[9] Soderholm also said that Sox players were self-conscious about the curtain calls to start with and only did them to please the fans. Meanwhile, he thought a tool that was used to inspire the team was turned around and employed against it.

Columnist Roeper conceded in 2006 that "we probably were the most obnoxious franchise — players as well as fans — in all of baseball."[10] But then he wrote in the same column that the players were not at fault for the curtain calls. He contended that it was the atmosphere created by the fans that demanded the players respond. "It was our fault," he wrote. "We were just nuts in the stands."[11]

Regardless, the White Sox had reignited their fan base, just as the Cubs had done in the late sixties. Not only did the faithful return, they cheered the club on in rabid fashion. Soderholm would remember a roar when he rounded second base after hitting a home run against Kansas City in the first game of that fateful late–July series. He described Comiskey as being a penned in, close-feeling ballpark. Maybe that is why Roeper thought it was so much noisier than U.S. Cellular in 2005. U.S. Cellular is open in the outfield and some of the noise can escape.

Or maybe the times were different. In 2005, jaded fans might have been afraid to get excited because of a feared collapse. In 2000, they watched their team go down meekly in the postseason after having posted the best record in the American League. They saw the Cubs blow their best chance to go the World Series yet by turning on one of their own. Fans had yelled and screamed and went fanatical only to experience a huge letdown and then realized they may have been partly responsible for the fall.

Cubs fans have 1969. Sox fans have 1977. Decades later, after division championships, a wild-card berth, and even a World Series, each fandom has a soft spot for clubs that have won nothing. Although fans of both Chicago clubs went through similar experiences, neither group will sympathize with the other. It only demonstrates that Chicago fans have their own identities.

When I began writing this book, my premise was that the fans on the opposite ends of Chicago were vastly different, at least when it came to their baseball tastes. Their experiences, traditions, and perspectives created two completely separate fan bases. Yet the attachment to two teams shows that these unique groups are eerily similar. The 1969 Cubs and 1977 White Sox both caused great excitement and long-standing nostalgia. In the late eighties an old-timers game was held at Comiskey, pitting the two former teams against each other. It had been a decade since the Hitmen had their fun season, and twenty years since the Cubs made a run at the World Series. But in the end, neither team won anything. Their somewhat-limited successes seemed to bring the wrath of other teams down on them for various reasons. And, at least to an extent, the fans turned on their team either from disappointment or what some perceived as player disloyalty.

With the passage of time, one would think that 1969 would simply fade into history. Many present-day Cubs fans have no first-hand memories of that season. Yet in 2006, almost four decades later, a baseball historian released a book on the club that had four future Hall-of-Famers (including manager Leo Durocher) but could not finish first in the initial season of divisional play.

Author Doug Feldmann was born one year after the championship that never was. Despite not having lived to witness the meltdown, Feldmann expertly chronicles the season in his book, *Miracle Collapse: The 1969 Cubs.* Feldmann is successful in writing a history that realistically sets the scene and atmosphere of Chicago baseball during the late '60s. "1969 still seems a year that provokes powerful emotions for Cubs fans," Feldmann wrote in an e-mail statement. "With high expectations, early season success and a late season collapse, it is perhaps the quintessential Cubs season."[12]

The 1969 season provided a novel experience for all Chicago baseball fans. The last World Series appearance by a Chicago franchise had been exactly a decade earlier and the only one in the post–World War II era. Chicago was obsessed with the idea that baseball might be played in Chicago in October.

"People weren't talking politics, war or economics in the summer of 1969 in Chicago," Ron Santo told author David Claerbaut. "They were talking about the Chicago Cubs. We were treated like rock stars; we would have to fight through the crowds just to get to our cars three hours after game time."[13] And this was something: Not talking about war or politics? The Vietnam War still raged for Americans and the violent Democratic National Convention was held in Chicago the year before.

Cubs fans around the country were having a great time, but the rest of the National League wasn't. There was the backlash against the Bleacher Bums, and then there was the Santo heel-clicking after the game. It seemed like the rest of the league was cheering for anyone playing the Cubs.

"Not to my knowledge" was Feldmann's response to the any supposed reaction to Santo's post-game celebrations. "I don't think the opposing teams cared if he did it or not."[14]

Yet Santo would later say he saw an increased number of inside pitches. "The rest of the league wasn't enthralled. Once they started to catch onto my

Oscar Gamble during the Hitmen year. He looks like he was ready to golf one of his 31 homers that year.

Ron Santo on the day his number was retired. His presence is a constant reminder of the new-found Cub hero worship of the late sixties.

act, the pitches seemed to get a lot closer to my head, the brush-back pitches seemed to get closer to my chin."[15]

In the end, the harshest lambasting of the Cubs came at the hands of their fans, who were bitter about seeing a rare chance to go the World Series vanish with the combination of a Cubs slump and a Mets hot streak. "It was brutal, most brutal I've ever heard," an unnamed Cubs player told Claerbaut.[16]

In 2006 the South Side Hitmen were still being written about and remembered. *Chicago Sun-Times* columnist Richard Roeper wrote in a July 4 column about the summer excitement at Comiskey. Roeper recalled that he went to about 30 games that year and stated that he "never heard crowds that loud, not in even in 2005."[17]

Roeper wrote of his July 3, 1977, experience when Jim Spencer homered in the first inning of the second game of a doubleheader against the Twins. Roeper — as others who were there have said — recalled how the fans wouldn't stop cheering until Spencer came out for his curtain call.[18]

The rest of the league wasn't as understanding. The curtain calls were criticized, and opposing teams gloated as the Hitmen began to unravel in

August. After an August 14 loss to Texas, Ranger pitcher Dock Ellis gleefully taunted both Sox and Cubs fans by saying there would be no Chicago World Series in 1977. By then the Cubs had fallen from first to third and would slip even further.

As with the Cubs at the end of 1969, White Sox fans felt a lingering bitterness after the failure of 1977. Rickie Zisk left the White Sox to sign a long-term deal with the Texas Rangers. During the Rangers' second trip to Chicago in 1978 during the Fourth of July holiday, Sox fans greeted Zisk and Bobby Bonds in a harsh way that would have made some of the Bleacher Bums proud. Bonds had started the 1978 season with the Sox and was traded in early May after getting off to a bad start. Sox fans were not ready to forgive former South Side Hitman Zisk for fleeing the team for more money.

"They threw ice at Bobby and everything from sparkplugs and hard candy at me," Zisk told *Chicago Tribune* columnist Rick Talley. "Firecrackers, too."[19]

Apparently, this treatment had Zisk a little psyched out. In his first four games at Comiskey as a Ranger, Zisk went 0-for-13. Those numbers didn't seem to concern him, however. He said there were more important things to do with his life than play in Chicago, and didn't want to end up "crippled." White Sox manager Larry Doby had a similar response to the outfield rowdiness that the Cubs had when they put their "basket" up in 1970. "I can see a day coming when we'll have to fence off the lower stands to protect the players," Doby said, prompting images of the basket at Wrigley.[20]

When the White Sox had their old-timers game, Zisk declined, citing family responsibilities. When the White Sox celebrated the 25th anniversary of the South Side Hitmen at their annual pre-season fan convention, Zisk wasn't around. When I contacted Zisk about doing an interview for a previous story about the 1977 team, the former right fielder didn't respond to phone messages, e-mails and regular mail. The 1977 campaign was his career year and during that season he couldn't say enough nice things about White Sox fans. But as time went on, he didn't even want to talk about those fans or a season that some White Sox fans don't want to forget, even in the wake of 2005.

The memories of both years can be very painful to both sets of fans and players. However, Feldmann doesn't think 1969 should invoke only bad memories, and that was not the intention of his book:

> My purpose in writing the book was not to remind people of the Cubs' collapse, or even of the Mets' ascension. Rather it was simply to recall the happy, fun moments from that season, such as Willie Smith's pinch-hit homer to win the game in the opener or "Billy Williams Day" in June against the Cardinals when he got several hits in a doubleheader.* Don Kessinger wrote the foreword for my book, and he

---

In the Cubs sweep of St. Louis, Williams went one-for-four in game one, and four-for-five in game two, which included two triples. More than 41,000 came to honor Williams, who was playing in his 895th and 896th straight games.

Richie Zisk during his only season with the White Sox. The 1977 season was his career year. Fans didn't forgive him for using free agency to go to Texas. He apparently didn't forgive fans for throwing things at him.

was very gracious. He was very willing to talk with me on any topic related to 1969. I truly believe that he feels (as well as other members on that team) that the city was behind them that summer, and they are remembered fondly.[21]

The 1969 and 1977 seasons were two more years that Chicago baseball teams didn't win championships. But Feldman doesn't believe that the squads are merely remembered because each franchise was having such a hard time winning at that point in baseball history. "The inclination is to say it's [fan nostalgia] a sign of a lack of success for those franchises. Rather, I tend to view it as an appreciation of lesser-known yet historic teams that might otherwise be forgotten."[xx]

12

Seeing the Game in a Different Way

"The rooftops are the worst experience. Not one person was watching the game. It was just an excuse to socialize. It was a phony experience."

— *Iowa City Cubs fan Andrew Shaffer.*[1]

"The Cubs are lucky."

— *Former Sun-Times columnist Ron Rapoport describing Cubs fortunes regarding the development of the neighborhood around Wrigley Field. Rapoport sees nothing wrong with being lucky and credits the neighborhood as one important factor in the Cubs attendance explosion.*[2]

"People come here to party and cheer on the Cubs. They want the Cubs to win, but if they don't, it's not the end of the world."

— *Roof-top owner Dave Abrams talking about the experience at Skybox on Sheffield.*[3]

In an early 1980s *Chicago Reader* article on the losing ways of the Cubs, there was an accompanying photo of an empty Wrigley Field in early September. Pigeons and other birds could be seen flying just under the roof of the upper deck and right above rows of vacant seats. In the horizon there was nothing but sky. Fans were absent, and that was the whole point of the story. After all, it was September and that meant the Cubs were playing out the string of another campaign when thoughts of contending for the postseason stopped shortly after Opening Day.

The seats are never empty now. As for the horizon, look out over the outfield walls and you'll see more fans. Wrigley Field, in the strictest and last sense, is a neighborhood ballpark. Apartment buildings and local businesses are almost on top of the place. And from the rooftops of the apartment buildings, fans can see the game live without going into the ballpark.

The Tribune Company became unhappy about the rooftop owners, and in a way, no one could blame them. The Cubs ownership thought their product was being stolen from them by a bunch of opportunists. Yet like the airing of Cubs games on TV, the team didn't suffer from overexposure. Wrigley remained packed. And the team got free publicity when the TV cameras pointed their lenses to the excitement that spilled out into the streets or climbed on top of a roof. That image only added to the mystique of Wrigley. The Chicago Cubs seemed to have fans everywhere.

I went to a Cubs-Marlins game on May 2, 2009, to check out the rooftop experience. Three hours before the start of a noon game, the streets around the ballpark were busy. Massive crowds hadn't arrived yet but the atmosphere differed from the pre-game transient-like crowds around U.S. Cellular. Fans were stopping in places to eat, drink, sell tickets, and buy tickets. The day centered on a Cubs game, and it was only beginning.

Car traffic is relatively light. Parking is at a premium at the ballpark. There is one small lot directly across the street and it is still empty. "Gold Parking" a sign read. The cost is $50. The lack of convenience is not stopping people from making their way to Wrigley.

There are two statues outside Wrigley. One is of Ernie Banks, one of the greatest players in franchise history. Banks is shown with his memorable batting stance, his bat cocked and ready so that his strong wrists can whip it through the strike zone. It is somewhat odd that there are no statistics carved into the base of the statue. Only "Mr. Cub" is inscribed. In the Tribune Plaza downtown on Michigan Avenue, a statue of Jack Brickhouse lists the announcer's milestones. The Banks sculpture seems a little bare. What about the younger fans who know little about Banks?

The other statue at Wrigley is of Harry Caray, holding out a microphone with all of Wrigley Field under his feet. His statue base reads, "Let me hear ya, a one... a two... a three" to recall his leading the singing during the seventh-inning stretch. Some do stop at the Banks sculpture, but the Caray statue draws the real attention. Younger fans may not recognize Banks, and maybe even some older fans are not moved. It is also a testament to a long-term TV strategy that constantly sold the whole Wrigley experience to Cubs fans. How many major league teams honor their broadcasters this way?

Waveland Avenue is somewhat famous. Directly behind the left-field wall, many a home run has been knocked out on the street. A fan will have a good idea how far the home run was hit if it is socked out onto Waveland.

In his "JoeBlog," on January 10, 2008, Joe Posnanski rates his "Twenty Greatest Home Runs Ever." Number 19 is the April 14, 1976, Dave Kingman homer discussed earlier. Posnanski claimed that the Kingman drive hit the third house on Kenmore, a street that intersects with Waveland and faces directly toward the stadium. Posnanski gave estimates of 550, 585 and 630 feet for the Kingman wallop.[4]

Posnanski didn't provide the source of these estimates nor does he say what side of the street the house is on. On the west side the third house sits behind one of the apartment buildings and is about 100 feet from the back of the bleachers. On the east side, the third house is about 40 feet closer and is somewhat blocked by trees that may or may not have been there in '1976. Regardless, it seems more conceivable that the east side house was targeted by Kingman's blast. On the other side, the house sits in the shadow of one of the rooftops. It would be some kind of feat to clear that building, even for King-man.

Posnanski wrote that it "banged on the porch."[5] That was the uniqueness about Wrigley. A fan can actually stand by the house, look up and imagine the Kingman drive. That person can see for him or herself just what estimate is the most accurate. Regardless, the moment can be relived without entering the ballpark, not that many Cubs fans want to remember a Met crushing one into an apartment building.

Rooftops line Waveland. One actually has bleachers and about twelve rows of wooden benches jutting out toward the sky. Ron Rapoport told me that some time during the mid–1980s someone from a rooftop signaled him to come up, have a beer and watch the Cubs.[6] No one just walks up to a rooftop now.

The other rooftop street is Sheffield Avenue. On September 7, 1969, Pirate great Willie Stargell homered against a stiff wind onto Sheffield with two out in the ninth inning to tie the game. Wrigley Field went silent as the ball arched out into the less famous of the two home run streets around the park. The Pirates went on to win in 11. Many Cubs players and fans looked at that game as another turning point in that fateful season.

Skybox on Sheffield is right on the line for the possible landing of the Stargell-like blast. Almost directly opposite the building is a square viewing section carved into the wall, allowing passers-by to see a tiny portion of the game. The panoramic view is up on the roof.

Wrigley wasn't always a neighborhood that was conducive to a festive atmosphere surrounding a major league stadium, according to Skybox on She-ffield owner Dave Abrams. He said the area was infested with dope addicts and pushers during the late eighties. Abrams said that an ex-cop who owned Mur-phy's helped change all of that:

> I would really credit the turnaround of Wrigleyville to Jim Murphy. It was his tenacity and his willingness to clean up the area that turned things around. A lot of his friends from the police department, as well as some political people said, "Let's change Wrigleyville. Let's turn it into a clean area and a positive experience."[7]

Abrams believes it is that neighborhood appeal and environment that makes the Wrigley experience unique in the major leagues: "There are no other stadiums like this. San Diego and Houston tried to emulate it but they couldn't. Only Wrigley and Fenway are still in neighborhoods."[8]

Abrams described the early rooftop businesses as merely taking people up to a roof and setting up a Weber grill. He now says it is a multi-million-dollar enterprise with fifteen rooftop owners catering to thousands of fans, and, as a direct result of legal actions, profits are shared with the Chicago Cubs ownership.

At Skybox on Sheffield, artwork lining the stairwells depicts the ivy and the dimension markers, as well as some caricatures of past Cubs players. The intention is to create some of the atmosphere of actually being inside the ballpark. "There are elements that are similar to being inside the park, and there are elements that are different," Abrams said.

> Obviously you are not in the park. It is almost like having your own private party and it just so happens that your party is across the street from the game. Our TV monitors are on an eight-second delay. So the beauty is that if people aren't watching the game, and they hear the crowd roar, they can look at the TV. It's almost like watching the game live.[9]

Abrams' skybox has three levels. The first is enclosed and includes a bar, a layout of wrapped sandwiches, a pool table, a business center where people can access the Internet and do things like print out boarding passes, and a lower view of Wrigley Field. During the Cubs-Marlins contest, three twenty-something guys huddled around the pool table with no apparent interest in the game. Three others sat at a dining table with drinks and food, with their backs to the field and the TV. Outside the sun was shining and a cool and gusty wind blew out over the outfield walls, providing a potential for one of those multiple-homer, high-scoring Wrigley games.

The next level is on the lower part of the roof. The smell of food is everywhere as caterers whip out hot sandwiches to fans. A small makeshift bar is a few steps up from the food area. It is all very efficient, and fans find that they are not experiencing long concession lines that are common in crowded ballparks. A person can almost eat and drink at will.

Almost immediately to the left is the next rooftop with another crowd so close you probably reach over the building and shake hands with a neighboring fan. Food aromas pass from one rooftop to the next. Looking across the rooftop skyline on Sheffield and Waveland, there is nothing but people creating a crowd that almost competes with the packed Wrigley Field. The scene resembles rows and rows of fenced-in and crowded backyards on the Fourth of July, with people grilling hot dogs and hamburgers.

That particular day the wind that is sending Wrigley flags flapping makes it somewhat difficult for the fan to juggle food and drinks. People party and glance up at the TV monitors should their view be blocked at any time.

Now for the view. You can look right over the shoulder of the pitcher warming up in the right-field bullpen. The pitch can be clearly seen as it nears the plate. Ground balls and low line drives are somewhat hard to pick up, but anything hit high in the air is easily seen.* Of course, anything hit close to the right-field wall can't be seen. That day, Cubs pitcher Ted Lilly smashed a double to right-center. Any fan knew the ball was hit well, but you would have to look at the monitor to see that it had been knocked up against the wall. Since the roof is not overly high and doesn't have a steep slant, fans don't get the scary feeling that is sometimes experienced in the upper deck in U.S. Cellular Field. Also, even though a fan doesn't have the intimacy of actually sitting in the stadium, the overall view is good and the action doesn't seem too far away.

The last level of the Skybox on Sheffield contains seats. They are actual stadium-type seats, not bleachers. Abrams said he wanted the stadium seating to create the in-stadium skybox atmosphere. The view is good, though he noted it was better before the Tribune Company extended their bleachers.

One drawback to the rooftop experience is the crowd. Finding a seat or even a ledge to put your food can be difficult. In addition, moving around can be just as difficult as it is on a crowded stadium ramp. And of course, as Abrams pointed out, the fan is not in the stadium. The crowd can be heard, but it is somewhat distant. A rooftop fan will not feel the emotions or enthusiasm of cheering fans.

Yet with the crowds and imagery of people everywhere around the ballpark, it is hard to imagine why the Tribune Company would want to fight the rooftop owners. Attendance records continue to be broken and interest in the ball club is nationwide. The rooftops can be looked upon as the average fan's skybox. Does that take away from corporate customers using skyboxes at Wrigley? Is the ball club's balance sheet hurt in other ways?

Regardless, the rooftops become more famous by the year. According to Abrams, people from all over the world have visited his skybox (even some White Sox fans.). He even appeared on a Japanese game show. The program was similar to the old *What's My Line?* where a panel attempted to guess the occupation of a guest by getting him to answer a series of questions. In the Japanese version, Abrams said, the panel consists of couples trying to identify people with somewhat different occupations. "It was interesting the way they described it," Abrams said. "They said I ran a baseball stadium outside of Wrigley Field."[10]

In contrast, at many major league venues, when sitting in the upper seats of the lower deck, a fan will look right up into the upper deck when trying to locate a pop up or well-hit but high drive.

The Cubs beat the Marlins, 6–1, the day I had my rooftop experience. In addition to hitting a double and knocking in a couple, Ted Lilly kept the Marlins off balance with some excellent moving breaking pitches. (I knew that because I could see this movement on the TV monitors.) The few times the Marlins made good contact, the Cubs' defense rose to the occasion. There were only three homers in this game; the wind didn't produce one of those Wrigley Field slugfests. Cubs fans in the Sheffield Skybox enjoyed the game but there wasn't the same kind of emotion that is usually felt inside the ballpark. Cubs fans are criticized for being party-going yuppies, but Abrams thinks that is a bad rap:

> The personality of a Cubs fan is all about having a good time, rooting for their team, and if the Cubs lose, they will still have a good time. Some of the other personalities of fans who have had success over the years with winning championships might be a matter of disappointment if their team doesn't win. In our case, if they don't, they don't. We kind of accept that.[11]

But Abrams also said he doesn't subscribe to the "lovable loser" theory. He described the environment on the rooftops as very lively when the Cardinals come into town and the White Sox venture over for the Crosstown Classic. During one of the three Sox games, the majority of fans on his rooftop were White Sox fans.

> They can come to Wrigley but not be inside the stadium. They like coming here and rooting for the White Sox. It's a great environment. It is a true rivalry. People are hyped up. In my opinion, it is similar to the Chicago Bear–Green Bay Packer rivalry. But it is a friendly rivalry too. It isn't a mean rivalry like a lot of people think.[12]

All in all, Abrams believes he and the other rooftop owners contribute a positive aura to everything surrounding the Chicago Cubs baseball experience. "All different elements of Wrigleyville contribute to the history of the club. And that includes the rooftops."[13]

13

Building a New Tradition

"All these so-called Cubs fans, ripping everything we do. I hope we get hot — just to stuff it to those 3,000 people who show up every day.If those are the real Cubs fans they can kiss my ass right downtown — and print it."

— *Cubs manager Lee Elia after an April 29, 1983, loss that put the team record at 5–14. This is a cleaned up version.*[1]

"About 85 percent of the world is working. The other 15 percent come out here."

— *Lee Elia still ranting. His comment wasn't well timed. The United States was still trying to rebound from one of its worse economic downturns in 50 years.*[2]

"I want gamers!"

— *A loud and angry Cubs GM Dallas Green yelling in a Cubs commercial during the early eighties.*

"If there are no lights, we'll have to think about playing in another ballpark."

— *Dallas Green summing things up for Wrigley Field community groups concerned about night baseball coming to the North Side.*[3]

"A lot of people think that Lee's my friend, so he won't get fired. That's not true. He'll get fired if he has to get fired."

— *Dallas Green describing the Cubs situation and his professional relationship with Lee Elia.*[4]

"I don't get ulcers; I give them."

— *Donald Regan, cabinet member and chief of staff to President Ronald Reagan.*

"No More Mr. Nice Guy."

—Title to early seventies song by Alice Cooper. The song tells (a man so socially ostracized that he is punched out by a minist(Sunday service. In late April 1983, the Cubs and their fans we1 duke it out.

On April 12, 1977, P.K. Wrigley died. Although it would tak four more years to disinvest itself of the Cubs, a truly historic era ended. The decade would only end with more losing. The 1969 sea: from forgotten, but the fans' memories of that milestone year wer(hazy. More and more Cubs fans were not even alive when the team last World Series appearance in 1945.

To say that P.K. Wrigley was not considered an activist owner like Reinsdorf or George Steinbrenner only states the obvious. He rarel) attended Cubs games. However, Wrigley maintained that he wasn't an abs owner, although he mostly lived in Lake Geneva, Wisconsin. In an inter\ that ran in a July 5, 1967, article in the *Chicago Sun-Times*, Wrigley told sp(editor James Mullen that he remained in constant touch with Cubs gene. manager John Holland and field manager Leo Durocher. He also said he rare. missed a Cubs game. Mullen asked Wrigley if that meant he watched man) games on television. Wrigley said he did.

Mullen had contacted Wrigley because the Cubs had finally started winning and vaulted into first place during the Fourth of July weekend. Fans had been turned away from a sold-out ballpark. Fireworks celebrated a key win. Cubs faithful were beside themselves, dreaming of a World Series. How was Mr. Wrigley spending his holiday weekend as Cubs fans drank from the pennant fever Kool-Aid? "I've been moving furniture and banquet tables around getting things ready," he told Mullen. "We're having 70 people over for a chuck-wagon dinner."[5]

Mullen was trying to be nice with his call to Wrigley. He told the Cubs owner he wanted to call when things were going well, after so many times trying to reach Wrigley when they were not going too well. Just how did Wrigley feel about his first-place Cubs? "I'm very pleased," he said. "I didn't see any reason why we couldn't move into first place. They are where they ought to be. Now we have to stay there."[6]

Very pleased? His team is in first, the fan base was going gaga, and he is very pleased? And what about that fan base, especially the younger part that Mullen said knew little about P.K. Wrigley? "The kids come out to see the Cubs because we play day baseball," Wrigley said.[7]

Fourteen years later when the Tribune Company bought the team, everything was going to change. Wrigley had been truly one of the last of the old-time family owners. Ironically, the Tribune conglomerate would almost become a more personal entity than the reclusive Wrigley. Owning a great deal of the

Donnie Moore pitching for the Cubs in 1979. Moore blew a save in the ALCS pitching for the Angels against Boston in 1986. Tragically, he committed suicide three years later.

local media made it more visible. And no lights? The Tribune Company wanted that to change. The corporation wanted the losing ways to change as well. But as it would be with the White Sox in the eighties, the Cubs would see that changing things would not be easy.

Dallas Green was hired as the new Cubs general manager in October 1981. Green came from the Donald Regan school of management. As manager, he rode the Phillies until they won the World Series in 1980. Green was proud of the fact that he was an in-your-face type of guy, a complete opposite of P.K. Wrigley. He wanted his players to be the same way.

Right-handed pitcher Dickie Noles was a Dallas Green type of player. In a game against the Reds in Cincinnati on April 7, 1982, Noles was not a happy man after he gave up a home run to Paul Householder. He hit the next hitter, Clint Hurdle, on the helmet with a fastball. A brawl nearly ensued. Noles told the media after the game he hadn't thrown at Hurdle, even though he had a long-standing grudge against Householder. "I decked him before and I'll deck him again if he comes after me," said Noles, describing a past confrontation with Householder.[8]

Yes, Noles was Green's type of guy. Even the Cubs' advertising in 1982 reflected the type of player Green wanted on the team and the new approach the organization was taking to "build a new tradition." Noles may have been that gamer that Green wanted, but he would not distinguish himself as a top-flight major league pitcher. His career record was pre-building a new tradition, like 36–53. And part of his aggression was due to a drinking problem. Noles is now working for the Phillies as an employee assistance professional. His main duty is to help keep players from abusing alcohol and other drugs. Apparently Phillies players have developed a trust for Noles since he was a player once himself.

The commercials were the direct opposite of the gentile women sitting around drinking tea and talking about Ladies Day during the mid-sixties. Even the cute little Cubs logo had a vastly different image.

The Dallas Green "I want gamers" quote at the beginning of this chapter was used. But he wasn't only yelling what he wanted. Green's fist pounded a table. The table shook under his fury. No more mister nice guy. Then again, did Green ever say he was a nice guy?

As for the Cubbie logo? It was a no longer a Cub. It wasn't smiling either. The Cub had become a ferocious-looking bear. In the new commercials, it ate a bat, chewing up splinters as it satisfied its appetite. If one hadn't known better, one would have thought he was watching a commercial for the Chicago Bears. At that time the Bears played in the NFC Central, known as the "black and blue" division. It was often said of the old-time Bears that, win or lose, a team knew it played in a football game when it went up against the Bears. Would the same type of mentality be associated with the Cubs?

In the early-eighties, WGN-AM, the station that carried and still carries Cubs radio broadcasts, aired a late Sunday afternoon show called *The Sports-writers*. The panel included *Chicago Tribune*'s George Langford and Bill Jauss and *Sun-Times* columnist Bill Gleason. The panel talked about how a new attitude was being projected by the Cubs. They spoke of a situation where Larry Bowa was on second and Bill Buckner was on first. Bowa took off to steal third but had to go back to second when the pitch was fouled off. But first he walked over to Buckner to complain that Buckner had not followed him to pull off a double steal. Apparently unmoved, Buckner stood up to Bowa, saying that he wanted to stay on first to force the opposition first baseman to hold him there. Buckner wanted the wider hole between first and second to remain.

Green also made it clear he wanted no connections to a losing past. He fired Ernie Banks, who had been a part of the organization as a player and front office person since 1953. Green wanted no one to hang onto memories of the losing years when Banks was piling up 40-homer seasons. And Green no longer wanted people pining over what happened in 1969.

While players were willing to get on with each other for the good of the club, and Green wanted to create a team history that only associated itself with toughness and winning, 1982 didn't show any concrete results of the new atti- tude. In the first full year of Tribune ownership, the Cubs were 79–83. It was

Bill Buckner batting against the Pirates on May 20, 1979, at Wrigley Field. The Pirates won that day, 6–5, and went on to win the World Series.

the team's fifth consecutive losing season. After the successful period from 1967 to 1972, the Cubs had returned to losing and complete non-contention, and there was nothing lovable about it. In fact, this period was the only time the team had put consecutive winning seasons together since the forties.

Ed Ivers of C.U.B.S. said he hated the phrase "new tradition." What he was really sick of was the old tradition of playing near the bottom of the standings. Apparently many other Cubs fans were not impressed with the new marketing and attitude. They seemed to be nonplussed by Dallas Green's tough-guy persona.

Cubs fans have been known for their optimism. "Hope springs eternal" is a phrase commonly associated with the Cubs faithful even in the midst of losing campaigns and post-season collapses. "Wait till next year" was another phrase linked to Cubs fans, and for many, it also had an optimistic tone to it. However, at the start of 1983, Cubs fans were not in a good mood and optimism wasn't reigning.

A banner was held up at Wrigley that read, "Hey Fans. Wait 'Til Next Year." But it was not draped over the upper deck at the last game of the season, or even in some contest held in September. The banner was soaked with sarcasm because it was displayed at the Cubs' 1983 home opener.

The attendance at that home opener said a great deal: 4,802. Nowadays you might have that many on the rooftops alone. It was the lowest attendance for a Cubs home opener since 1944. Wrigley Field was returning to the olden times when the team needed to beef up attendance with Ladies Day promotions. (It must be pointed out that rain washed away the original opener, and day two would see a drop in attendance. But 4,802?)

Things only worsened for the Cubs when they lost their home opener and the next five as well. Frustration was building everywhere. The players couldn't have been happy with the horrible start. The fans couldn't have been impressed with new slogans and a supposedly new attitude as long as the losing continued. These two groups headed for a collision course.

On April 29, the Cubs lost, 4–3, to the Dodgers. From the score, it doesn't appear to be that deflating a defeat. It was a winnable game for the Cubs and that was a good point. At least they were not humiliated by tape-measure home runs and a lopsided ending. Yet this frustration and anger reached a boiling point and it almost led to a physical confrontation between players and fans.

This was no ordinary loss. First the Cubs dropped the game, even though their pitching gave up a mere four hits. The winning run scored on a wild pitch. But the worst part was that the Cubs still had not gotten going after losing their first six games of the season. Their record was 5–14. Manager Lee Elia was angry because he thought "some jerk on TV will say the Cubs are 5–14 with the worst record in baseball. That's lovely."[9] Well, the Cubs did have the worst record in baseball, but not by much. San Francisco was 6–14. Regardless, the media was not the real target of Elia's wrath. He aimed most of his anger at the fans.

Only a little more than 9,900 attended the game. Some who stayed afterward had a few things to say to the Cubs as they walked down the left-field line toward the clubhouse. Cubs players, especially outfielder Keith Moreland, didn't appreciate the feedback. *Gary Post-Tribune* sportswriter John Mutka would write about the intense Moreland: "Say that he isn't putting out an effort and you'll be eating mush for a week."[10]

"I saw it," Dallas Green said the next day. "They were drunk. There were three guys with their hands full of beer and Keith tried to get over the dugout."[11] The confrontation led to the now-famous Lee Elia outburst. The tirade aimed at the fans was so full of profanity that even Elia was embarrassed about it. Still, was there anything that unusual about the Elia outburst? Arizona Cardinals head coach Dennis Green nearly had a seizure after this team had outplayed the Bears and still lost a game in 2006. There is a video of Hal McRae on the Internet showing him throwing an absolute fit when he was manager of the Kansas City Royals in the early-nineties.[12] You wouldn't want to talk to Mike Ditka after a loss. Various managers, coaches, and players have sworn, cursed, and thrown furniture in times of stress. Many have said things they wanted to take back, or at least forget.

What was truly different about Elia was the intensity of anger directed at Cubs fans who didn't know what it was like to see their team in a World Series. Maybe those fans taunting the players were way out of line. But according to Green there were only three of them. Was it wise to lash out at a whole group of people for the actions of so few? Or was it a few? Were the sarcastic banners and other fan behavior getting to the Cubs?

The Cubs immediately went into a spin mode, beginning with an Elia apology. "My frustrations just peaked," he said. "It's obvious the fans have the same frustrations and I was out of line."[13]

"We're not performing," Green said. "We're not doing the job on the field. And the players and Lee Elia and Dallas Green are responsible for that. The fans are not. The fans have a right to expect more from us because we popped off and said more was going to come from this team."[14]

"Our enemies are not the people in the stands and our enemies are not the people who walk around pencils and pads," said Cubs board chairman Andy McKenna.

> Our enemies should be the nine guys in gray uniforms on the other side of the field. I wish we would channel our aggressions towards them. This was a terrible, terrible thing that happened. The worst thing we can do, in view of Lee's remarks and our won-lost record, is panic. No, on second thought, the worst thing we can do is alienate the public, and I'm afraid we've done that. In any business, you must treat people right.[15]

Cubs fan Kasey Ignarski wrote to Dallas Green telling him that he didn't appreciate the comment about unemployed Cubs fans. Here is Green's reply, as posted by Ignarski on his Internet site:

> There aren't any more words than what Lee and I have already uttered to let you know how we feel about what he said recently. We feel terrible about his comments, have not swept the incident under the table or backed off from the issue and have apologized. I know words don't mean a lot in these situations so we are looking for positive actions on his part and the part of the ball club. We've all made mistakes in our own lives and in our own businesses and we all do what we can do live them down and better ourselves. Lee and I will do this in this case.[16]

When Green assumed his job in October 1981, he warned that he was "no Messiah." However, he did assure fans about his work ethic and that he expected everyone in the organization to put in the long hours needed to build a successful team. "Any losing team has attitude and work dedication problems, like the Phillies did when I became responsible for player development in 1972. Changing that outlook is a matter of pride."[17]

No, Green didn't promise any quick fixes. He even emphasized that any rebuilding would take time because the Cubs needed to retool their farm system and bring their own players along. Going out and buying a team through free-agent acquisitions was not going to happen.

Yet he did promise that the face of the team was going to change and results would follow. He wanted patience, but that is a hard thing to ask of a fan base that witnessed so much losing over a four-decade period. And by the beginning of 1983, there were few signs that the losing tradition was going to be replaced by a new tradition.

Elia's tirade not only took a shot at fans but aimed some verbal missives at the concept of day baseball. P.K. Wrigley thought it was an excellent way to build a fan base that would last for decades. The Tribune Company and the new Cubs management looked at day baseball as an impediment to long-term winning and success. Fan reaction? You want a strong fan base? How about winning a few games?

In March 1982, Green stated that the possibility of lights at Wrigley Field was not a matter of *if,* but *when.* The GM didn't think the Cubs could be competitive if they continued to play all their home games in the day. This simple policy statement incurred the wrath of another organization that used the acronym C.U.B.S. Citizens United for Baseball in Sunshine vowed to fight any move toward night baseball for the Cubs.

"He kept telling us how honest he was," said Mark Hanselmann, vice president of C.U.B.S. in response to Green. "He talked about what an advantage day baseball is."[18] But Green now said night baseball was something that had to happen, even if it was merely looking at the possibility in the somewhat-distant future. Architects were looking into Wrigley to see if lights were structurally possible. If not, Green said the Cubs would have to look into playing elsewhere.

"There are too many more important pressing issues now than whether we have lights or not," Green said. "I'm just saying, someday, somehow, we have to play night games to be able to compete."[19]

"He got an awful of people mad," Hanselmann said. "But it is just as well it happens now so we can mobilize."[20]

Seven months later, Green faced another public relations crisis. A day after the '82 season ended with another sub–.500 mark, the Cubs carried out what *Tribune* columnist John Husar described as "the biggest front-office purge in Chicago sports history."[21] Twelve people had been relieved of their duties. In addition, the team ridded itself of three coaches, including long-time favorite Billy Williams.

The front-office employees were described as devastated and in tears. Dallas Green was angry that the names of the front-office people were leaked to the media. He didn't think the media had any right to print those names since they weren't players or coaches. Green labeled the media actions as "demeaning" and "downright cruel." *Tribune* reporters Robert Markus and Peter Fuller doubted that Green wanted to keep the names private for "humanitarian reasons."[22] Columnist Husar took it a step further, accusing the Cubs of possessing a caveman mentality where the weak are exposed and left to fend for themselves.[23]

By the end of 1983, the family-owned Cubs had truly turned into the corporate-owned Cubs, and its image took a real beating. One fan group still wanted input into decisions regarding trades and player development. Another accused the Cubs of taking steps to destroy the neighborhood. Employee firings didn't put Dallas Green or the organization into any kind of a good light. A manager rips the fans and a player wants to climb into the seats to take matters into his own hands. Hardly anyone described Wrigley Field as the "Friendly Confines." The one person who liked to use that phrase had been shown the door as well. Yet there was so much more that was wrong.

In 1982 and 1983, the first two full years of Tribune ownership, the Cubs finished a combined 36 games under .500. They were more laughable than lovable. Yes, it takes time to turn a team around, but the team seemed to be regressing. The new tradition looked like the old one.

To go along with the Cubs' failure was the White Sox's success. Jerry Reinsdorf and Eddie Einhorn had their public relations problems as their fans also struggled with change. Yet the Reinsdorf and Einhorn group had owned the Sox for only a slightly longer time than the Tribune Company owned the Cubs and the Sox had already won a division title. Yes, the team flopped in the playoffs, but the Sox were young in most spots, their division was weak, the club actually went over the 2,000,000 attendance mark, and suddenly the future looked like nothing but sunshine was ahead. Would the Cubs become Chicago baseball's second-class citizens?

Dallas Green turned down an interview I requested. Through a Phillies spokesman, he said his association with the Cubs "was a long time ago."[24] His eventual departure from the Cubs in 1987 has been described in two ways: He resigned due to philosophical differences with the team, or he had been pushed out by a well-designed corporate purge. Regardless, his Cubs legacy is an important one, as he had been willing to be the force behind changes that were met with stiff resistance. After various legal haggling, lights were installed in Wrigley Field in 1988. Wrigleyville is a very different neighborhood today. And in 1984, the turnaround finally came and it helped the Cubs stave off the short-term success of the White Sox and preserved their place in Chicago baseball history.

14

1984 — George Orwell Was Right — Love Was Hate

"Now, the Cubbies! There's a pitching staff! Reuschel, Rainey, Ruthven, Jenkins, Trout, Noles — immortals merely stopping off in beautiful Wrigley Field on the way to Cooperstown. Just ask Dallas Green — he'll back up everything I say."

—*William E. Carsley*

"Going into a season when three of his four-man rotation have the names Rainey, Ruthven, and Sanderson has to arouse some emotion, however weak. Is pity an emotion?"

—*Warren Lonngren*

"I am fed up hearing of the Cubs with the little trades they have made up to now. It's getting tiresome to hear the words 'Wait until next year.'"

—*Charles Caine*

All three men had these comments printed in a pre-season column published by Tribune *columnist Steve Daley. None sound too optimistic.*

The Cubs' spring training record after 21 games was 3–18. Most baseball observers will say that spring training means nothing. Veterans are working themselves into shape in various ways. Young players are trying to play their way onto a major league roster. Some may not play one major league game that year, or ever. So how can fans or experts truly make any real observations about a team in the spring? Actually, in a sense, they can, but not by the spring training won-lost record.

But 3–18, which included an 11-game losing streak? One would think a team would win a few games by accident. Regardless, this was by far the worst spring training record of any team and in either league. Cubs fans could not have felt good when they picked up the paper every morning just to see another loss. In fact, spring training fans were apparently already in mid-season heckling form when the losing streak hit nine. According to *Tribune* reporter Fred Mitchell, Keith Moreland was "spotted by several witnesses" attempting to climb a fence in the right-field corner to go after some loudmouths. Moreland had been taken out of the game in the top of the seventh. His action was reminiscent of the day in 1983 when he tried to climb over the Cubs' dugout to get at some hecklers. Lee Elia's tirade followed.[1] "I think too much is being made of our record," Moreland told Mitchell; "It's blown out of proportion." Moreland didn't seem overly concerned, but Dallas Green was not too happy. In a clubhouse meeting, Green let his team know his feelings. Cubs catcher Steve Lake said that "he really let us have it."[2] "What I said to them is between me and the team," Green said publicly. "Our record doesn't count until the season starts April 3, but you know me. I want to win everything, whether it's tiddlywinks or whatever. I'd like to see us play a little better. Jim [manager Jim Frey] is playing a lot of people and trying to get a feel for what's going on. That's fine, but we have had no consistency."[3]

If the Cubs were establishing a new tradition, it didn't appear that most Cubs fans were ready to buy into it, as the letters to Steve Daley indicated. The team had completed a miserable period from 1973 to 1983 when it had no winning seasons. The first three seasons under Tribune control were only a part of that process. Yes, Dallas Green had asked for patience at his hiring, but progress seemed nonexistent.

Letter writer Carsley had also poked fun at the White Sox's starting rotation, saying that the staff came from other teams and were not homegrown. However, he was really comparing two staffs and found the Cubs' staff truly inferior.[4]

Cubs fans claim they don't care what the White Sox do. But one couldn't blame Carsley or any other Cubs fan for their jealousy about the White Sox. The Sox had won their division the year before by 20 games, and though it was unrealistic to think they would have such an easy time again, the Sox were favored to repeat. Cubs fans couldn't have wanted to relive a season where the South Siders went to the playoffs and their team started on another decade of losing.

Dallas Green apparently didn't want "Building a New Tradition" to be an empty slogan. As the spring training record hit that dubious 3–18 mark, the Cubs general manager traded reliever Bill Campbell and catcher Mike Diaz to Philadelphia for outfielders Gary Matthews and Bobby Dernier and pitcher Porfirio Altmirano. To Green it was a simple matter of getting players in the outfield who could catch the ball.

After the trade, the Cubs won four out of their next six to salvage a nearly lost spring training. They scored 35 runs in their victories, and a lively offense always makes a team look interesting. But was this team any good at all, and did it have any real chance to compete in the National League East?

According to an excerpt from the *Bill James Baseball Abstract 1984* that ran in the *Tribune* on April 1, the Cubs were an average team that had an opportunity to have a "miracle" season. James theorized that the Cubs could win the National League East because of several factors. First, he felt that the Cubs' run differential in 1982 should have allowed them to win eight more games, thus making them nearly a .500 club—not the 91-loss team shown in the standings. James also felt that the more laid-back Jim Frey was an improvement over what he called the "high-pressured" Lee Elia. He further stated that the difference between the top and bottom of the division was not significant and that the defending division champion Phillies had problems of their own. Finally, he wrote that the Cubs had shored up their pitching in the offseason, which "was something that all miracle teams do."[5]

This little story might have been comforting for Cubs fans, but was their team really going to improve on their miserable '83 record? They seemed to answer that question when they opened the season in San Francisco.

The Cubs edged the Giants, 5–3. They received a solid performance from starter Dick Ruthven, who went deep into the eighth, allowing only two runs. They got homers from the heckler-hating Keith Moreland and Ron Cey. Jody Davis had a two-run double. It was only the third Opening Day win in the last 11 seasons for the Cubs.

"The Cubs and the media get carried away with spring training," Giants manager Frank Robinson said. "The Cubs have a fine team, a lot like ours."[6] It was a good thing Robinson's comparison didn't ring true for the Cubs. San Francisco ended up in last place in the West with a 66–96 mark in 1984.

No, the Cubs were nothing like the Giants in 1984. On May 25, they were shut out, 3–0, by the Reds. The loss ended a six-game winning streak. More important, the Cubs were in first place, two games ahead of the second-place Phillies. In addition, Dallas Green made another one of his trades that would define the Cubs' 1984 season.

Wanting more pitching and no longer needing Bill Buckner to play first, the Cubs sent Buckner to the Red Sox for pitcher Dennis Eckersley and infielder Mike Brumley. Eckersley had won 20 games in 1978 and 17 the following year. After those stellar seasons, the right-hander had fallen on some hard times, posting records of 12–14, 9–8, 13–13, and 9–13, and was 4–4 at the time the Cubs picked him up. But pitching is always at a premium, and Buckner had become the odd man out with Leon Durham taking over at first.

Eckersley lost three of his first four starts with the Cubs, and by the time June 17 rolled around, the team had fallen out of first. They slipped down to third and were two behind the first-place Phillies. But Dallas Green was not done trading. He sent Mel Hall, Joe Carter, Don Schulze, and Darryl Banks to the Indians for Rick Sutcliffe, George Frazier, and Ron Hassey. Sutcliffe was the big person in this trade.

Sutcliffe was a big right-hander who won National League Rookie of the Year honors with 17 wins in 1979 while playing in Los Angeles. He had some problems with Dodger manager Tommy Lasorda and was sent to Cleveland, a baseball never-never land in the early-eighties. He picked up 14 wins in '82 and 17 more the following year, but he seemed to be languishing with the Indians in '84, having won only four out of nine decisions. His ERA was an unimpressive 5.15. He wanted out, and the Indians were happy to oblige him.

Sutcliffe won his first start with the Cubs, going eight innings and giving up one earned run in a 4–3 win over the Pirates at Pittsburgh. He then made his first Wrigley Field appearance five days later against St. Louis, beating the Cardinals, 5–0. Sutcliffe was dominating as he picked up 14 strikeouts. He lost his next start on June 29 when he didn't get past the fifth inning. Sutcliffe would not lose another game in the regular season, winning five in July, six in August, and three in September.

Another turning point in the season was the "Sutter game." In this contest, Ryne Sandberg homered twice to tie the game against Bruce Sutter, the one-time Cub and premier reliever for the Cardinals. The first homer came in the ninth when Sandberg led off and tied the game at nine. The Cardinals went ahead with two runs in the tenth. But Sandberg responded with another shot into the left-field seats, this one a two-run homer with two out. Sutter slumped in frustration on the mound as soon as Sandberg laced into his pitch.

The Cubs won in the eleventh. It was one of those Wrigley Field games that, for once, the Cubs emerged victorious. Sutcliffe followed the next day with one of his best performances of the year. Cubs fans were delighted with a three-game sweep over the hated Cardinals. The Cubs were now only a half-game out of first and seemed to be on the right track again.

One of the longest-running debates about the Cubs and their inability to close out seasons centers on day baseball. Does playing in the afternoon all summer drain them? There was no such controversy in 1984. In July and August the Cubs were a combined 38–20. No one was tiring this time. At the end of play on September 1, the Cubs stood at 81–54, five games ahead of the second-place Mets. There would be no surge by the Mets or folding act by the Cubs this time. Dallas Green had wanted fans to forget 1969. The 1984 Cubs did a lot to accomplish that, or at least dampen the pain of that year.

The clinching win came on September 24 in Pittsburgh, and fittingly, Sutcliffe got the win. The Pirates had a grand total of one runner left on base, because hardly any of them reached base to start with. Joe Orsulak, who had a triple and a single, was the only Pirate to get a hit off Sutcliffe. Orsulak scored on a ground out after his triple, and then was picked off after his single. When

Bruce Sutter in his early days with the Cubs. In 1984, there was something labeled as the "Sutter game." Ryne Sandberg knocked two late-inning home runs off Sutter to help the Cubs topple St. Louis. Sandberg won the MVP award and the Cubs took their first division crown.

Orsulak struck out to end the game, Sutcliffe had faced only one man over the minimum, as he had eight innings with only three men coming to the plate. It was the first title for the Cubs since division play began in 1969.

It had all been so unlikely. The Cubs hadn't recorded a winning season since 1972. Nothing in the pre-season indicated that they were going to win the division fairly easily. Bill James had been right. The Cubs did put together a "miracle" season, or just a solid season by a team that had been transformed by trades. Now only the San Diego Padres, a first-time playoff participant themselves, stood in the way of a Cubs appearance in the World Series.

The conditions for the first game of the playoffs were ripe for one of those Wrigley Field slugfests. The wind was blowing out. Homers were going to be hit. But this time only one team was going to hit the homers, and they hit five of them. That team was the Cubs.

It was their first post-season game in 39 years. Bob Dernier, who had 45 stolen bases during the regular season, was needed to get on base for the RBI men to bring him home. Dernier instead started the game with a homer into the left-field bleachers. One out later, Gary Matthews homered as well. The two key players that came over in the pre-season trade got the Cubs off to a 2–0 lead.

Sutcliffe, a good hitting pitcher, homered to start the third inning. The Cubs added two more runs that inning, and with the eventual Cy Young Award winner on the mound, it looked like a win was a sure thing.

But in the next inning the Padres loaded the bases with two outs. Carmelo Martinez hit a sinking line drive to right. Keith Moreland came in and made a shoestring catch to end the threat. "When he first hit it, I thought it was a line drive over Ryno's head for a base hit," Moreland said. "But it stayed up."[7]

"No question in my mind that was the turning point in the game," Sutcliffe said. "If Moreland doesn't make that catch, I'm in a struggle."[8]

Moreland didn't fully understand the importance of his catch until he ran off the field. What if the ball had gotten past him? "It was not until after I got in the dugout that I thought about it being dangerous," he said. "I said to myself, 'Lord, it could have been 5–3.'"[9]

But the score remained 5–0 and ended up 13–0. It was the most lopsided win in playoff history. The five homers set another playoff mark. In 30 league championships up to that point, 21 teams that won the first game went on to win the series. And, oh, it was the first post-season win for the Cubs since 1945.

The second game at Wrigley was more conventional. Bob Dernier set his usual tone for the contest when he led off with a single. He then went from first to third on a ground out by Ryne Sandberg. Dernier scored on a ground out and the Cubs felt they had the momentum with another lead. They wanted to get the lead and keep it going into the late innings in order to prevent Padres reliever Goose Gossage from having an impact on the game.

Yet the real key was the starting pitching. For the second straight game, the Padre starter couldn't get past the fourth inning. Lefty Mark Thurmond left after 3⅔ innings, trailing, 4–1. On the other side of the field, Steve Trout pitched into the ninth inning for the Cubs. He gave up five hits and kept the ball on the ground. First baseman Leon Durham had 14 putouts. "Having a sinkerball pitcher for our team in this ballpark is a big plus," manager Jim Frey said. "Trout pitched a monster of a game for us."[10]

The 1984 season was the last year of the best-of-five game format in the League Championship Series. No team except for the 1982 California Angels that won the first two games of the series ever lost one. *Tribune* reporter Fred Mitchell worded it this way in his game story: "Barring a minor miracle and pending notification of next of kin, the San Diego Padres can be pronounced dead. Check the Padres' vital signs, doctor. They've floundered for the past two months despite a mammoth division lead."[11]

It is one thing for a sportswriter to sound like he is taking things for granted, but how about the Cubs? Did the team that had so many doubts about it during spring training just assume it was going to the World Series? When did a Chicago baseball team ever do that? "It was surreal," Les Grobstein told me. "Those first two games, the Padres looked like they were dead meat. But the Cubs didn't look over-confident or cocky."[12]

Yet according to author John Kuenster, who looked back at the series 17 years later, shortstop Larry Bowa said he heard talk on the trip to San Diego that some Cubs players thought the series was all but over.[13] From his experience on the Phillies, Bowa knew that wasn't true.

According to Grobstein, Padres fans didn't feel the series was over. He said an estimated 3,000 greeted the Padres on their return to the San Diego airport, and that support "pumped the Padres up."[14]

The Padres won the third game in convincing fashion, 7–1. The Cubs actually led, 1–0, going into the bottom of the fifth, but the Padres scored three that inning and four in the sixth. The Cubs only picked up one hit in the last four innings. The Padres finally received a good start as Ed Whitson threw eight innings of five-hit ball. The series was not over.

In the eighth inning of game four, the Padres looked like they were in great shape. In the top of the eighth, they led, 5–3, and had closer Rich Gossage on the mound. In those days, Gossage oftentimes came in the eighth and went two innings for the save. During his early career with the White Sox, he sometimes entered during the seventh. However, the Cubs made the best out of three hits, scoring two runs and tying the game. With the game even, the Padres were forced to pinch-hit for Gossage in the bottom of the eighth. Now it looked like some momentum was on the Cubs' side.

And for a moment it looked like the Cubs could break the game open in the ninth if they would get a clutch two-out hit from Ron Cey with the bases

Ryne Sandberg, the icon player of the eighties for the Cubs. Here he is ready to take a cut in his MVP year in 1984.

loaded. But Cey grounded out to second to end the inning. What followed was a nightmare image that Cubs fans will never forget.

In the Padres' ninth, the Cubs had their big-man reliever, Lee Smith, on the mound. Smith had also come on in the eighth. With one out, Tony Gwynn singled. Then Steve Garvey stepped up to the plate.

The sight of right fielder Henry Cotto trying to scale the right-center-field wall and the ball disappearing into the San Diego night is a dark memory for Cubs fans watching that game or even seeing it in a highlight film. Garvey shooting his arm into the air as he rounded first cannot be a pleasant recollection, either. The Padres had evened the series with a 7–5 win. Sportswriter Fred Mitchell had been wrong. There was plenty of life left in San Diego.

Eric Show started game five and was just as ineffective as he was in the first game. He gave up a two-run homer to Leon Durham in the first inning, and a solo shot to Jody Davis in the second. Two batters later, pitcher Sutcliffe singled, and Show was history. The number-one pitcher for the Padres couldn't get past the second inning.

Everything seemed to be in the Cubs' favor. They had an early lead, and their pitcher with a 17–1 record was on the mound. Jack Brickhouse, who was in the radio booth with Harry Caray, was yelling "Hey! Hey!" in response to Davis's homer.*

The Cubs' problem was that their offense went to sleep for the rest of the game. From the third to the seventh, they went three up, three down. During one inning, there was a walk, but that runner was erased when he was caught stealing at the end of a strikeout. Three Padre relievers had given up nothing.

Then came the seventh inning, and the Cubs' lead was down to one. But they were still ahead, and needed only nine more outs to face the Detroit Tigers in the World Series. There was a ground ball through the first baseman's legs, and a ground ball that ate up the second baseman, which became a double instead of a double play. Before the Cubs knew it, the Padres were ahead, 6–3. Six Cubs outs later, the San Diego comeback was complete.

The word "choke" was thrown out by the Chicago media in the post-series analysis. Leon Durham, who had let a routine grounder skip through his legs to score the tying run, wondered about fan reaction. "Are they are going to rip my ass all winter?" Durham was overheard saying on the plane home.[15]

Then there was the criticism that Jim Frey had left Sutcliffe in too long. "The first five innings, Sutcliffe threw pitches you couldn't hit," Tony Gwynn told John Kuenster. "Then it looked like he was starting to get tired."[16]

"In the sixth inning, Rick's ball began to straighten out and lose some of

---

*WGN-TV was not broadcasting the playoffs. Ironically, White Sox announcer Don Drysdale was doing the play-by-play nationally.

its movement," Garvey told Kuenster. "And his location wasn't as good as it had been earlier. It was a hot day, and you could tell he was losing it. I thought they were going to lift him then, but they left him in. They shouldn't have."[17]

Sutcliffe told Kuenster that he had been slated to pitch the fourth game of the series. He added that the reason he had been taken out after the seventh inning of the 13–0 first-game romp was to help save him for a fourth game start. But Frey didn't want to move Sutcliffe up and have his ace working on three days' rest while derailing the pitcher's routine.

Kuenster cited unnamed "dissenters" who claimed that Sutcliffe would have fared better pitching in the cooler night game on Saturday. And even if he failed to put the Padres away, Steve Trout could pitch game five. Instead, the dissenters said, Sutcliffe wilted in the sun and the Cubs' number-two pitcher received only one start in the series.[18]

What about the charge in Kuenster's story that the Cubs had become overconfident after the two wins at Wrigley? Though Kuenster wrote that post-season veteran Larry Bowa was concerned, it was never stated how the Cubs showed this arrogance. Loud talking? Dismissing the Padres as unworthy opponents? A laid-back attitude that was totally out of place? In the third game they had been beaten by a good pitcher. They had come back in the late innings to tie the fourth game against a tough reliever. They were ahead until the seventh inning in the fifth and deciding game. They hit nine home runs in the five-game series.

Regardless of the speculation, something important happened in 1984, even if the Cubs missed a great shot to go to the World Series. Remember the small but angry crowds at Wrigley? Remember Lee Elia? Remember Keith Moreland wanting to get in the stands so he could beat up a loud mouth? Remember when Moreland wanted to go after another heckler in spring training?

After the last regular-season game held at Wrigley, fans wanted the Cubs to come out for a curtain call. Now Wrigley was packed and there wasn't a heckler in sight. Instead of sarcastic and bitter signs reading "Wait 'Til Next Year," being held up on Opening Days, Cubs flags were being waved.

"I was undressed in the clubhouse, drinking a cup of beer when the game ended," Leon Durham said that day. "But I got dressed and went back out to see the fans. I had to get me some of that."[19]

"It was totally unexpected," recalls fan Kasey Ignarski, who had started buying season tickets that year. "The whole thing was overwhelming. The Cubs came out and thanked their fans."[20]

And what of Dallas Green? When he left the Cubs after the 1987 season, the local media blasted him as a lousy GM and a bully. They wrote that the Mel Hall–Joe Carter swap for Rick Sutcliffe was short-sighted and wrong. A bully he might have been, but his trades built the 1984 Chicago Cubs. In addition to the acquisitions of Dennis Eckersley and Rick Sutcliffe, six of the eight regular everyday players were Green acquisitions.

"He rankled a lot of people," Ignarski said. "He was trying to make his mark. As far as the Sutcliffe trade, I had no problem with that. It helped bring about '84 and '89."[21]*

Imagine this scenario: The White Sox winning their second straight division, as most expected, and the Cubs continuing to lose while Green talked about a "new tradition." It could have been a turning point in Chicago baseball history. Instead, the Cubs had their first 2 million attendance season and then rounded out the decade with another division title. The White Sox had only one winning season for the last half of the decade, and their fans were not happy about the threats of moving the team elsewhere. The Cubs regained their popularity.

No, Dallas Green wasn't the best GM in baseball history. But his go-for-it-now trades helped the Cubs regain and solidify their spot as the number-one baseball team in Chicago.

---

*Sutcliffe won 16 games when the Cubs won their second division title in 1989. Carter had some big years with Cleveland, including a 200-hit, 121-RBI season in 1986. But the Indians didn't win a division title until 1995 and by then Carter was in Toronto.

15

Another New Tradition

"Eddie Einhorn was a fast-talking outsider and a big forward thinker."
— *Ex-Chicago television sports reporter Mike Leiderman.*[1]

"They wanted to change the image. That doesn't show disregard for the fans."
— *Long-time Chicago TV and radio reporter and current media consultant Tom Shaer regarding the strategy of Jerry Reinsdorf and Eddie Einhorn when their group of investors purchased the White Sox in 1981.*[2]

"I run this team, not the fans."
— *Or words to that effect. Jerry Reinsdorf in response to criticism during the 1981 season.*

"They wanted it to be more than a South Side team."
— *Tom Shaer in reference to the new owners' strategy in building a larger White Sox fan base.*[3]

"I have great memories of the last five years at Comiskey Park. Bill Veeck made going to the old ball game a fun experience. Win or lose, the Sox and Veeck's many promotions turned South Side baseball into the best entertainment value in town. Thanks for the memories. We'll miss him."
— *Letter to the editor published in February 11, 1981, edition of the* Chicago Sun-Times. *The writer is Ginger Rapsus of Oak Lawn.*[4]

"I just heard about Harry Caray being the new broadcaster for the Cubs, and I am infuriated. He is a big mouth. When I watch the White Sox on television, I turn down the sound and just watch the game. What is wrong with Milo Hamilton? I guess you could call me a Republican because I'm not really comfortable with changes, and I am not comfortable with Harry Caray."
— *Thirteen-year-old Jeff Wilhoit in a letter to the* Chicago Tribune *published on November 25, 1981.*[5]

An end of an era. The common phrase is often used in describing significant historical change. However, to use that simple phrase to describe Bill Veeck's exit from baseball in early 1981 is inadequate. His legacy was huge. Additionally, baseball was changing with or without him. In fact, it had already changed. Free agency forced Veeck into a "rent-a-player" system that could only work in the short run. Baseball is a business, had always been a business, but the money stakes were getting higher. Even for teams that drew well, advance sales became more important. Teams wanted the fans' money earlier and for longer periods of time. For fans, there was no more getting up and seeing that it was a nice day and deciding a day at the ballpark would be a good idea. To do so would risk getting bad seats or no seats at all. The corporate owner was becoming the in-thing, whether in structure or in resources. Men like Bill Veeck or P.K. Wrigley were a large part of Chicago baseball history, but they were part of a past to be remembered and no longer experienced.

On the South Side, White Sox fans would experience some of the same growing pains that their Cubs fan brethren would endure with the Tribune Company. Jerry Reinsdorf and Eddie Einhorn, the leaders of the investment group purchasing the White Sox, were not the shy, reclusive Cubs owner P.K. Wrigley had been. They were ready to do things differently, regardless of what critics or fans thought.

That first year for Reinsdorf and Einhorn was as eventful as any season of their ownership. The seeking of their own baseball identity, their inability to hold onto Harry Caray but retaining Jimmy Piersall, and the optimism that the on-field play generated had major short- and long-term impacts on the franchise. If anything was happening in 1981, it was a new way of doing things. Strong reactions followed, both in the near and distant future.

Doing It Their Way

While the title of this chapter refers the new Cubs slogan of the early '80s, a new tradition was also starting on the South Side, and its philosophy was not always welcome.

Throughout 1981, the White Sox announced the following changes and plans as the new ownership sought to take control:

- The removal of the center-field shower, which symbolized the 1977 season and the last years of the Bill Veeck era.
- The creation of something called a golden box seat with a golden price.
- A proposal to create a family section in Comiskey where no drinking would be allowed.
- The construction of a new stadium. The new ownership didn't feel it could compete as a major league franchise as long as the Sox played in a stadium that opened in 1910.

- The eventual moving of Sox games off free TV.
- For some odd reason, deciding that White Sox fans wanted or needed mascots by the name of "Ribbie" and "Roobarb."
- The acquisition of catcher Carlton Fisk and outfielder Greg Luzinski.

The family proposal seemed harmless enough, but there was something substantial behind the move. During the late '70s Comiskey Park had become known more as one big tavern than a ballpark and the new owners wanted nothing to do with that image. The White Sox may have been considered a blue-collar team, but they weren't going to be a drunken blue-collar team if Reinsdorf and Einhorn had anything to say about it.

Chicago radio sports reporter Les Grobstein told me the following story. There was a ruckus in the upper deck behind home plate during a late-'70s game and a White Sox employee was getting roughed up by a couple of fans. Sitting in his box, owner Bill Veeck put his cigarette out and placed the butt in his stump. Veeck, who was in his mid-sixties, hobbled over, grabbed the biggest guy, got him in a headlock and threw him to the ground. Having defused the situation, Veeck returned to his box, lit another cigarette and resumed watching the game. Grobstein said that Veeck enjoyed a certain amount of rowdiness.[6]

Eddie Einhorn and Jerry Reinsdorf were not about to break up any fights themselves, but they weren't going to put up with the brawling and other outright obnoxious fan behavior at Comiskey. They tightened security by hiring off-duty cops to put an end to the real and perceived troublemaking at the park.

"They (Reinsdorf and Einhorn) gave security the license to beat the crap out of people," Grobstein said. "A few of these fans sued and the judges had no sympathy for them. Word got around and a lot of these people stopped coming to games."[7]

I was at a game in the early '80s and witnessed a security man escort a fan out of the stadium. Actually, escort isn't the right word. The security man had the fan by the back of the collar, and when he got the fan by the cement steps that led under the stadium, he sent the fan flying. The fan was thrown with such force that he cleared the steps with considerable ease. Yet only more cement was waiting, and the landing had to be painful.

Alienating fans that can make the atmosphere at the ballpark hostile cannot be looked at as a bad thing. While the troublemakers may decide to take their business elsewhere (like Wrigley Field or their local bar), other fans and their families were grateful to be able to attend the game without being subjected to swearing, rowdiness, or a punch in the face. In this case, the admired Bill Veeck was a contradiction. He wanted to create a fun atmosphere for the baseball fan and regarded a crowded baseball stadium as a piece of heaven. Yet Comiskey's reputation as a drinking hole couldn't have jibed with many fans.

Veeck may have liked breaking up a fight on occasion, but most people don't go to a game to get in the middle of a fracas. Fans will always drink at a ball game, but there are limits to everything, especially when other fans don't want to expose themselves or their kids to anti-social idiots.

While making the ballpark safer is a positive development, other changes made by the new owners were met with some lukewarm response and even outright hostility. Eliminating the center-field shower? Who could forget those hot summer days and humid nights when the South Side Hitmen were swatting the ball all over the place? The shower was a symbol of the heat, emotion, and a new found fanaticism. Fans yanked that chain and let a circular stream of water pore down on them. And these guys were going to take that away?*

Yes, Comiskey Park was old, yet that was one of its biggest assets. There was history there. And despite its enormous size, it still had an intimacy about it. Would a larger stadium with fans seated further away from the action provide that same type of intimacy? Eric Soderholm remembered rounding the bases after hitting a homer during the '77 season. He said he could feel the roar of the crowd. And now the place where that happened was going to be torn down?

Mascots? Yes, fans did have fun at the ballpark, but what White Sox fan ever expressed the need to see grown men dress up in goofy-looking outfits? The kids may like it, but how many Sox fans thought back to their childhood and remembered wanting a Barney-like character or two roaming the stands?

And a new TV deal? Was Eddie Einhorn a TV man or a baseball man? Did he care more about fans watching the game at home on pay TV or at Comiskey? Would fans cut down on going to the park because they laid out money to watch the Sox at home, thus defeating the purpose of raising additional revenue? The pay–TV concept was winning over very few fans.

Harry Caray

As ownership transferred from Veeck's group to the one headed up by Reinsdorf and Einhorn, Einhorn was asked if Veeck would have any role in the franchise. Einhorn basically said no; he and Reinsdorf wanted to put their own stamp on the team. That made sense, and one way to put your stamp on the team is who you have in your broadcast booth. After all, the new ownership said they wanted to change the image and one way to do that was to control your media.

They quickly signed Jimmy Piersall to return, but the negotiations with Harry Caray didn't go so smoothly. Caray, with all his popularity, thought he

---

The shower now is on display behind the left-center-field seats. Eventually there was also a room of streaming water where fans could douse themselves on hot days.

had some real leverage. Eddie Einhorn, the experienced TV man, didn't want any kind of deal rammed down his throat. At one point in mid–February 1981, Einhorn told Irv Kupicent of the *Sun-Times* that the Sox thought he had a deal with Caray.[8] Things changed when Caray's agent came back and said they still wanted more money. "If Einhorn says there was a deal, he's a lying bastard," Caray told *Sun-Times* reporter Phil Hersh. "Who's pushing him? He's the one doing the pushing when they get quoted in Kup."[9] Caray also told Hersh he was angry that Einhorn had taken some of the negotiations to the newspaper even though he had requested Caray not to do so.

The announcer then made some threats about not returning to the broadcast booth at all. He thought out loud about doing "talk shows and sports shows."[10] Caray thought he could even make more money.

During the immediate post–Hitmen era, the White Sox as a team did little to generate excitement. It seemed that if there was real interest in the team, it was generated by events like Disco Demolition or something that had been said in the broadcast booth. Mostly it was the latter. The announcers were getting more attention than the players during the bleak years, from 1978 to 1980.

"We want to get it resolved," Einhorn said while defending himself to Hersh, "but I want to draw the line when people start taking advantage of us. We want to spend money on the field. These guys are getting bigger than the team. We're not going to get pushed around."[11]

The two warring parties realized they needed each other and came to terms two weeks later on a one-year deal. When the two met with the media, a reporter asked Caray if he wanted to give his new boss a kiss. The kiss never happened, but they gave all the appearances of being in love with each other, at least professionally. "I know we'll get along well," Einhorn told the media. "We both have a great love for baseball, and especially for the White Sox."[12] "There is no feeling of animosity," Caray chimed in. "Eddie said some things that I misunderstood and I said some things that he misunderstood."[13]

Caray must have been referring to something that had been said in private. It is hard to misunderstand when a person is being called a liar or the other is being labeled as self-important enough to think he is bigger than the team. The partnership was going to be a tenuous one, and the ownership and Caray would meet again after the season ended.

In meeting with Reinsdorf and Einhorn at the season's conclusion, Caray expressed his doubts about the Sportsvision concept. First, he didn't think it would work without the Cubs. Second, he explained to the owners that with the Cubs already broadcasting 150 games and adding games aired on NBC on Saturday afternoons and on ABC on Monday nights, there would be approximately 200 free baseball games in the Chicago market. Why would anyone want to invest the Sportsvision market? "I made a fortune off of television sports," Caray remembered Einhorn saying. "Who the hell are you to tell me what will or won't work?"[14]

In a subsequent meeting, Caray played one more card. Still fearing that Sportsvision wouldn't attract many viewers, Caray wanted a multi-year deal for at least three years, and maybe five. He feared that without a long-term commitment from the White Sox, he would be out after one season. The negotiations stalled, and Caray decided to make an overture to the Cubs.[15] A few days later, it was announced that Harry Caray would be doing play-by-play for the Cubs.

The *Tribune* conducted a poll over a two-day period in mid–November that was published on the 21st. Of the 2,500 fans who responded, 44 percent identified themselves as White Sox fans who were so angry Caray had moved to the Cubs that they had decided to take their allegiance with them. Agreeing with the letter writer quoted at the beginning of the chapter, 77 percent of those identified as Cubs fans voiced strong displeasure at the idea of Caray doing Cubs play-by-play. Only a negligible amount said they would stop being Cubs fans as a result of the move.

Was this an overreaction or did Sox fans make good on their threat? In the two years preceding the Cubs' division-winning year of 1984, it didn't appear so, at least at the gate. In 1982 and 1983, the White Sox drew 1,567,787 and 2,132,821, respectively. The Cubs drew 1,249,278 and 1,479,717. Any effect Caray had by making the move (and I believe there was some effect), it didn't happen in the short term.

Jimmy Piersall

It should have been a great night, and in many ways it was. On May 31, 1981, the Sox split a doubleheader with the California Angels. More important, the team drew a total of 52,493 to its ballpark. The paid attendance was just a little more than 40,000, but the idea of that many people in Comiskey was astounding, especially in the light of almost everything that happened in the seventies.

In third inning of the first game White Sox first baseman Mike Squires was called out on strikes on a pitch he thought was outside. Jimmy Piersall agreed with Squires. According to Piersall, he stood up in the broadcast booth and spread his arms to show how far it was out of the strike zone. First-base umpire Dale Ford noticed and claimed that Piersall had leaned out of the booth to get fans riled. Ford then stated that Piersall made an obscene gesture toward him. Piersall said the only finger gesture he made was with his thumb, adding that he was having fun. Harry Caray backed up Piersall, saying that his broadcast partner made no obscene gestures. Caray also wondered why the umpires were looking up at the booth when they should have been concentrating on what was happening on the field. No wonder they were blowing calls, he said.[16]

Ford apparently told Sox first-base coach Vada Pinson that a forfeit could occur if Piersall incited the crowd. On hearing this, manager Tony La Russa told Ford that wasn't a wise move. Although Ford backed down, he said he would walk off the field if the Piersall act continued.[17]

It is hard to know who is telling the truth. Umpires can be tyrants, and Piersall was never inhibited in actions or words. Piersall may have gone too far; the umpire may have overreacted. Regardless, the team didn't need the controversy, at least as far as the ownership was concerned.

"He can't control himself," Jerry Reinsdorf said. "He's too much of a fan. I feel sorry for the guy. The attraction is out there [on the field]. We don't need any attention on the booth. I don't think announcers should be communicating with umpires during the course of a game."[18]

A little more than three months later, Piersall was involved in another controversy that nearly cost him his job. He appeared with Caray on a Sunday night television show in early September hosted by *Sun-Times* columnist Mike Royko. The discussion turned to the players' wives and how they react to game broadcasts. Caray thought that a wife or girlfriend getting involved in her man's career may actually be a detriment rather than a help. In his book, *Holy Cow!*, Caray quoted Piersall as saying, "There are a lot of horny broads on the circuit."[19] Caray wrote that Piersall wasn't being offensive and the comment shouldn't have been taken that way. As it turned out, Caray's book was a little short on details.

According to Richard Dozer of the *Tribune*, the transcript of the show quoted Piersall as saying this: "I think each ball club should have a clinic once a week for the wives. I don't think they know what baseball is. First of all, they were horny broads who wanted to get married. They want a little money, they want a little security and a big strong looking ballplayer. I traveled, I played, I got a load of them broads, too."[20]

Caray maintained the show received no negative feedback as a result of the remarks and that Piersall had said more controversial things on other occasions. He felt that the controversy was stirred up by the White Sox players and organization as an excuse to get rid of Piersall. Eddie Einhorn took a different viewpoint. "You'll never have a winning team like this. I'm not knocking them, but this is unprecedented — a broadcasting team that upstages the team on the field. Our organization is not well thought of because of things like this. Here we've had a team in the race all year, and we haven't been on national television yet."[21]

The White Sox suspended Piersall with pay for the remainder of the season. Eddie Einhorn said it wasn't just the Royko show but a series of things that Piersall had done. Caray wrote in his book that the team stirred the controversy only as a means to get rid of Piersall.[22]

The Sox players were more than willing to see Piersall get fired. The general reaction from the fans (at least in print) and the print media was just the opposite. *Tribune* media critic Ron Alridge wrote the strongest rebuttal to the suspension in a September 11 column:

> It would be nice to think the Sox players were equally upset that their wives had been called broads, a sexist slur, but that seems unlikely. Remember, we're dealing with a macho sport that still treats females with contempt, ridicule and harassment. If you don't believe it, ask some of the women sportswriters who try to cover major league baseball.[23]

In the end, the White Sox kept Piersall, a decision at least partially influenced by Caray's bolting to the Cubs. In late November the team held a press conference to announce their new media lineup. Although Jimmy Piersall would remain, he would not be in the broadcast booth. He would work out of the Sportsvision studios and provide pre-and post-game analysis. Manning the booth would be Don Drysdale and Ken Harrelson. Drysdale had been doing Angels broadcasts and Harrelson was coming to Chicago from Boston. Drysdale would do the play-by-play, with Harrelson doing the color. Joe McConnell would be the radio play-by-play announcer, with a partner for him to be named at a later time.

Ken Harrelson in his playing days with the Indians, shown here hitting on the last day of August 1969 at Comiskey. He hit his 26th home run of the season that day but it is not known if it was this at-bat. Except for a brief time during the late '80s, Harrelson has been connected with the White Sox since 1982. He has done the TV play-by-play since 1990.

Piersall was the big story, however. Fans wanted to know if he was going to return after his suspension. In the stories written in both the *Sun-Times* and the *Tribune*, barely a word was devoted to Harrelson and Drysdale. The story centered on the controversial Piersall. "Nobody is going to hide Jimmy Piersall," Piersall said. "At the end of the game is when you'll enjoy me. They damn well better play good. The Sox have some exciting players and some not so exciting. They promised to get rid of some of them for me. I'm going to make people mad. What the hell do I care?"[24]

In the photo that accompanied the *Sun-Times* story, Piersall appeared to be having a great time. Sitting directly in the middle of the on-air personalities, he leaned forward with a huge grin. The majority of attention seemed to fall on him, and Piersall even felt confident enough to take a pot shot at his old pal Harry Caray. He said Caray "had some odd ideas. Fans who watch free TV don't go to games. What do you want them for?"[25]

From the way Piersall was carrying on, he made it sound like he had full rein to say just about anything he wanted, and in reality, his contract allowed him to be outspoken and opinionated. He was going to be the controversial Jimmy that many White Sox fans came to love. Nevertheless, after Piersall took his swipe at Caray, Einhorn stepped in to do some damage control. Piersall had yet to analyze even one game. "He (Caray) represents Chicago and is a people's person," Einhorn said, trying not to offend the leftover Caray fans.[26]

The re-signing of Piersall was an act of political convenience. By everything they said publicly, Einhorn and Reinsdorf really didn't want Piersall. They had to know they couldn't control him if they already had to deflect what he said at a press conference five months before the next season was to begin. Yet with Caray gone, they did not want to lose Piersall as well. Having owned the White Sox for less than a year, the two didn't want to alienate a fan base that feared Einhorn and Reinsdorf were going to destroy White Sox tradition.

In the last analysis, it might have been better to swallow some bitter pills and accept the backlash of a Piersall firing. His remaining only led to more public infighting, embarrassments, and bitterness.

The Season on the Field

Then there was the practical side of winning and losing on the field. When purchasing the team, Jerry Reinsdorf spoke about building a solid farm system and building the club from the ground up. While there isn't anything inherently wrong with this philosophy, the White Sox had just gone through one of their worst periods in team history. From 1968 to 1980, the team had only two winning seasons. Promising players had their careers sabotaged by off-the-field injuries, a superstar left when he was still an imposing presence, and free agents fled to other franchises because the past White Sox ownership had no means to keep them. The team never really came close to going to a World Series during this dubious 13-season period, and at times was completely overshadowed by the Cubs. It was hoped that a new infusion of capital would turn the team around quickly, at least in relative terms. Building a farm system sounded like a long-term approach, and that could mean several seasons of continued losing and non-contention. White Sox fans already had plenty of that, and from their early actions, the new ownership had a good grasp of that concept. "We haven't gotten any new players that the fans can identify with the new owners," Einhorn was quoted in a March 5, 1981, *Tribune* column by David Israel. "We have to do something before the season starts so the fans know we mean business."[27]

Einhorn told Israel that two main priorities for the White Sox needed to be accomplished before the 1981 season began — acquiring newly designated free agent Carlton Fisk and trading for a long ball hitter to add some punch to the White Sox offense.

Fisk was a long ball hitter of sorts. Twice during his Boston career he had hit 26 homers and he may have hit more in Fenway Park if some of his line drives off the Green Monster had been allowed to complete their trajectory. Home runs had become a scarce commodity since the Hitmen were disbanded. From 1978 to 1980, no White Sox player hit more than 20 home runs.

Yet Fisk could provide so much more than power, namely World Series experience. Few fans will ever forget Fisk using his body language in an effort to keep his 12th-inning leadoff drive from going foul in Game 6 of the 1975 World Series against the Reds. That homer won one of the most dramatic games in post-season play, and the memory of Fisk's triumphant trot around the bases had to create similar fantasies for White Sox fans.

Additionally, the White Sox had a developing pitching staff, and Fisk took pride in calling a good game:

> The young pitching staff very definitely played a part in my decision. I enjoy that part of the game. That is the part of the game I enjoy the most. Home runs are fun, base hits are fun, and they're essential. But behind the plate, that is the part of the game that's a real thrill for me. I think I can help them [pitchers] as far as their approach to get batters out, the ways to handle them. There are certain times to get a batter out and certain times to let him think he can do something.[28]

Now that they had Fisk, the White Sox turned their attention to the other need that Einhorn thought they had to address — an imposing power hitter. Greg Luzinski had three 30-homer and .300 seasons playing in Philadelphia. In late March the Phillies were willing to part with him, yet they wanted young left-hander Steve Trout from Chicago. The White Sox were not willing to part with Trout or any of their other starting pitchers. Trout was flattered that the Phillies were interested in him but he was happy the White Sox wanted to keep him. "I would be disappointed if I was traded. There's a lot of excitement on this club right now. This is a pretty solid team. And I want to be a part of it."[29]

As it turned out, the White Sox didn't have to part with Trout or anyone else. Five days later Luzinski was obtained in a straight cash deal. Though his power numbers had declined some in 1979 and 1980, Luzinski still had that hulking frame and domineering presence in the batter's box. He vowed he would be a major contributor to the White Sox. "I'm out to prove that I can still hit at the age of 30. I'm going to bring the White Sox a winner. I swear that from the bottom of my heart."[30]

The cost of the deal, including the purchase price and Luzinksi's salary, was estimated at $500,000.[31] In those early days of free agency, that was a lot of money. The White Sox had backed up the earlier Einhorn statement that new ownership had to demonstrate to the fans that they meant business. Adding the Veeck acquisition of base-stealing Ron LeFlore, the White Sox had a veteran presence with name recognition. The pre-season optimism was at it highest since the appearance of Dick Allen for the 1972 campaign.

This optimism was demonstrated by the home Opening Day crowd on April 14, when 51,560 made their way into the old ballpark to see the Sox take on the Milwaukee Brewers. The White Sox already had a dramatic season-opening win at Boston when Fisk hit an eighth-inning three-run homer to help knock off his old teammates, 5–3. In the home opener, the newly acquired free agent would do it again.

In the fourth inning Fisk capped a six-run inning by hitting a grand slam. The Sox had an easy 9–3 win. In three games, Fisk already had eight RBIs. But as hot as his start was, it was the return of the fans that added to the great feeling generated by a team on the rise. That Tuesday afternoon crowd was a Chicago Opening Day record that will only be broken if a large-capacity ballpark is built in Chicago.

"It was some crowd all right," Einhorn said to *Tribune* columnist David Condon.

> When I first stared counting the house I was convinced that we would be short of capacity. Then after being occupied with opening ceremonies, I looked around again and saw them hanging from the rafters. They were standing on the catwalks around the scoreboard. I think that because we got a better weather break than had been forecast, lots of fans made last-minute decisions to come out.

And the impressive thing is that they've been ordering for dates far into the future, not merely for Wednesday's game.[32]*

---

*I attended the May 20, 1973, Bat Day doubleheader that attracted a crowd of 55,555, the largest attendance of any Chicago baseball event. There is something about a crowd when fans are sitting in aisles and standing wherever they can. The new, larger stadiums can't produce this atmosphere. The White Sox, backed by home runs from Bill Melton and Carlos May, won the first game, also by the score of 9–3.

And for that game, the new owners did something that Bill Veeck would have endorsed. Fans presenting home Opening Day stubs for the Wednesday game would get that ticket for half-price. It was a smart move because Chicago traditionally had small crowds for the second home game of the year.

And the fans would keep coming. In a four-game stretch that began on May 31 and ended on June 4, the Sox drew 160,357. At the end of play that day, Chicago stood in second place with a 27–19 record, two games behind division-leading Oakland.

One week later the White Sox played their last game of the first half of this interrupted season. A players' strike over free agency put major league baseball on hold for almost two months. This was one work stoppage that was not going to be blamed on newcomer Jerry Reinsdorf. However, like with other work stoppages, it came at a bad time for the Sox. In 1972, an owners' lockout wiped out an anticipated huge Opening Day gate for the club. Then, of course, there would be the 1994 strike that would do some heavy damage to two franchises: the Montreal Expos and the Chicago White Sox. In 1981, the team lost some of its momentum in reconnecting with its fan base.

When baseball resumed in August, the split-season concept utilized in the minor leagues was put into effect. Division winners of the first half would play the division winner of the second half, with the winner advancing to the League Championship Series. If the team won both halves, it would play the second-half season runner-up in a wild card-type of setup.

Chicago baseball fans were desperate for post-season play. Although the logical thing would have been to resume the season where it had left off, the split season gave the team a chance to get into the playoffs without having to endure the 162-game schedule. The trouble was the Sox returned to action with a 15-game road trip. It appeared they were experiencing some Chicago baseball-type luck.

As it turned out, the Sox went 9–6 on the road trip and returned home in first place. Their first game at Comiskey in two-and-a-half months was against the Yankees and was beset by repeated rain delays. The game was score-less until the eighth when Dave Winfield doubled in a run off reliever LaMarr Hoyt. In the bottom of the inning, Greg Luzinski crashed a three-run homer. The rains came down again, and this time the game was called. What was left of a crowd of 30,000 went home happy knowing their team was in first place and looking good going into the last month of the season.

It all fell apart quickly, however. The White Sox lost their next three to the Yankees by a combined score of 23–4. One game was a 12–2 shellacking that had the Yankees laughing in their dugout. What was not funny was the Sox then dropped six of their next seven. After a 3–1 loss to Toronto, the Sox had slid all the way to fifth. It was obvious that the postseason wasn't going to happen for Chicago.

The White Sox split their final six at home, including a dramatic last-day victory when they overcame a 12–5 deficit with four in the eighth and four more in the ninth. However, having been eliminated from the playoffs, attendance for those last six games never topped 8,000. It looked like a normal late September or early October on the South Side.

Yet interest had returned on the South Side despite the season nearly being ruined by a strike that never should have happened. The situation with the White Sox franchise stabilized and there was even hope of some great things to come. The fans didn't think they would have to wait a century for a World Series championship to come to Chicago.

16

1983 — Breaking Through

"Where are the detractors now?"

— *General manager Roland Hemond after the White Sox clinched their first Western Division title.*[1]

"Wherever you're at, Harry and Jimmy, eat your hearts out. I hope people realize what scum you are."

— *Jerry Reinsdorf during the celebration of the clinching. He, of course, was referring to Harry Caray and Jimmy Piersall.*[2]

"Take that, Bill Gleason."

— *Eddie Einhorn on the owners' radio show the day after the clinching. Einhorn was referring to former* Chicago Sun-Times *columnist Bill Gleason.*

"We didn't pay attention to that. We pulled a game out of our butts and he said we won ugly. We just laughed because we knew how mad he was."

— *Outfielder Tom Paciorek describing the White Sox's reaction to Texas manager Doug Rader saying they won ugly. "Winning Ugly" eventually became a fan rallying cry.*[3]

"Personally I think the White Sox success this year is simply a devious plot designed to embarrass the noble Cubbies."

— *William Carsley in a letter published in the Chicago Sun-Times a day after the White Sox clinched their first division title.*[4]

The date was September 17, 1983. Fireworks were shooting into the late-summer night sky, seemingly dividing the air space between the griddle-iron stadium lights in half. Directly below stood the center-field scoreboard that still celebrated home runs and victories. However, it no longer looked like "the Monster." Times had changed and the square scoreboard now had a JumboTron screen that provided electronic images to the fans. At this time the image showed fans running across Comiskey Park. This was not an out-of-control, angry crowd or a disco-hating mob. They had been part of a group that had pushed the season attendance past 2 million for the first time in Chicago baseball history. And they were celebrating something that hadn't happened in 24 years in Chicago baseball history. To the right of the happy image relayed on the scoreboard was an announcement spelled out in tall letters: 1983 A.L. West CHAMPS.

From the bitter comments from Hemond, Reinsdorf, and Einhorn, one would never know that the White Sox became the first Chicago baseball team to win a title since division play began in 1969. One would never know that the team had taken over a city after the rest of the major league franchises had spent the last decade winning just about nothing. One would never know that everything went right (at least before the playoffs) for a Chicago baseball team after years of everything going unbelievably wrong.

There were rooftop home runs. At times, especially during the second half, there was a pitching staff that was unhittable. The team had speed and base stealers. The club also had a homegrown home run hitter with a working-class background who seemed to epitomize what many thought was the long-standing White Sox fan base. More important, there was no late-season swoon, there was nothing that resembled a choke, or a team that petered out in September because it didn't have enough players to finish off a season in first place.

Yet there was controversy from the very beginning, which essentially started when the ownership purchased the White Sox in early 1981. Two letters to the editor in the *Chicago Sun-Times* that ran the day after the clinching demonstrated the polarizing effect the season had on White Sox fans despite the team's success:

> Now that the White Sox are nearing a Division title, it will be interesting to read and hear what Messers. Schulian, Rapoport, Piersall, Caray, and other members of the "Hate Tony La Russa Club" will have to say about this excellent Sox manager. Will they "eat crow" and admit they were wrong? Don't bet on it.[5]
> John Craddock, Glenview

> Hip, hip, hooray and three cheers for Bill Veeck for standing by his guns and refusing to be "bought out" by the present owners of the Chicago White Sox. Pennant fever or not, as a lifelong Sox fan, I feel all Sox fans have been betrayed and exploited by a greedy ownership. Give our White Sox back to the fans.[6]
> Galen Banashak, Western Springs

So why the animosity amidst the good feelings? Many issues that caused some of the feelings expressed in the second letter had nothing to do with the 1983 White Sox squad that won the division title. The new owners had improved the team and won many fans over with fairly quick results. Yet they still struggled to win over the baseball city as a whole, even as the team moved up in the standings steadily and capped it with the historic clinching night.

Go back just a little more than a year and one could see there was still plenty of baseball angst on the South Side of Chicago. It appeared that the honeymoon the new ownership experienced through their initial months of running the club was over. It also was apparent the White Sox felt the same on-going frustration in competing with the Cubs for the city's attention. "We're three games out going into the All-Star break, and everybody says we stink," outfielder Ron LeFlore said in the early part of July 1982. "If the Cubs were three games out now, they'd be having a parade."[7]

The angry-sounding LeFlore was quoted in a July 11 column by the *Tribune's* Bob Verdi. Accompanying the story was a photo of a sour-looking Tony La Russa. From that awful look, one would have thought the White Sox were last, not third, two games behind the Kansas City Royals and California Angels. Although the White Sox were not exactly where they wanted to be (they were barely over .500), the team had come a long way from the 90-loss clubs of the late seventies. However, true optimism, the optimism that had been generated earlier by the acquisitions of Fisk and Luzinski, had dissipated. The Sox had started the season 8–0 and had a seven-game winning streak in May. But their inconsistent play pushed them down to third place and created doubt that the team was a true contender.

Verdi tried to convince Sox fans in his July 11 column that Jerry Reinsdorf and Eddie Einhorn were decent guys who really wanted their team to win. The columnist even praised the ownership for doing some things that irritated the fans, although nothing specific was mentioned. He basically wrote that taking decisive actions that offended some people was better than having the laid-back attitude of an absentee or uninvolved owner.[8] The absentee owner statement seemed to be a jab at Edward DeBartolo, who had tried to purchase the Sox prior to the Reinsdorf-Einhorn group. DeBartolo was turned down by the American League for various reasons, including his Ohio roots and residency. The "un-involved" owner? Was that a poke at the late P.K. Wrigley?

Regardless, White Sox faithful showed impatience during the 1982 season. La Russa was not a fan favorite, and the feeling was mutual. They lashed out at each other during and after a game on June 23 against the Twins. The fans booed La Russa when he took starter Dennis Lamp out of the game with none out in the ninth. The Sox led, 3–0, and the Twins had a runner on first who had walked to start the inning. La Russa then let the fans have it after the game, even though his decision to bring in reliever Salome Barojas led directly to a 6–3 Twins comeback win.

> If they want to hoot me and my club after we blow a 3–0 lead, I'll take my hat off to them. They paid their buck and they can boo all they want. Just don't try to tell me they're true Sox fans. I guarantee they weren't as upset losing this game as my club and I were.

It was not exactly a Lee Elia rant, but it sounded similar. The White Sox blow a game in the ninth and the manager lashes out at the fans? Just what is a true Sox fan? What was a true White Sox fan was debatable, but La Russa had two more vocal critics. They, of course, were Harry Caray and Jimmy Piersall. By 1982 Caray had moved to the other side of town, but Piersall was still around. In an August 8, 1982, *Tribune* article by Skip Myslenski, Piersall talked about his work approach as a game analyst. Piersall maintained his right to speak his mind regardless of whether it might offend a manager, a player, or an umpire. The story appeared after La Russa and Piersall had a confrontation in the Sportsvision studio that Piersall said was physical. He claimed coach Jim Leyland and La Russa were screaming at him. Piersall also claimed that Leyland was acting like a wild man, and was trying to provoke a fight. He stated he wasn't going to get into anything like that because that was what La Russa and Leyland wanted.[9]

La Russa described it this way to author Rob Rains: "Piersall had been saying certain things about me and my club and I wanted to talk to him face to face. I did it the way I think it should be done. There was nothing physical."[10]

"I care about what the fans say, what they want, not what the players want, not what the managers want, not what the owners want," Piersall told Myslenski. In essence, Piersall, as Caray had so expertly done throughout the seventies, was attempting to paint himself as the fans' media guy. Like the working class stiff, Piersall only wanted his money's worth, whether it was from his baseball team, a restaurant where he ate or the place he bought his groceries.[11]

Jerry Reinsdorf and many in the White Sox organization were not buying the political posturing, especially when it came to the treatment of La Russa. "They [Caray and Piersall] tried to destroy him," Reinsdorf told La Russa biographer Rob Rains.

> I could never figure what Harry had against him. They had a lot to do with the public perception. I had no problem resisting the public perception. We had been 20 games under .500 in 1980 and in 1981 we were two games over .500, so I couldn't figure out what was wrong with the guy."[12]

La Russa and the Sox felt the hostile atmosphere at Comiskey was so bad that the Sox manager couldn't come out of the dugout. In the early part of the 1983 season, Roland Hemond asked for some compassion from the fans. "If the fans and media are patient with Tony, this team will produce for him. It's not easy to be patient when things go bad, but that's what it takes to build a winner."[13]

Another person on the Sox who had issues with the fans and the media was Greg Luzinski. Luzinski had been the symbol of rebirth and rebuilding in the early stages of transition in 1981. But he was mired in a 3-for-53 slump in May of '83 and the fans let him have it. "Fans yelling abuse don't help when a team isn't getting the job done," Luzinski said in response to the fan hostility.

> Everybody's squeezing the bat too hard right now. I'm trying to pick the whole team up and so is Carlton Fisk. Then we start making errors, the fans get on us even more, and the pressure grows. Slumps are mostly mental. It's harder to relax when you keep thinking about them.[14]

The trouble was that fans had high expectations in the beginning. In December 1982, the Sox signed left-handed free agent Floyd Bannister to a long-term deal. Pitching for the Mariners in '82, Bannister was only 12–13. However, as usual for that era, Seattle was not a good team. The Mariners were 10 games under .500 that year and their run production was mediocre, although they played in a bandbox of a domed stadium. However, Bannister led the American League in strikeouts with 209, threw three shutouts, and had a respectable ERA of 3.43. With the developing Sox pitching staff of LaMarr Hoyt, Rich Dotson, and Britt Burns, fans felt the ownership was keeping its promise of building the team by aggressively dipping into the free agent market to sign a power pitcher. And power pitchers, like power hitters, are all the more exciting.

Yet the season started out like so many other underachieving campaigns. The Sox began their year on the road in Texas and lost the season opener, 5–3. Losing one game is not a big deal, but rookie first baseman Greg Walker made two errors on the first two balls hit to him in the first inning. The White Sox once again came under attack from Jimmy Piersall for putting the inexperienced Walker into a situation that he wasn't ready to handle.

Reinsdorf and the White Sox felt that Piersall went too far in criticizing the organization. Piersall was relieved of his Sportsvision duties. He continued a talk show gig at WMAQ-AM, a frequency that now houses the round-the-clock sports station WSCR-AM.

Reinsdorf wrote to Piersall:

> On the very first telecast of the baseball season this past Monday night, you again exceeded the boundaries that you yourself had acknowledged. The White Sox has just completed the most successful spring in their history and had the best spring training record of all 26 major league teams and after 2 errors in the 1st inning by one of our young players you launched a vitriolic attack on the manager and the organization that was totally unwarranted and unprofessional. You continued the attack throughout the telecast and later on your radio show.[15]

Was the Piersall attack any more out of line than any past criticism toward the White Sox organization? Or did the team finally have a real excuse to rid themselves of someone they didn't feel comfortable with in the first place? Was the firing due, as *Tribune* columnist Steve Daley speculated, to Piersall directing his arrows too closely to the front office?[16] Did Piersall get too close to the truth? Had Piersall been retained only to help sell Sportsvision?

The White Sox lost the next two games as well. Starting out 0–3 is not something that can't be overcome.* But more bad things were on the way.

Bannister, who was hailed as the next left-handed superstar, was 2–6 by May 26. In two of these losses he couldn't get past the fourth. In the last loss, he actually put in a respectable performance. The lefty went 7⅓ innings and gave up three runs in a 3–1 Sox defeat. But he was not matching the hype of his signing and the White Sox were a miserable 16–24.

Frustration was setting in with the team and it didn't have anything to do with the media or the fans. Outfielder Tom Paciorek stated the obvious when he said the early 1983 White Sox were not the 1927 Yankees.[17] Owner Jerry Reinsdorf was grateful there was more attention being paid to Lee Elia's anti-Cubs fan tirade than the White Sox's bad start. Yet even he knew that distraction was not going to take attention away from the Sox in the long run if the team didn't do something significant in 1983.

Then two things happened that helped turn the season around. One was the trade of second baseman Tony Bernazard to Seattle for another second baseman, Julio Cruz. Cruz was put in the ninth batting position in hopes that his speed would create some opportunities as the lineup turned over. Cruz's annual stolen base totals since 1978 were 59, 49, 45, 43, and 46, and he had already had 33 at the time of the June 15 trade. But Tom Paciorek thought there was another part of Cruz's game that was just as important. "What a terrific defensive player. He was so acrobatic. He could get a jump and make plays that you didn't think were possible."[18]

The other development was the move of Carlton Fisk into the second spot in the lineup. The conventional wisdom after the season was that Fisk saw more fastballs when Rudy Law (another base stealer) was hitting in the leadoff spot. Regardless, Fisk would end up matching his then-career-high of 26 homers. It was quite an accomplishment considering that Fisk had only one home run on May 10. Many believe Fisk's move to the second spot in the order was the true turning point in the season.

"Pudge wasn't afraid to hit behind in the count," Paciorek recalls, and said it in admiration as if he hadn't liked hitting behind in the count himself. "He helped Rudy out too."[19] Paciorek agreed with the conventional 1983 wisdom that Fisk saw many fastballs because base stealer Rudy Law put pressure on opposing defenses. In addition, since Fisk was willing to take pitches and hit behind in the count, Law had more chances to steal. Law set a franchise record of 77 stolen bases.

By the All-Star break, the White Sox were 40–37. Not a great record by any standards, but they had played 11 games over .500 since the Fisk move to the second spot. More important, the White Sox were only 3 behind the first-

---

*In their first championship season, the Bulls actually started out 0–3.

place Texas Rangers, hardly an impossible deficit to overcome. The 0–3 start that put the Sox three games behind the Rangers didn't seem all that important now.

The All-Star game was held at Comiskey Park on July 6, the fiftieth anniversary of the first All-Star game, also held at Comiskey. Babe Ruth's two-run homer in the right-field upper deck in the third had provided the difference in the American League's 4–2 victory.

An old-timers game was played at Comiskey the day before. Ex-Cub Billy Williams got the crowd to its feet when he launched a home run deep into the right-field upper deck. This drive would have sailed deep onto Sheffield Avenue if it were hit at Wrigley. The scoreboard went off for the Cubs great, and even White Sox fans had to be impressed that the old guy still had that great swing eight years after he retired.

There were some ceremonies in between the old-timers game and batting practice for the present-day all-stars. When Jerry Reinsdorf and Eddie Einhorn were introduced to make a presentation, they were met with some boos. They smiled sheepishly at the anger from fans that didn't fully understand or trust them yet. (And the feeling was probably mutual.) But Einhorn was happy not only with the result of the All-Star game (the AL won, 13–3, on the strength of a Fred Lynn grand slam), but the reputation the White Sox organization gained in hosting the game. "The success of the All-Star game was very important to us," he said. "It established credibility for the White Sox operation and let everyone in baseball know that we could deliver on our promises."[20]

More important to Sox fans, the promise of a successful season came to pass in the second half of the '83 campaign. Everything went right that could go right in that second half. Four games in particular demonstrated the kind of run the Sox had in order to take their division title.

- On August 4 at Comiskey against the Tigers, the White Sox picked up only one hit in the first five innings, but scored four runs in the sixth and won, 4–2, behind eight strong innings by Rich Dotson. The key hit was a line shot RBI double by Julio Cruz down the left-field line.
- On August 22 in Kansas City, Greg Luzinski led off the second by hitting a tape-measure home run that came very close to clearing the left-field bleachers in Kaufmann Stadium. A center fielder named Dave Stegman singled with two outs in the next inning. Through two outs in the eighth, Royal starter Paul Splitorff didn't allow a base runner, and then Scott Fletcher rolled what appeared to be an easy two-out grounder to shortstop U.L. Washington. The usually reliable Washington muffed the ball, giving the Sox an extra out. Julio Cruz did it again by following with a drive that barely cleared the left-center-field fence. His homer counted just as much as Luzinski's big swat. From the painful look on Splitorff's face, it appeared the lefty knew the game was over, and maybe even the divisional race. With LaMarr Hoyt on the mound, the game was over. The Sox won, 3–1, with Hoyt going the distance.
- Nine days later, the Sox and the Royals were tied 2–2 in a night game at

Comiskey. Ron Kittle reached out and knocked a Dan Quisenberry breaking pitch on the outside part of the plate into the left-field seats for a three-run homer. The Sox won, 7–3. "That young man hit a good pitch," Kansas City manager Dick Howser said after the game. "I can't criticize the pitch."[21]

- In the first game of a doubleheader against the Twins on September 21, Harold Baines lined a seventh-inning single to center and knocked in a run, giving the Sox a 2–1 lead. LaMarr Hoyt again was on the mound and once the Sox had the lead, the fans had to know the game was safe. Hoyt faced the minimum six hitters in the last two innings and picked up his 22nd win. The winning was becoming routine. Suspense didn't exist.

The White Sox won the second game of the doubleheader, 7–6, when Scott Fletcher doubled in the winning run off the bottom of the left-center-field wall in the bottom of the ninth. After the win, Sox players gathered on the pitching mound to salute their fans. They were on the road for the remainder of the season, so they wouldn't return until after they played the first two games of the playoffs. Clinching the division title so early gave them the opportunity to say good-bye in a truly victorious way. It was quite a turnaround for the franchise. Since 1967, it had been rumored that the team would be moved to Milwaukee, Seattle, New Orleans, or Denver. Now they seemed to reaffirm their place in Chicago.

So maybe Hemond, Reinsdorf, and Einhorn had the right to make their critics eat crow in the aftermath of the clinching. Many had called for La Russa's head, saying the White Sox would never win anything as long as he was manager. There were the doubters who didn't think the White Sox could ever really draw. And finally there were the critics, led by Jimmy Piersall, who thought the White Sox organization was completely inept and couldn't accomplish a thing. During the last part of 1983, all had been proven wrong.

Stunned silence. That was how '83 alumnus Tom Paciorek reacted when I asked him to respond to this information: The White Sox record during the last 30 games was 24–6, and they had outscored their opponents 174–91. Just before being given that little piece of data, Paciorek was speculating as to why the White Sox had failed in the American League Championship Series against Baltimore. He thought part of the reason was the early clinching. Playing two weeks of meaningless games didn't help, he said. Paciorek also mentioned that the Sox had been no-hit. (Oakland pitcher Mike Warren did the trick in a 3–0 A's win on September 29.) But the Sox won 11 of the last 14 games of the season even with the no-hitter. Paciorek thought the Sox couldn't have played well against the Mariners the day after the clinching celebration, but the Sox won that game, 6–0, behind a complete-game performance by Rich Dotson. In fact, in that four-game series, the White Sox shut out the Mariners three times. "I never heard that statistic before," Paciorek finally said regarding the 24–6 mark and the outrageous way the Sox had outscored their opposition.[22]

He was still in awe of the statistic, not fully realizing the White Sox had played that well even thought he had been part of the whole process. Or maybe he didn't realize it *because* he was part of the process.

However, the way the White Sox played in the last two months of the season didn't carry over to the playoffs. After winning game one, 2–1, at Baltimore, the Sox were dominated in the next two games, losing 4–0 and 11–1. But even as they faced elimination in game four, there was still optimism. If they pulled out a win, Hoyt would pitch game five. Including his 2–1 win in game one, Hoyt had won 22 of his last 26 decisions.

Every person has probably had a nightmare or paralyzing fear that he will do something to embarrass himself. The worst fear usually centers on some professional blunder that not only humiliates but sabotages others as well. For Sox shortstop Jerry Dybzinski, that fear was realized in the seventh inning of the fourth game.

The game was still a scoreless tie in the seventh. Greg Walker led off with a single, and Mike Squires was sent in to pinch run. Vance Law singled Squires to second. It all looked so promising. Britt Burns was pitching the game of his life, and if the Sox could push a few runs across, they could also push the series to a deciding fifth game. But then the unfortunate Jerry Dybzinski came to the plate.

The situation called for a bunt. Dybzinski was adept at bunting, but this time he failed. Oriole catcher Rick Dempsey pounced on the ball and fired to third, forcing Squires. Then came a play that defined the Sox's fortunes for the eighties and well beyond.

Julio Cruz hit a sharp single to left. Vance Law was stopped at third as the hit was corralled by Gary Roenicke in short left field. Yet for some odd reason, Dybzinski kept running and got hung up between second and third. Law decided he might as well head home, as the Orioles were chasing down Dybzinski. Law was an easy out. The Sox had three hits out of their first four batters, yet now there were two out. To Dybzinski's credit, he didn't shy from reporters after the eventual 3–0 loss. However, his explanation of his baserunning gaffe didn't make sense:

> All my instincts told me to keep running because there was going to be a play at the plate. I was hoping they would throw to third to get me while the run scored. I know I can run the bases and bunt, but I didn't do either of those things when the team needed it the most. I'll just have to live with it, hoping I get a chance to make up for it.[23]

A play at the plate was not a given, especially the way the ball was hit. The play was also in front of Dybzinski and there was no way he should have been heading to third unless he saw a throw to the plate going all the way through. Also, at that point why should the Orioles have conceded a run?

Ron Kittle is not happy after getting hit by a pitch in the third game of the American League Championship Series in 1983. Kittle was not able to play the next day and the White Sox dropped the series because they completely lost the ability to score a run.

Burns was on top of his game and one run could have been all he needed. And why even give himself up when there was still a potential for a big inning? Comiskey Park deflated; the whole inning deflated.

Even so, Dybzinski was being too hard on himself. He singled with two out in the ninth to keep things alive, and was ninety feet away with the winning run when Rudy Law struck out to end the inning. Greg Luzinski went 0-for-5 and never put the ball in fair territory. He struck out three times (all called third strikes) and fouled out twice. The White Sox hit .211 as a team for the series, hit no homers, and had only two RBIs. In that heart-breaking fourth game, the Sox had 13 runners on base and scored none of them. Ron Kittle had been hit by a pitch in the third game and wasn't available for the fourth. His presence could have made a difference. Scapegoating Dybzinski, by saying he let the team down, was not fair since the team let itself down, especially when it was outscored 19–3.

In their post-game celebration, Baltimore rubbed it in the Sox face. They sang the "Na, na, na" song as they drenched each other in champagne. The World Series appearance was their sixth in 17 years. The Sox had had only one in 64 years.

Despite the playoff loss, the new White Sox ownership had to be pleased. The Cubs seemed to become Chicago's second-class citizens. No new tradition had yet to be built on the North Side, unless you call fans and players wanting to beat each other up a new tradition. With their youth, it appeared the Sox would be contending for years, and that they would have a new tradition of their own. The White Sox could finally build their fan base and bury the hapless Cubs in the process. What happened instead was the Cubs solidified their place in Chicago sports while the White Sox spent the rest of the decade imploding.

17

The "Magical" Year

Craig Biggio, Derek Bell, Jeff Bagwell, Jack Howell, Moises Alou, Brad Ausmus, Jeff Bagwell, Jack Howell, Moises Alou, Dave Clark, Ricky Gutierrez, Shane Reynolds, Jeff Bagwell, Jack Howell, Moises Alou, Dave Clark, Ricky Gutierrez, Brad Ausmus, Bill Spiers, Derek Bell.

Solo off Ryan Dempster,(yes, that Ryan Dempster), three-run homer off Oscar Henriquez, two-run homer off Livian Hernandez, two-run homer off Jim Parque, solo homer off Carlos Castillo, three-run homer off James Baldwin, solo homer off LaTroy Hawkins, two-run homer off Mark Portugal, solo homer off Cal Eldred, solo homer off Cal Eldred, solo homer off Cal Eldred, solo homer off Bronswell Patrick, solo homer off Carlton Loewer, two-run homer off Carlton Loewer, two-run homer off Matt Beech, three-run homer off Toby Borland, solo homer off Tyler Green, solo homer off Seth Greisiner, solo homer off Brian Moehler, solo homer off Alan Embree.

There must have been something about the number 20 for the Cubs in 1998. The list at the top comprises the 20 Houston Astro strikeout victims of Kerry Wood on May 6, 1998. He was still 20 years old when he recorded one of the most dominating pitching performances in baseball history. Wood went out to a restaurant to celebrate his win that night, and if he was served an alcoholic drink, the restaurant would have been in danger of losing its liquor license.

The second list comprises 20 home runs hit by Sammy Sosa. Sosa hit 609 in his career; so what would be so significant about these dingers? They came in one month. At the beginning of June 1998, Sosa had 13 homers. A good amount for that point in the season, but the number was no indication of what kind of year Sosa was going to have. He had five multi-homer games in June and went into July with 33 homers, a good season for many hitters. There was one other startling stat for the month: The Cubs were only 12–15.

It has been said that after the 1994 work stoppage Sosa and Mark McGwire saved baseball in 1998 with their dual assault on the 60-homer standard set by

Roger Maris and Babe Ruth. It also can be said that Kerry Wood and Sammy Sosa, in a sense, saved the Cubs, or at least reversed a post-strike backlash that even affected a franchise with a fan base that extended well beyond the Midwest.

At the beginning of 1998, the Cubs were not ready to fold their tents and leave Chicago. However, their fans, like almost all baseball fans, felt betrayed by the 1994 strike. The Cubs were in last place at the time of the walkout. However, I can recall talking with many Cubs fans afterward. Pain was deeply embedded in their faces as they recalled 1994. No, they had not been in position to head into the playoffs as the White Sox had been, and they headed into 1995 knowing they had spent the last five decades without going to a World Series. But they felt betrayed nevertheless. It didn't matter whether the owners or the players did the betraying. Baseball had been taken from them, and a betrayal was a betrayal.

Interestingly, the Cubs outdrew the White Sox by more than 100,000 when the Sox won the Western Division title in the last year of two-divisional play in 1993. The Cubs won 84 games that year, but that was only because of a strong September that made the season look more respectable than it really was. When the strike halted play in 1994, the Cubs had already drawn more than 1.8 million and looked like they were going to match or exceed the '93 total of 2.6 million-plus despite being in last place. The White Sox were not only the better team, but the Cubs looked like they had regressed to the laughable early sixties. Yet at Wrigley the vines were green, and the sun seemed warmer. Right outside the stadium, the rooftops were filled and the restaurants and bars were overflowing.

The 1994 season began to change all of that, at least in the short term. Attendance at Wrigley in the immediate post-strike era didn't suffer as badly as it did on the South Side. The club still drew a little more than 1.9 million in 1995 but that was their lowest total attendance in nine years. Additionally, from the sound of many crowds, there were many no-shows at Wrigley, so that attendance figure would have been less if they counted only fans that did show and not total ticket sales. It helped that the team almost crept into a wild-card spot in 1995, and there was some excitement at Wrigley that last weekend. However, their most prized star, Ryne Sandberg, had left the club in mid-season '94, and the team seemed rudderless.

Only 15,758 showed for Kerry Wood's twenty-strikeout game. True, it was a mid-week game and the kids were still in school. Yet today a small crowd like that would be a major news story and a signal that something was seriously wrong with the club. When was the last time the Cubs drew under 20,000 for any game at any time?

It helps any professional team to have an identity. Having a city's name or team nickname plastered on a shirt or jersey doesn't give any franchise an identity. During the '80s many media people outside of Chicago were amazed by the popularity of the Chicago Bears. True, a great deal of that popularity came as a result of their 1986 Super Bowl win over the New England Patriots. And in a championship-starved town like Chicago, that lone title among decades of letdowns went a long way. Yet, the Bears had a strong image in the city that went beyond winning one championship. They were like throwbacks from the old black-and-blue NFL Central Division in the sixties and seventies. Opponents used to say that when they played the Bears, they knew they had been in a real football game. The Bears of the '80s represented the toughness that had been missing from the club for so long. That was why even defensive and offensive linemen had their own radio shows in the '80s. Hardly any player on the Bears was anonymous.

The Cubs developed a strong identity with their fans, and that partly came from the fact that players stayed with the team for most of their careers. In the late '60s and early '70s this included Banks, Santo, Williams, Jenkins, Kessinger, and Beckert. In the '80s it was Sandberg, Sutcliffe, and Grace. Now in 1998 it would be Wood and Sosa.

Who was Kerry Wood in 1998? He was a young pitcher that looked like he had a world of talent. But teams on both sides of town seemed to have those players from time to time. Was this guy for real? On May 6, it appeared that he was, and then some.

One has to look at the details of the game to see how amazing it was:

- Wood struck out the side four times; he retired the side in order seven times and faced only two hitters over the minimum. During one inning, all three Astros took called third strikes.
- All eight starters other than the pitcher struck out at least twice, two of them three times.
- Wood hit a batter (Craig Biggio, who made a career out of getting hit) and walked no one.
- Only two outs left the infield. There was a sacrifice accounting for another out. A line out to third showed that one ball was at least hit hard. The remaining outs came on two grounders and a pop out. The Cubs' defense barely broke a sweat as they just stood there and watched Wood pitch. It was similar to a Little League game when some over-grown kid strikes out just about everybody and the nerd in right field is thankful the ball wasn't hit to him.
- The Astros had one hit, a Rickey Gutierrez infield single. Gutierrez did reach third, but that was partly due to a Wood balk, one of the pitcher's few mistakes that day. Otherwise, the Astros didn't threaten at all, as no other runner reached second. It seemed like the Cubs walked away with the win, even though they only scored two runs on eight hits. Houston starter Shane Reynolds went all the way and picked up 10 strikeouts. Reynolds pitched well but no one seemed to talk about what a hard-luck guy he had been in a game where there were 30 total punch-outs.

The first-place Astros flailed away at breaking balls. They were overpowered by fastballs. Other times they just watched the ball go by. There was even a little debate about if their hit was truly a hit. "He deserved a no-hitter, and I'll go up there [to the press box] and tell them to change it to an error," said third baseman Kevin Orie, who had tried to snare a grounder hit by Ricky Gutierrez. Orie added:

> I figured maybe I had a chance at it, but it died. It came off the bat quickly, but it's always a tough read when this grass slows the ball up. So I ended up trying to stretch for it and it stayed outside. I was thinking of diving. Diving's not my style, but maybe if I dived I could have got up and made the play.[1]

Houston's Jeff Bagwell tried to put an end to the whole discussion. "It was a hit," Bagwell said. "Everybody can look back now, but it was a hit to me. But if it's in the sixth or seventh inning, that one's an error. But you can't go back and say it wasn't a hit."[2]

"I don't care if it was a five-hitter," Wood said. "We won."[3] The only other thing that Wood was concerned about was that he finished the game. For the rookie it was only his fifth major league start. On entering the game he had pitched a total of 18⅓ innings in the big leagues, with a so-so mark of 2–2. At least one player compared him to Nolan Ryan. Ryan had finished his career five years earlier and ended with 324 wins, six seasons with 300 or more strikeouts, 5,714 career strikeouts, seven no-hitters, and 12 one-hitters.

The Cubs had gone into the game only one game over .500. Would Wood's performance be a catalyst to something bigger? The team did finish the month of May with a 17–11 mark. But there was something else on the horizon that would eclipse even Wood's near-perfect and staggering performance.

Sammy Sosa came to Chicago via a trade to the White Sox on July 29, 1989. The Sox had sent Harold Baines and infielder Fred Manrique to Texas for Sosa, infielder Scott Fletcher, and young lefty pitcher Wilson Alvarez. The White Sox were rebuilding and Alvarez was considered a big part of the deal. Like Wood, Alvarez had some great success in the early part of his career. In his second career start, on August 11, 1991, Alvarez threw a no-hitter against the Orioles in Baltimore. He also won a 1993 playoff game against the Blue Jays, throwing a complete-game seven-hitter in a 6–1 victory in Toronto.

Sosa looked different when he played for the Sox. He was twenty-one at the time of the trade from Texas. Much trimmer, he was never thought of as a player who would hit home runs. In fact, in early 1992 he was traded to the Cubs for George Bell, a guy who had some good home run years, including 1987 when he hit 47. Bell hit 25 homers for the Sox and knocked in 112 in 1992. But he slumped to 13 in 1993 and then left baseball.

Sosa gave some indication that he could be a big-time power hitter in 1996. By August 20, Sosa had already hit 40 homers and knocked in 100. He was then hit on the hand by a pitch from Florida's Mark Hutton. Sosa's hand was broken and he was out for the season. The Cubs had only 38 games left and reaching 60 home runs would be a tough task. But 50 was attainable and would have made Sosa a household name. Sosa had a good year in '97 but he hit a relatively few 33 homers and still flew a little under the radar until 1998.

It was early evening but the sun still shone prominently. The heat and humidity were searing in the crowded stadium. The home team had a so-so record and almost no chance of getting to the playoffs. However, there was palatable excitement in the crowd. Mark McGwire was set to resume his chase at the Maris home run record. What the rest of the St. Louis Cardinals did really didn't matter much.

In the first inning McGwire launched one toward the left-field upper deck, right down the line. From the seats the ball was lost in that hot, yellow sun. Finally it could be spotted as it hooked to the wrong side of the foul pole. The drive smacked off a window of the skybox-looking structure with a loud thud. The Plexiglas window didn't shatter. Unlike in the movie *The Natural*, the ball didn't crash through a scoreboard or short out the stadium lights. It did have a chilling effect in the midst of the heat. The crowd, which was on its feet at the crack of the bat, sat down with a collective disappointed sigh at the realization that the long clout was nothing but a foul ball. McGwire didn't hit a home run that night, but history still awaited him.

McGwire had been known as one of the "Bash Brothers" when he played with Jose Canseco on the Oakland A's during the late '80s and early '90s. He won American League Rookie of the Year honors by knocking 49 home runs in 1987, swatted 52 homers in 1996, and hit a combined total of 58 homers playing for the A's and Cardinals in 1997. It was assumed that McGwire would assault the home run record in 1998.

Few expected Sosa would be chasing the record with McGwire. But after June, he was. McGwire had an imposing figure, standing at 6'5". His swing was vicious, and his homers seemed to range between no-doubt-about-its and some tape-measure job. Sosa, though not as tall as McGwire, had bulked up by then, and his swing was intimidating. He had his hands down on the bottom of the bat, which he held away from his body and out over the plate. Sosa looked like he could hit the ball as far as he wanted at any time. As with McGwire, his home runs were things to be seen and remembered. The ball shot off his bat and soared over the wall. There was little doubt where the ball was heading when Sosa connected with his hard but level swing. He would soon adopt his homer-hop. Like Mantle and Maris in 1961, the double chase was on, but this time fans were convinced both players would break the record. It was only a matter of who would do it first.

On September 8, the Cubs played the Cardinals in St. Louis. McGwire had already tied Maris at 61 and Sosa stood at an amazing 58. McGwire came up in the fourth and faced Steve Traschel. The Cubs were leading, 2–0, but the score hardly mattered. McGwire laced a low line drive down the left-field line. The ball skimmed the top of the wall and kept going. The former Bash Brother had become the first player to hit 62 home runs in a season.

Busch Stadium went berserk and Sosa politely applauded from his right-field position. As prolific as Sosa had been, he just couldn't keep up with McGwire. Although it seemed as if McGwire would pull away, Sosa got hot and got back into the chase to see who would establish the record.

By September 13, Sosa had hit the 60 mark. McGwire ran into a little slump, going 1-for-14 since hitting number 62. Sosa responded by hitting two more against the Brewers at Wrigley. Both were typical Sosa shots onto Waveland Avenue. Both were estimated at lengths close to 500 feet. Now Sammy Sosa was the second player in major league history to hit 62 home runs.

McGwire hit five homers over the last weekend of the season to reach the 70 mark. It had to be somewhat frustrating for Sosa to hit 66 round-trippers and not even win the home run championship. However, coming in second in the greatest home run race ever didn't diminish his landmark season. Sosa ended up only two hits short of 200, knocked in 158, scored an incredible 134 runs, and hit .308. He became the first Cub since Andre Dawson in 1987 to win the National League Most Valuable Player award. Saying that he had a career season doesn't come close to describing the year Sammy Sosa had in 1998.

What is almost forgotten about 1998 is that the Cubs made the playoffs for the first time since 1989. The San Francisco Giants could have clinched a wild-card spot on the last day of the season, but they blew a 7–0 lead against the Rockies in Colorado. Losing that game, 8–7, San Francisco was forced to come to Chicago for a one-game playoff to see who would win the last National League playoff spot.

Fans converged on Wrigley on that Sunday afternoon to see if they could get tickets for the Giants game or soak in the atmosphere of Wrigley after such an historic season. Many said their team was going to the playoffs. The Cubs were not there yet, but their fans wanted to grab any excitement they could. Nothing much really had happened with their ball club since they had taken the Eastern Division in 1989.

The Cubs took a 5–0 lead into the last inning against the Giants. Steve Traschel, the man who gave up the record-breaking homer to McGwire, allowed only one hit in 6⅓ innings. San Francisco pushed across one run in the ninth when Barry Bonds came up with the bases loaded, representing the tying run. Bonds was still three seasons away from cracking the 70-home run barrier himself, although he was dangerous enough. Bonds had hit 37 homers in 1998 and had 122 RBIs. He picked up only one RBI with this at-bat on a sacrifice fly. Joe Carter, one of the players traded for Rick Sutcliffe in 1984, came up with one runner on and the Giants now behind 5–3. Carter will be most remembered for hitting the game-winning home run off ex–Cubs and then–Phillies reliever

Mitch Williams to win the final game of the 1993 World Series for the Toronto Blue Jays. This time Carter provided no heroics and popped up to first to end the game. Ironically, it was Carter's last at-bat in his major league career.

The 1998 playoffs are not something most Cubs want to remember. Atlanta swept Chicago in three straight, outscoring the Cubs 15–4. Sosa hit no home runs. Kerry Wood missed the whole month of September with what would be the beginning of many physical problems for him. He gutted out five innings of three-hit, one-run ball, but ended up taking the loss in a 6–2 Braves win in the third game. The loss ran the Cubs' post-season losing streak to six. The Cubs had also lost 10 of their last 11 playoff contests.

Sammy Sosa didn't only help Mark McGwire revive the popularity of major league baseball. Sosa and Wood helped revive the Cubs. Attendance was still somewhat good on the North Side in the immediate post-strike years. The 1998 home attendance returned to the pre-strike numbers as the Cubs drew more than 2.6 million, which was almost the exact total in 1993. The team had someone called "Kid K," and a guy who had passed up Babe Ruth. The pain of 1994 was forgotten. The Cubs have not slid under the 2 million attendance mark since then, and now routinely top the 3 million mark. A great deal of that can be attributed to the 1998 turnaround. The franchise has Wood and Sosa to thank for it.

In 1994 the White Sox were the better team in Chicago. As in the mid '80s, they seemed on the verge of real Chicago baseball history. Instead, the strike ended all of that. Try on these big ifs: What if the White Sox won the World Series in 1994 and became a perennial playoff contender during the remainder of the '90s? What if Sammy Sosa hadn't cracked the 60-home run barrier? What if Kerry Wood had struck out 20 in a game for some other team? Would the White Sox still have such a hard time competing for the baseball entertainment dollar in the city? Would the Cubs have worn down their fans with non-contending baseball, and would the attendance with the golden egg vanish? Would the rooftops not be as crowded? Would the rivalry between the fan bases have lost its intensity because one team was clearly superior to the other?

But the strike did happen, as did something called the White Flag Trade. Sosa and Wood also happened. By the time the White Sox won their World Series in 2005, the Cubs had once more solidified their place in Chicago and beyond. And part of it happened because the Cubs had two players who did some things that were so special that their fans forgot a betrayal. They returned to Wrigley, to the rooftops, to the restaurants, and to the bars. The Cubs were more than lovable losers. They had become one of the most popular franchises in the history of professional sports.

"Baseball has been berry-berry good to me." This phrase is known to most *Saturday Night Live* fans from the skit mocking Latino players' efforts to articulate themselves and the major league's attempts to make all their athletes politically correct. In fact, the less political opinions they have the better. Just go out and say how everything is great and that way the fans will love everyone.

Sammy Sosa fell far. He went from a player that dwarfed his own sport and who helped revive his own franchise to being called a cheat and a self-centered creep who didn't know the meaning of the word "team." Sosa went before a congressional committee investigating steroid use and said he had problems with the English language. The *Saturday Night Live* Garret Morris character could be laughed about as a naïve illiterate. The real 600-homer-plus Sosa was derided for hiding behind a supposed language barrier that few people really believed existed.

In a sense, it was not surprising that Sosa couldn't handle the adulation that had to overwhelm him. It had happened with the biggest of baseball's home run hitters. Babe Ruth was embittered by the fact that he never was chosen to manage the Yankees and his considerable feats didn't seem to comfort him during his last years. He died in his early 50s. Roger Maris had been hounded by fans during his record chase and preferred not to talk about his 1961 history-making season. He also died in his early fifties. Henry Aaron handled his home run march the best but had to endure racism and death threats.

Mark McGwire was humiliated during those congressional hearings. He has been passed over in the Baseball Hall of Fame voting and it is debatable if he will ever be elected to Cooperstown. Barry Bonds has had many legal problems, is liked by virtually no one, and is shunned by major league baseball. Rafael Palmeiro never threatened the single-season home run record, but how much credibility do his 569 homers and 1,835 RBIs have? Palmeiro has 3,020 hits, but how much consideration will he receive for the hall with the suspicion of steroids hanging over his head?

What will Cubs fans really remember about Sosa? Will it be his one known corked bat incident? All his bats that are in the Baseball Hall of Fame were x-rayed and found to be cork-free, as were the other bats he had in his possession at the time of the incident. Will fans remember him more for when he walked out on his team hours before the last game of the 2004 season ended? He said after the 2003 playoffs that he had wanted to retire as a Cub. But his final season was in 2007 and he went back to Texas, where he had started. Sosa actually had a decent year with 21 homers and 92 RBIs. He was able the cross the 600-homer threshold. But when he retired, hardly anyone noticed.

There was the "homer hop" that got old when hits didn't turn out to be home runs. Instead of getting doubles off some deep fly balls, Sosa was either thrown out at second or held to a single. Then there was White Sox shortstop Jose Valentin who ridiculed Sosa's kiss blowing and chest thumping post-homer routine after Valentin had homered at Wrigley during one of the Cross-town Classic games.

Somehow it doesn't seem likely that Sosa will be at a Cubs fan convention any time soon. If he did, would he be willing to face fans who would want to know about possible steroid use and corked bats? Or would Sosa say he doesn't understand English?

"I choked. That's the bottom line. I choked. I let my teammates down, I let the organization down, and I let the city of Chicago down."[4]

This harsh self-assessment was made by Kerry Wood after the seventh game loss to the Florida Marlins in the 2003 National League Championship Series. Wood had been given the role of stopping the Marlins after Florida had come back from a three-games-to-one deficit. He couldn't do that; the Marlins won, 9–6, and went on to win the World Series against the Yankees. It was the Marlins' second world championship in six years. The 2003 campaign marked the 95th straight season without a world championship for the Cubs.

Wood had won two games in the Division Series against the Atlanta Braves, 4–2 and 5–1. In the 4–2 win, it was Wood's two-run double that made the difference. The 5–1 win was the deciding game of the best-of-five series. The series victory marked the first time a Chicago baseball team won a post-season matchup since the White Sox took the World Series from the New York Giants in 1917.

The Cubs line up before their first game against the Florida Marlins in the NLCS in 2003. Dusty Baker has his son standing next to him.

September and October are crunch times. In the September stretch run, Wood pitched seven innings of two-run ball in a 9–2 win over the Brewers. He then threw a complete-game four-hit shutout in a 2–0 victory over the Mets. His next outing was a six-inning, five-hit, one-run performance against the Reds. The Cubs eventually won that game, 7–6. Wood then beat the Reds by allowing one hit over seven innings. The Cubs took that contest, 6–0. In the third game of the League Championship Series against the Marlins, Wood had a substandard performance, at least by his own standards. He went 6⅔ innings and gave up three runs. The Cubs won in extra innings, 5–4.

From September 7 on, the Cubs had won seven straight games in which Wood started. He had lost on September 2 when he threw seven innings and gave up four hits and two runs, one of which was unearned. The Cubs lost that game, 2–0, hardly Wood's fault.

In the disappointing game seven against the Marlins, Wood allowed a three-run homer in the first to give the Marlins a quick lead. But Wood hit a two-run homer in the bottom of the second to tie the game at three. It was the first time a pitcher had hit a home run in the postseason since Rick Sutcliffe homered in the first game of the San Diego series in 1984.

The 2003 season had been a breakout year for Wood. He won a career-high 14, stayed healthy enough to pitch 211 innings (while giving up only 152 hits), and picked up 266 strikeouts. Add in the two playoff victories and Wood had the season that many expected after his historic 20-strikeout game.

Yet Wood, like many other Chicago baseball players during the last three or four decades, didn't fulfill fan and team expectations. Maybe his success came too quickly and the expectations were too much. By the seventh game of the Marlins series, Wood was a young 26. A *Chicago Tribune* photo shows him rubbing his eyes in an effort to control his emotions after Florida took the lead in the fifth inning. Despite assurances from his team after he was pulled in the sixth, Wood was described as physically shaken after the game. The young man seemed to still have a bit of the Little Leaguer in him, and was unable to come to terms with significant disappointment.

By 2008, Wood had been turned into a full-time closer. It was believed that he could stay healthy with less innings pitched, even with more appearances. In '08, he had a good year, saving 34 games. Yet the Cubs chose not to re-sign him for '09 or beyond, and Wood moved over to Cleveland.

After moving on, Wood took out full-page advertisements in each Chicago daily newspaper. Superimposed over a picture of Wood following through with his delivery, the former Cub thanked fans for all the good times he had enjoyed during the past decade.

It has been an honor to have been a Chicago Cub for the last 13 years, and to have played in the greatest ballpark, Wrigley Field. My deepest thanks go to my teammates and the Cubs organization for taking a chance on a kid from Texas and welcoming me into the Cubs family. Thank you Cubs fans, the greatest fans in all of baseball, for believing in me and supporting me over the years. I will always be proud to have been a Chicago Cub. Although I'm a member of a new "Tribe," I will forever be a Chicagoan.[5]

The Cubs' decision to not re-sign Wood caused the usual fan debate. But how many times has a player decided to say a real good-bye when he signs with another ball club? Kerry Wood will probably always be remembered as a Chicago Cub.

18

What Might Have Been

"There are few words to describe how awful I feel and what I have experienced within these last 24 hours. I've been a Cubs fan all my life and fully understand the relationship between my actions and the outcome of the game. I had my eyes glued on the approaching ball the entire time and was so caught up in the moment that I did not even see Moises Alou, much less that he had a play. Had I thought for one second that the ball was playable or had I seen Alou approaching, I would have done whatever I could to get out of the way and give Alou a chance to make the catch. To Moises Alou, the Chicago Cubs organization, Ron Santo, Ernie Banks and Cubs fans everywhere, I am so sorry from the bottom of this Cubs fan's broken heart. I ask that Cubs fans everywhere redirect the negative energy that has been vented toward my family, my friends and myself into the usual positive support for our beloved team on their way to being National League champs."

— *Steve Bartman's statement as released in the Chicago Tribune, October 16, 2003. Bartman's hopes were dashed as the Cubs lost the seventh and deciding game of the series, 9–6.*[1]

"It isn't fair."

— *Fictional character Tessie Hutchinson in the Shirley Jackson 1948 short story The Lottery. Hutchinson had "won" her hometown's annual lottery. Her winning was actually a death sentence in which all of the townspeople took part in her killing, including members of her own family. The family of Cubs fans were ready to turn on Steve Bartman, and he was fortunate to have escaped a similar fate.*

"I welcome your death threats."

—*Writer and humorist Jay Pinkerton after analyzing the Bartman-Alou snafu. Pinkerton, after looking at the several stills of the incident, came to the conclusion that Alou had no chance of making the catch. He thought it was time for Cubs fans to recognize Bartman's innocence and seemed unconcerned about the consequences of holding that opinion.*[2]

"The ball was in the stands. It was clear. I just zeroed in on the ball,
and it was an easy call."
— *Left-field umpire Mike Everitt explaining why he had not made a fan
interference call in regards to Steve Bartman.*[3]

"You cost us the World Series!"
— *One of the cleaner fan taunts thrown at Bartman.*

"He wasn't leaning over. He was behind the rail; he didn't know
Alou was coming. It looks like I touched the ball, but I didn't. I got
50 hate calls already. The firehouse I work at is being bombarded."
— *Firefighter Pat Looney. Looney sat next to Bartman that strange night.*[4]

Cubs fans, as their White Sox counterparts, have struggled to find answers
to some of the crushing disappointments over the decades. For the Cubs faithful, there have been numerous debates about what happened in 1969 and the
decades of discussion have not brought closure. There have also been discus-
sions regarding the final playoff game against San Diego in 1984 and decisions
that led up to the circumstances of that game. But in October 2003, they
found a real explanation, a quick conclusion that seemed to forestall any debate.
They found a Tessie Hutchinson-type scapegoat, or in this case, a loyal Cubs
fan named Steve Bartman.

Bartman sat in the front rows, down the left-field line, hoping his team
would hold onto a 3–0 lead with one out in the eighth inning of game six of
the National League Championship Series against the Florida Marlins. Bartman
actually sat further down the line where the wall rises by the bullpen. It is one
those seats close to the field, as he could look down and see the chalk of the
baseline right below even though no fan is able to interfere with anything hit
on the ground. Still, Bartman's proximity to the field is one thing that makes
Wrigley Field unique, especially in the age of giant cookie-cutter stadiums that
push fans away from the action. Only this time Bartman was a little too close.

Even the most casual of baseball fans know the story about Bartman supposedly interfering with a foul fly down the left-field line. Left fielder Moises
Alou ran over, hoping he could scale the side of the wall and steal an out from
the Marlins. The Cubs had their 3–0 lead, their best pitcher was on the mound,
and they needed only five outs to play themselves into the World Series. However, Alou never got a chance to make the catch as Bartman deflected the ball.
Alou kicked at the wall in frustration and threw his mitt to the ground. (Lou
Piniella would say that he never saw anything like Ted Lilly throwing his mitt
to ground when he gave up a homer to Chris Young of the Diamondbacks in
the second game of the 2007 playoffs. Didn't he ever see this film clip?) Cubs
pitcher Mark Prior kicked at the grass as he stood in between the mound and

the third-base line and pointed to Bartman, trying to get the umpire to call fan interference. Cub fans began to direct their wrath at Bartman, who had to leave with a security escort and a jacket over his head. He was the object of debris and verbal attacks as he headed down the exit ramp. There were even chants of "Kill him, kill him." Underneath the stadium, an angry fan tried to get past the Cubs security people who had surrounded Bartman. Bartman looked small. With his face covered, he could have been mistaken for some shamed criminal being taken to trial.[5] For some reason, Cubs fans had already assumed they had lost the series, and that Bartman was the reason.

What happened next seemed like a self-fulfilling prophecy. There were walks, an error, four more hits, and a wild pitch. By the time the inning was over, the Cubs saw their 3–0 lead turn into an 8–3 deficit. Their eighth and ninth innings were three-up, three-down affairs. Florida had forced a seventh game. There is a photo of a young female Cub fan, still in her Wrigley Field seat and wearing a Cubs stocking hat, crying her eyes out. That sums up what happened in game seven for the Cubs.

It had been a stunning development. The Cubs had gone 19–8 during the month of September to win the National League Central. They clinched by winning a doubleheader against the Pirates on September 27. The Wrigley crowd was subdued and quiet that day, as if it hadn't sunk in that the Cubs were going to the playoffs. They then beat Atlanta in the first round in five games. The Braves routinely had beaten the Cubs in the '90s and won 101 games in 2003. The Cubs even had a chance to win the series in four games, but Sammy Sosa's ninth-inning two-out drive that would have tied the game had it gone just a little further was caught by the center-field wall. That first playoff round looked like a changing of the guard in the National League. Suddenly the Braves didn't appear to belong in the Cubs league. The overall closeness of the series shouldn't fool anyone. The Cubs were the better team, or at least playing better at that time of the season. Atlanta never really challenged Kerry Wood in the fifth and deciding game of the series. It was the first time the Cubs had won a post-season series since their world championship in 1908, and the first time a Chicago baseball team won a post-season series since the White Sox World Series title in 1917.

Against the Marlins in the League Championship Series, Chicago took a 3–1 advantage by scoring 33 runs in those four games. Yes, the Cubs got shut out on two hits in game five but talented pitchers like Josh Becket can do that to a team. Coming back home for the deciding two games had to be an advantage for the Cubs. The Friendly Confines were always considered to be an advantage for the Cubs.

Sometimes it is easy to find someone like Tessie Hutchinson. For the second time, the Cubs lost a National League playoff series with a two-game advantage. For the second time, the Cubs had a 3–0 lead in what could have been the deciding game. For the second time, their best pitcher ran out of gas in the latter innings in what could be the clinching game. And for the second time in nineteen years, fans were left looking for explanations as to why history had passed their team by again when victory seemed inevitable.

But actually there had been 95 other times prior to 2003. During a 1929 World Series game, the Cubs had an 8–0 lead only to see it erased by a ten-run inning by the Philadelphia Athletics. (The A's picked up 10 hits in the inning, including an inside-the-park home run, and the A's wrapped up the Series two days later. The Cubs' best pitcher of that year lost that game, too.) There was a called shot by an opposition slugger that may not have been a called shot at all, although it haunted a quality pitcher for years. But the 2003 defeat seemed to overshadow Cubs post-season history, and nothing seemed to explain why the losing continued into the twenty-first century.

In reality, there is a believable, though painful, explanation for the 2003 setback. The Cubs let themselves get riled by a common baseball occurrence, lost their collective concentration and composure, and blew it.

First of all, by looking at photographs and replays, it is difficult to decipher if Bartman actually interfered with the play or if Alou even had a real chance to catch the fly. Besides, how many times have outfielders caught foul balls in that part of Wrigley? It almost never happens because there is so little foul territory. Second, if the ball lands in the seats, there is no interference in the truest sense. Once a ball is out of play, the fan is entitled to it. And besides, the left-field umpire was adamant with his no interference call no matter how many tantrums the Cubs threw.

After the game, Cub manager genius Dusty Baker said that Bartman must have been a Marlins fan. There was Bartman, wearing a Cubs hat, with earphones listening to the Cubs radio broadcast of the game. Some Marlins fan.

What was Baker doing in the immediate aftermath of this alleged Marlin fan deliberately sabotaging the Cubs? He remained in the dugout. Shouldn't he have come out, convened his whole infield on the mound, and calmed everyone down? The goal of the World Series was in sight. Instead, he watched Prior walk Luis Castillo with a wild pitch and his reliable shortstop boot one. By the time Baker came out to change pitchers, the game was over. Maybe he should have taken Prior out earlier. As with Rick Sutcliffe nineteen years earlier, maybe the starting pitcher was tiring and was taken out one or two batters too late.

Cub fans had reacted with what can be called "Chicago Baseballitis." Any time something strange or bad happens in a playoff or pennant race, it is automatically assumed that the team is finished. It is as if pre-destiny had been cast against the Chicago teams. However, with the Cubs, fans are still preoccupied with the superstitious notion that bad luck will follow them forever.

"I think they're done now," Cubs fan Chris Barr said after the game. "It's the curse, no question."[6]

Dusty Baker sharing his wisdom with the media.

"They've got no chance after this," Mark Krier said, agreeing with Barr. "How do you come back after that?"[7]

Then Ralph Harlander, who according to the *Tribune* was pretty angry, chimed in.

"Just like '84, just like the last time," Harlander said. "I don't want to live through the nightmare again."[8]

If Harlander thought he was living a nightmare, what was Steve Bartman going through? At this stage, Bartman had not been identified by name, at least not by the *Tribune* and certainly not by the Cubs organization. But some fans at Wrigley knew who he was, if not his name.

"We got him out for his own safety," said Mike Hill, manager of Wrigley Field security. "He was kind of scared."[9]

Kind of scared? The diminutive Bartman was not kind of scared. From the videos shown on YouTube, he looked terrified. He got caught up in a moment similar to the one experienced by Tessie Hutchinson. In that stark story, Hutchinson was swarmed by a peaceful group of townspeople who had turned into a hateful mob.

Bartman must have felt that way. Unlike the helpless Hutchinson, Bartman was at least surrounded by people providing protection. It was a good thing he had the protection. From his demeanor and his overall defensiveness, it is doubtful that he would have been very successful in defending himself if some angry Cubs fan got hold of him.

In the beginning Bartman was at least anonymous. That didn't last once his name was broadcast over the radio, on the Internet, and by the *Chicago Sun-*

Times. After issuing his apology, Bartman went into hiding. Meanwhile, Cub Nation had embarrassed itself in front of the whole country with its overreaction.

With the Cubs' loss in game seven, it was the first time in 14 attempts that year they lost back-to-back games in which Prior and Wood had started.[10] The 2003 season was only the second time Wood had thrown more than 200 innings in a season. With the added work in the playoffs, was Wood beginning to tire? How about Prior? He had just turned 23 and was barely into his first full season at the major league level. Even if the Cubs reached the World Series, would he have been spent?

Yet, as years went by, the speculation about Bartman continued. The ball he tried to snare was eventually destroyed in an attempt exorcise the club of billy goat-type demons. It didn't work. The Cubs actually won one more game in 2004 than they had in 2003, but that didn't even earn them the wild card. Chicago lost seven out of their last nine, including three extra-inning defeats. Houston took the wild card by winning three more than the Cubs.

There was more scapegoating in 2004. Some Cubs players thought TV announcers Steve Stone and Chip Caray were too critical in their on-air analysis. Left-handed pitcher Kent Mercker even called the broadcast booth during a game to complain. On another occasion he and Stone had words in a hotel lobby. Moises Alou, who would have one of his best years with 39 homers and 106 RBIs, didn't even want Stone and Caray on the same plane with the team. His previous wrath at Steve Bartman had been re-directed at the broadcast booth.[11]

On September 30, the Cubs picked up only seven hits in a 12-inning loss to the lowly Cincinnati Reds. With their playoff hopes were all but dead, Stone saw no reason to go easy on the team.

"The truth of the situation is that an extremely talented bunch of guys who want to look at all directions except where they should really look, and kind of make excuses for what happened. This team should have won the wild card by six, seven games. No doubt about it," Stone said.[12]

Winning the wild card by that much would have put the Cubs a game or two away from 100 victories. Were they that good? And if they were, was the late–September collapse more mind boggling than the Bartman incident? Or were they just a very good team that waited for something bad to happen and then shifted the blame elsewhere? Baker said Bartman was not to blame for that horrendous inning. The Cubs, as an organization, almost immediately released a statement that had exonerated Bartman and asked for other Cubs fans to understand the situation. Kerry Wood had tried to take all the blame for the game seven loss with no mention of Bartman. So why were Baker and some of his players so pre-occupied with statements originating in the broadcast booth? Shouldn't they have wanted to erase the bad memory of the Marlins series by getting to the 2004 postseason?

Considering Steve Stone's continued popularity today, (he now does TV color for the White Sox,) Cubs fans weren't buying the scapegoating of 2004. While some may blame Bartman for 2003, rarely is it heard that Stone's TV commentary was to blame for the team's failure to go to the postseason in 2004. The Bartman incident still hangs over the team and only a World Series championship will erase that memory.

It is ironic that Stone ended up leaving the broadcast booth because of a perceived negativity. For so long TV had played such a prominent role in making the team popular. Maybe the Cubs really didn't want their broadcasters to be too honest or harsh? Did any Cubs player ever get into a shouting match with Jack Brickhouse?

In 2003 and 2004, there had been no black cats or billy goats. There were only the two Steves: Bartman and Stone. Who would have thought that these two men would ever be linked in any way? In reality, the two Steves had only one thing in common: They each witnessed the Cubs march toward a century without a world championship. Other than that, they couldn't be blamed for anything else.

There has been no real end to the Steve Bartman debate since 2003. In his column the day after the incident, Jay Mariotti of the *Sun-Times* blamed Bartman for the defeat. He didn't refer to Bartman by name since the media was still in a protective mode. Instead, he called the guy the "Idiot Fan" and labeled the incident as the "Revenge of the Nerd." Mariotti wrote that if it wasn't for Bartman, "the Cubs probably would be preparing for a World Series right now. He should have gotten out of the way and let Alou do his job."[13]

Mariotti held this opinion even though his own paper that day had the following headline on the front page: SCAPEGOAT? Years later, he would apologize for heaping blame on Bartman. The nerd wasn't at fault after all.

Moises Alou, the man who thought he had the ball in his sights, hasn't helped clear the murky waters that muddy the Bartman incident. In spring 2008, he told AP reporter Jim Litke that he wouldn't have caught the ball anyway. Then he recanted, claiming that he had no memory of saying that to Litke.[14] At times Alou seemed to be forgiving and other times not. If Alou was confused or simply had a faulty memory, how were Cubs fans supposed to put this painful memory behind them?

"I don't remember that," Alou was quoted in the *New York Post*. "If I said that, I was probably joking to make Bartman feel better. But I don't remember saying that."[15]

Then the *Post* quoted Alou as saying that Bartman should be forgiven even though his statement didn't actually pardon the Cubs fan.

"It's time to forgive the guy and move on," Alou said. "I said that the night it happened."[16]

Actually, this is what Alou said the night it happened: "Hopefully he won't have to regret it for the rest of his life."[17]

He also said, "I timed it perfectly, I jumped perfectly. I'm almost 100 percent sure that I had a clean shot to catch the ball. All of a sudden, there's a hand in my glove."[18]

At this writing, the Cubs have a nine-game losing streak in post-season play. They have been swept two times in a row. They have lost six out of seven post-season series since 1984. Their combined record in those series is 9–22. If the Bartman incident has caused Cubs fans to search for answers, the experience in the 2008 playoffs only made matters worse. Big things were expected after a 97-win regular season. Most Chicago sports pundits couldn't imagine any National League team stopping the Cubs. Yet the Cubs were swept by the Dodgers and were outscored 20–6 in the divisional series. The first two losses came at Wrigley Field, a place where the team has never clinched a post-season series. As that composite score indicates, only one game was close. In game one, a solid starting pitcher couldn't find the plate. In game two, every player in the infield made an error. In game three, a potent offense couldn't muster any runs and lost a low-scoring contest. Nothing made sense. How could a team that had played so well over a 162-game period just fold their tents and go home? Whatever the answer, the Cubs had completed their century-old cycle of not winning a World Series.

And what of Steve Bartman? A family friend who also acts as his spokesman has told the Chicago media that he is not in seclusion, and is still living a normal middle-class life in a Chicago suburb. A fan that needs a spokesman? This was an indication that his life isn't normal. Regardless, Bartman has never tried to profit from the incident; he has neither taken any money nor made any public appearances. If he has returned to Wrigley Field, he hasn't been recognized. No matter how innocent he may be, remaining a Cubs fan can't be fun for Bartman. His team still has not played in a World Series. He was not forgiven by many, and is still connected to a crushing defeat that led to a huge disappointment.

The Chicago Cubs could do one thing to vindicate both themselves and Bartman: Stop their century-long slump and win the World Series. Yet at this writing, they remain underachievers, including fading from contention in the National League Central when many had made them the prohibitive favorites for the 2009 season. Fans, again, are left looking for answers, and will continue to until the team finally does what it hasn't been able to do for more than 100 years.

19

Into a Wilderness of Their Own

"I'm a hawk."
— *Jerry Reinsdorf regarding his stand in the baseball owners' negotiations once the players went on strike.*

For the White Sox, the 1990s began with a mixture of hope and controversy. One of the last old- time parks hosted its final season in 1990. Although it had seen only three World Series, Comiskey still held memories for millions of fans. Maybe its demolition was inevitable. Yet even for fans who looked forward to the new ballpark, saying good-bye to the old one was difficult. They realized that they would never be able to sit in a place where they saw a dramatic home run or a well-pitched game. Their first major league experience may have been at Comiskey. After 1990, Comiskey was going to be no more.

As with the C.U.B.S. fan organization in the late seventies and early eighties that wanted their team to actually contend, the Sox had a grassroots group that fought the building of a new stadium. S.O.S. stood for Save Our Sox. S.O.S. was adamant in its opposition to the new Comiskey Park primarily on two fronts. First, S.O.S. members thought the subsidy for the new stadium was corporate welfare and that the old park could have been renovated. Second, the group believed the stadium could have been placed at a different location slightly to the north but wasn't because it would have dislocated white citizens.

Forty-five South Side residents joined in a class-action suit against the Illinois Sports Authority, the City of Chicago, and the State of Illinois to stop the construction of the stadium at its current site. They claimed a different location would have dislocated fewer residents and businesses. The resident group felt that their civil rights were being violated, but their claims were denied.[1]

From a strict fan's viewpoint, some thought the new stadium was a symbol of the sport changing for the worse.

"There was no reason to subsidize baseball," activist and fan Doug Bukowski said in the late nineties. "In fact, it's (the new park) going to be an inferior replacement. People are not going to be able to see baseball as they have for the past 80 years.[2]

"The last row of the upper deck in old Comiskey Park, the very last row behind home plate, was closer to the field than the first row in the new Comiskey Park," Bukowski said.[3]

S.O.S. activist and Sox fan John Aranza had a hard time facing the passing of Comiskey. He and friend and co-activist Hank Trenkle actually sat in what was left of the old Comiskey Park bleachers late at night during the park's demolition.

"And we were up there with half the park demolished," Aranza told authors Joanna Cagan and Neil deMause. "We were looking out at 35th Street with all the cars, looking down, and with sunflowers growing in the middle of the field and some bunches of the sunflowers were bigger than us. And the jangled tubing of the railing, the wreckage out there, and we're just thinking of what was. And I know you can't live on those feelings, but it was just kind of bitter and soothing at the same time."[4]

No matter how bittersweet fans felt about the new ballpark, they took solace that the last season in the old park was a memorable one. The team had suffered through four consecutive losing seasons in the late '80s, including the last-place finish of 1989. Few expected the still-young and rebuilding 1990 team to do much. But instead of having another losing campaign, the White Sox enjoyed their best season since the Winning Ugly team of '83. The 1990 squad somehow won 94 games, but had the misfortune of being in the same division as the Oakland A's, who won 103 that year. In the entire history of the franchise, the White Sox have never won more than 100 games in a season. Seriously contending for the division title was only a fantasy for the White Sox, despite having the third-best record in all of baseball that season.

"Doing the Little Things" was the slogan attached to the overachieving 1990 White Sox. The team had to do the little things, such as moving runners along and turning double plays. With little power and many young players still learning the game, the 1990 club was not going to overwhelm anyone. But they made sure to hit the cutoff man, made a habit of bringing in a man from third with less than two outs, and had a career season from their closer. In the present-day set-up, they would have coasted to a wild-card berth.

"The 1990 club never beat themselves," Sox fan Dan Dorfman recalls. "They squeezed all the talent out of themselves."[5]

The last game at old Comiskey symbolized the 1990 season and many of the other "Go-Go White Sox" seasons. With a little luck of a tricky-hop triple, the Sox beat the Seattle Mariners, 2–1. Closer Bobby Thigpen recorded his 57th save, a season record that would stand until 2008.

The 42,289 in attendance that day pushed the season mark past 2 million for the first time since 1984. They stayed afterward to say good-bye, displaying signs that read, "Thanks for the Memories," "Good-bye Old Friend," and "Years from Now, We'll Say We Wuz Here."

"That last game of 1990 I walked around the place for two hours," fan Gerry Bilek said. "I found all kinds of hooks and craneys I didn't know about."[6]

No matter how sad some fans were at the loss of a friend, attendance increased with the novelty of the new stadium. Additionally, the team on the field was very good. From 1990 until August 1994, the White Sox had five straight winning seasons, including two 90-win seasons and a divisional title. Young players like Frank Thomas, Robin Ventura and Jack McDowell began developing into real stars. Then beginning on August 12, 1994, just about everything went wrong for the White Sox and continued during the remainder of the decade.

In January 1995, the White Sox ran the following advertisement in the Chicago daily newspapers:

> We've heard from the players.
> We've heard from the owners.
> We even heard from Ted Koppel.
> It's time we heard from you.
> Write us what you really think.
> Write us if you miss baseball.
> Write us if you don't.
> Write us about going to games as a kid.
> Write us and tell us to go to blazes.
> Write us how Uncle Bernie likes his trailer home.
> Write us something.

What prompted this advertisement? Major league baseball was in the middle of one its biggest public relations debacles in its history. The players' strike that ended the 1994 season prematurely was still going on and threatened the 1995 season as well. Replacement players were being lined up for spring training. Whether or not they would have been utilized in regular-season games is not fully known. Regardless, by the beginning of 1995, it appeared that major league baseball was willing to threaten its future instead of coming to some kind of agreement with the players union. Many fans felt the players union was at fault and it should be more compromising. Regardless of who was to blame, the sport suffered.

I was one fan who wrote the White Sox. Using a pro-union slant, I stated that Chicago was not only built by industrialists and businessmen but by craftsmen and laborers. I further explained that although the players union didn't resemble many modern-day unions, it was still a union and breaking a union ran against everything I believed in. I told the organization to get back to the bargaining table, hammer out some kind of compromise, and return to playing baseball.

The response I received from public relations man Rob Gallas demonstrated that my letter was read closely. He said that I had made an impression with my pro-union leanings. What actual impact my letter and the others had will probably never be known.

What is also not known is the volume and type of response the White Sox received. Jerry Reinsdorf had made it clear in 1981 that the profane letters he received then had no impact. Was there enough anti-player union sentiment that Reinsdorf felt the owners' hard-line stance was vindicated? Was there enough anger at both sides to go around? How angry were fans for a missed chance at a World Series? Did the letters give the organization an idea of what would happen once the strike was settled?

As a result of responding to the White Sox advertisement, I was sent four tickets to the July 12 White Sox game against the Brewers once the strike ended. The seats were in the upper deck, but were in the lower section just to the third-base side of home plate. An accompanying letter mentioned that I could come to a White Sox game in 1995 without "buying a ticket." It appeared that the organization understood some of the consequences of the strike. If it hadn't realized it from the letters it received, the Sox organization must have learned it from the attendance in 1995. The gate dropped off almost 1 million from 1993, the last full season before the strike. It also didn't help that the Sox finished 32 games out of first place that season.

The players also were learning about fan backlash. White Sox catcher and player representative Mike LaValliere was taken aback by some bitter fan mail. One letter included ashes of burnt tickets.

Ozzie Guillen lashed out at fans, saying the "players don't owe the fans anything."[7] In a 1999 interview with me, Guillen made it clear that his verbal assault came as a result of racial slurs thrown at Frank Thomas in Toronto. Yet a quote like that can get lost and misinterpreted, especially when it accompanied a news photo of an angry-looking Guillen standing by the batting cage. Guillen didn't back down from his statement during his 1999 talk with me. Although Guillen is to be admired for sticking up for a teammate in the face of racial taunts, his bitterness and choice of words added to the game's deteriorating relationship with its fans in 1995. As time went on, the relationship between the White Sox and their fans only worsened.

"The 15,000 or 20,000 people that are going to come, they're going to see good baseball and we appreciate them. Those people really want us to win."[8] That was the opinion of White Sox infielder-outfielder Dave Martinez as quoted in a Phil Rosenthal story. The *Sun-Times* piece ran in September 1996 and dripped with anti-fan bitterness. Attendance at Comiskey was still lacking—at least according to some in the Chicago media and some White Sox players. At the time Martinez spoke, the White Sox were falling further behind the first-place Indians. The wild card seemed like the most plausible way to get into the playoffs, and the Sox had a decent shot at that goal.

Rosenthal agreed with Martinez. In his story, he wrote that 40,000 fans should have been attending these important late-season games. Both Rosenthal and Martinez, however, seemed to be unaware of two things. First, the wild card was still a new concept. Many fans weren't getting excited about a team competing for the best second-place finish, even if it meant a playoff berth. Up until 1995 baseball had been the only professional sport that had only first-place teams in the postseason. Many traditionalists wanted to hold onto that practice.

Second, although the club was having a respectable season, it wasn't enough to bring back a still-angry fan base. The novelty of new Comiskey had worn off, and the White Sox were not in first place. Many were not willing to sit in the far regions of the upper deck to see an average team. The Sox ended up winning 85 games in 1995 and failed to make the playoffs. They won exactly that same number of games 11 years earlier. In 1985, the team drew 1,669,888. In 1996, it drew 1,676,416. What were they complaining about? White Sox players and Phil Rosenthal seemed to be out of touch.

"Anyone who thinks this White Sox team will catch Cleveland is crazy." One thing you can say about Jerry Reinsdorf: At times he is extremely quotable. However, this is one quote he would probably like to take back. This unforgettable sentence would be held against him for years, at least until the 2005 World Series. It still may be.

Reinsdorf was defending what has become known as the White Flag Trade. On July 31, with the White Sox only 3½ games behind the first-place Indians and third baseman Robin Ventura due to return from injury rehab, Reinsdorf declared the 1997 season over. Ventura said he didn't know the season ended on August 1. An irate Ozzie Guillen smashed a TV with a baseball bat. Fan reaction — both for and against the trade — was strong. The bitterness and rancor would surround the team for the next several years.

Listed below is a sampling of letters to the *Chicago Sun-Times* published on August 10, 1997, in response to the trade:

Well, Jerry Reinsdorf, you've done it again. Thanks for nothing. I have returned the remainder of my White Sox season tickets now that you have rendered them worthless.

You seem to have forgotten one of the largest segments of your customers: the corporate client. We hand over an enormous amount of money even before the season starts, contributing greatly to your cash flow. The only reason for buying the season tickets is to pass them along to our customers as a gesture of our appreciation to them.

By throwing in the towel on this season, the enthusiasm to attend a Sox game is gone. My clients would consider it a joke and an insult to be handed these tickets now. As for next season, why would I want to put money up front for what might turn out to be another fiasco? I hope you have included less revenue for next spring in your budget.

Building for the future should always be a part of the equation. But giving up on the current season never should be. Baseball has always been a very enjoyable vehicle for entertaining clients — until now! You have pushed us into finding an alternative route. After all, you are not the only sport in town. — Scott Collins, Downers Grove, IL[9]

This letter is intended for all of the whining, sniveling crybabies out there who are complaining about White Sox management throwing in the towel. Give me a break! I've been a White Sox fan long enough to know what false hopes are, and anyone believing this was a team worth keeping together until October should watch their baseball on the North Side of town.

I'll endorse Jerry Reinsdorf's comment by saying: I didn't like this team (nor did I like the '95 or '96 versions, either). I applaud Sox management for making a move when other teams were willing to deal and not perpetuating the "contending" myth.

So what Hall-of-Famers did the Sox trade away? Wilson Alvarez? An average pitcher at best. The main thing that he had going for himself was being a left-handed starter. Roberto Hernandez? The second coming of Bobby Thigpen. Can anyone recall if Hernandez ever pitched a three-up, three-down inning? I can't. Danny Darwin? A nice guy, but not someone who gives you pennant fever.

Doesn't anyone remember trading Cy Young pitcher LaMarr Hoyt for an unknown infield prospect years ago? There was wailing and gnashing of teeth. A year and a half later, Hoyt was out of baseball while that unknown prospect, Ozzie Guillen, has been the Sox shortstop for more than a decade. This is baseball, folks; trades (and patience) are all part of the game.

Hey, guess what? We're talking White Sox baseball! I'm pumped. I think I'll actually go to the ballpark to see some of these youngsters in action. Do lower salaries mean lower ticket, parking and concession prices? — Curt Krill, East Dundee[10]

I was glad to see Carol Slezak come out with a column sticking up for the recent moves made by Jerry Reinsdorf. Even Dennis Byrne weighed in with a complaint about all the Jerry-bashing fans, the same "fans" that have not bothered to fill all those empty blue seats at Comiskey Park even before the trading got under way.

As Slezak pointed out, the Sox have been an undisciplined and underachieving team all season. That's not the fault of Reinsdorf, but a combination of poor performances by Sox players and bad leadership by manager Terry Bevington.

Instead of whining and moaning about Reinsdorf, true Sox fans should be applauding him for cleaning house and making way for some minor leaguers to move up to the majors and put some zest into a listless, tired, overpaid, and underachieving team. And while Reinsdorf has the broom in his hand, he also should sweep Bevington out the door. — Bill Ceceran, Chicago[11]

You don't need a dipstick to figure out the reason baseball is on a decline when one of the most influential guys in the game is Jerry Reinsdorf. — Joseph Stachowksi, Chicago[12]

In his book, *Sox and the City,* Richard Roeper had this to say:

Would the Sox have won the division if they had kept the veterans and maybe added a couple of solid players? Maybe not. We don't know. All we know is that the owner surrendered — and he didn't ask the fans if they'd like a refund of the tickets they had purchased for the remainder of the season.[13]

And, of course, Reinsdorf-hater and *Sun-Times* columnist Jay Mariotti weighed in:

> So now, we see the Roberto Duran of owners, the man who may have ruined the White Sox forever, claiming an "80 percent" approval rating for his Great Cowardly Purge. If so, Jerry Reinsdorf kept the fax machine on only long enough to hear from the following: his wife, his four children, Hawk Harrelson, the Wimperoo, and the family dog.[14]

In 2009, Sox fan Dan Dorfmann still felt the trade was the right thing to do.

"It didn't bother me," Dorfmann said. "Reinsdorf was right. They weren't going to win. Alvarez was never the pitcher we thought he was. Even with him, the White Sox wouldn't have finished any closer."[15]

Dorfman also felt that the personal animosity toward Reinsdorf was unfair and that Reinsdorf was treated shabbily in comparison to other team owners in the city.

Regardless of the baseball side of the trade, its effects on the White Sox were devastating. The ball club entered its own kind of wilderness during the latter part of 1990s. Team-fan relations were just as bad or worse as baseball union-management relations. The Cubs, a team that was pretty bad for most of the decade, would recover and keep its fan base. Team attendance rebounded at Wrigley, especially with the emergence of Sammy Sosa and Kerry Wood. The White Sox weren't just the number-two baseball team in the city. They were relegated to even a worse position than the Cubs in the early sixties. The Cubs were laughed at then; the late '90s White Sox generated little reaction. The team suffered from a fan disinterest that, in a sense, was worse than in 1970 when they lost 106 and drew few more than 495,000.

"It's as bad as I have ever seen it," veteran *Tribune* sportswriter Bill Jauss told writer Sridhar Pappu. Pappu's story about the White Sox plight ran in the *Chicago Reader*, a weekly newspaper, on September 18, 1998.[16]

"It's absolute apathy," Jauss continued. "It's like a relationship. If there's anger, at least there's emotion there. With time, nurture, and good luck, sometimes you can turn that emotion from hate into love. But if you're in a relationship where neither party cares about the other, that's just about the end of the road. I'm afraid this is where the White Sox have come."[17]

Attendance, as always, is one of the best ways to analyze fan interest, or in this case, overall response to events of the nineties. The 1999 season mark of a little more than 1.3 million was the worst since 1989 when the team finished dead last. The White Sox lagged behind the league average by slightly more than 935,000.[18] The 1998 season had been only slightly better. After the White Sox clinched their division in 2005, tickets to their fan convention quickly sold out. In 1999, fans could show up on any day of the convention and not worry about a sellout. The combination of the strike and the White Flag Trade had sent the team reeling. But observers said winning would bring the fans back, wouldn't it?

The White Sox won the American League Central in 2000 with relative ease. Young players were developing in front of the fans' eyes. The timetable for success was ahead of schedule even with White Sox management. Attendance increased by about 600,000. Good times were back again, weren't they?

A closer look demonstrated that the good times weren't really back yet. Season attendance still didn't crack the 2 million mark and still was almost 300,000 under the league average. Attendance in 2000 didn't come all that close to the other division-winning years of 1993 and 1983. And in '83 attendance might have been even better if the team had gotten off to a good start. Additionally, attendance in September, when the team was wrapping up the division, wasn't very impressive. The Cubs, who had another losing season, outdrew the White Sox by 800,000. The local media wondered why the fans still weren't coming back.[19]

The White Sox clinched the division title on the road. *Tribune* columnist Skip Bayless pointed out that about 300 people greeted the team on its return to Midway Airport. Bayless compared that to 25,000 who went to Midway after the White Sox won the American League pennant in 1959.[20] This lack of fan warmth wasn't lost on the players, either.

"I'd like to say I expect a packed house (for the next home game), but I also thought that a couple of other times and it wasn't there," relief pitcher Bobby Howry said. "If we don't see it, I don't think we ever will."[21]

A mere 23,319 showed for that first game. The Cubs also happened to be in town and drew 26,055 for a meaningless game between two non-contenders. Winning hadn't even helped.[22]

In 1983 and 1993, I purchased playoff tickets on the street from scalpers. In 2000, I was able to buy them at the ticket window. Pennant fever wasn't running that rampant, at least in a relative sense of ticket availability.

The aura of the division championship still didn't bring out the fans in 2001. Starting pitcher David Wells lectured fans about their apparent apathy in the early going. He didn't want to hear any excuses about cold weather and told fans to bring their coats.[23] The White Sox had a disappointing 2001 season largely because of Wells, and their overall attendance dropped again. Yet in 1984, when the team had a bad season, the White Sox surpassed the attendance record set in the '83 title year. If the 1994 season had been allowed to continue, attendance would have equaled or surpassed the 1993 division winners. Even in 2007, when the team lost 90 games, attendance was better than the 2005 World Series year. But the success in 2000 didn't create the same goodwill in 2001 as past and future successes had done. Fan alienation still ran deep. Things weren't going to turn around without a world championship.

At the center of the controversies was team CEO Jerry Reinsdorf. Every

Dan Pasqua trying to break up a double play during the 1993 American League Championship Series against Toronto. The Blue Jays won the series by beating the White Sox three times at the new Comiskey Park.

Chicago sports fan has an opinion of him. Starting in the late '80s, Reinsdorf put a face on the White Sox organization. He has become one of the most controversial figures in Chicago sports.

On the Internet there are many complimentary stories about the White Sox CEO. Loyalty is important to him, and people who work for him have that quality, both to him and his organization. Past players such as Ozzie

Guillen, Kenny Williams, Greg Walker, Harold Baines, Joey Cora, Chris Singleton, Tim Raines and Darrin Jackson have worked for Reinsdorf after their playing days were over.

Since 1981, the White Sox have won five divisional titles (excluding the meaningless one in 1994) and a World Series. The team has enjoyed six 90-win seasons. During this time, White Sox pitchers have thrown four no-hitters, including a perfect game, two pitchers won a Cy Young Award, and one reliever set a major league record for saves that stood for 18 years. Frank Thomas won two MVP awards. In a rare feat, the team hit four consecutive home runs, and home attendance records were set. A new stadium was built to mixed reviews at best, but alterations have been made to the stadium, making it more appealing. With time and some success, history has been made at the new park to give it an identity of its own.

On the debit side, the White Sox have suffered 12 losing seasons since 1981. Other than their 2005 championship year, the team lost all its postseason series with a combined record of 4–13. An historic stadium was turned to rubble and the franchise didn't seem to understand how that affected some fans. For some reason the team signed players like Jose Canseco and Wil Cordero. From the beginning, the fan-team relationship was shaky, and it hit rock-bottom during the late '90s. The White Sox still have to work to compete with the Cubs.

In the summer edition of the *Baseball Research Journal* published by the Society of Baseball Research, writers Norman Macht, Richard Crepeau and Lee Lowenship delve into the reasons why baseball didn't integrate before 1946.[24] Jerry Reinsdorf has led the way with minority hirings of general managers, managers, coaches and broadcasters. His record on this issue will be a great legacy, no matter how the team performs on the field.

Richard Nixon struggled to compete with the ghost of John Kennedy, a charismatic man with deep flaws. Reinsdorf struggles as he still competes with the memory of Bill Veeck, a man who charmed many even when he was failing.

But Chicago sports broadcaster and media consultant Tom Shaer believes Reinsdorf has succeeded in many ways that Veeck didn't, including the ongoing competition with the Cubs.

"Upon resumption of the Crosstown Classic exhibition in 1985, the Sox clearly wanted to win very badly," Shaer wrote in an e-mail. "Richie Hebner of the Cubs told me their players couldn't believe Tony La Russa was using so many relievers trying to win, which he did.

"The attitude is totally different now. The Sox have had their ballpark for 19 seasons and make tons of money from broadcasting and ballpark sponsorships. They draw well. They are proud and secure as a franchise, and I rarely hear much from their staff about the Cubs. Really, very little. In the early-to-mid–1980s, it was always there. Not now. The White Sox have closed the gap tremendously."[25]

Shaer maintains the gap closed even before the World Series win in 2005. Attendance increased slightly in 2003 and 2004 before exceeding the 2 million mark in the World Series year.

"Being a very strong and successful number-two baseball team in the number-three (media) market in the country is a pretty nice place to be," Shaer wrote.

That may be. And with the likes of Buehrle, Konerko, Dye, Jenks, and Pierzynski, the White Sox have established a real identity. Attendance is much better even though it has not surpassed Cub attendance, and it never will. Yet to reach this point of relative parity in the Chicago baseball market, the White Sox had to find their way out of a massive wilderness that nearly destroyed their franchise.

20

Finally

The following quotes are excerpted from a book by George Bova entitled *Dedicated to…What Winning the World Series Means to Chicago White Sox Fans.* White Sox fans express their emotions after 2005 World Series championship. Each entry is preceded by the words "Dedicated to…"

To My dad and his dad—"To my dad (1920–1999) who only saw one World Series in his lifetime.

"I remember him calling me into the living room (late '50s and early '60s) whenever the animated Hamms Bear beer commercial was on TV between innings. And I remember sitting out in the backyard with him on hot summer nights listening to Bob Elson.

"After the clincher in 1959, he popped open a Hamms, and he slipped me an ice cream bar to celebrate.

"He took me to my first game—a twi-night DH with the Red Sox in 1965. We went to many more, including the final game in Old Comiskey.

"When I was a teenager and young adult, we had our differences, like all fathers and sons. But when it came to White Sox, we stood on common ground."[1] Sage of the Sox

"To my grandma who took me to see Carlton Fisk, the greatest player a six-year-old could ever see and Harold Baines, who will always be grandma's 'boyfriend.' Watching the White Sox win Game One of the 2005 World Series was one of the most special things of my life, especially when I think of all the other parents and grandparents who weren't here to see the greatest season of White Sox baseball. Ever."[2]—Mike Harrison

"To Fidel Castro who had Jose Contreras and El Duque pitching 20 hours a day ever since they were six years old."[3] Jenks4Pres

"To my daughter, who in her zest to be the best Sox fan at age 15, cried right alongside her long-suffering mother in seeing the impossible dream achieved."[4] Digdagdug23

"To my dad who took me to my first Sox game in August 1960. As a result I now have a lifetime of memories.

"Also to my daughter Leah. The 2005 campaign will go down as my favorite season not only because of the World Series title. Leah enjoyed everything about going to a game, from the home run fireworks to yelling 'charge' and being entertained by the scoreboard in between innings. She enjoyed the game only as a happy child could, and there is a child in every one of us who cheers for the White Sox." The author[5]

"Now a quote from Ozzie Guillen in a pep talk to his team as they began the playoffs: "Don't be happy just to be here. Win this thing. Win this thing.""[6]

Small Ball

From 2001 to 2004, the White Sox averaged 223 home runs a season. Despite having all this power, the team never won more than 86 games and came close to making the playoffs only once. In 2003 the White Sox finished in second, four games behind Minnesota. But the Sox sabotaged themselves by losing five straight to the Twins in mid–September. In one game, their starting pitcher, Estaban Loaiza, went out to the mound even though he was ill and had thrown up before the game. Sox field management didn't realize how sick he really was until Loaiza had given up four runs in 2⅓ innings. There was even some speculation on the Internet that a White Sox base runner had admitted to a Twins first baseman that the race was essentially over and that the White Sox were done. Manager Jerry Manuel didn't survive this 2003 debacle. Fans called for his head on a daily basis. The White Sox concurred. Manuel was fired after the season was over.

In 2004, the homer-happy White Sox hit 242 round-trippers. They also scored 865 runs, good for third in the league. But these impressive power stats only netted the team 83 wins, and they finished nine games out of first. The Twins, a team that seemed devoid of big-name players, had beaten them again. They even clinched the Central Division title at U.S. Cellular Field.

For the 2005 campaign, second-year manager Ozzie Guillen and GM Kenny Williams wanted the club to take a different direction. No one had anything against a crowd-pleasing homer, but the club wanted a more balanced offense able to score without the benefit of the long ball. Carlos Lee, who had clubbed 31 homers with 99 RBIs in 2004, was traded to the Milwaukee Brewers for base-stealer Scott Podsednik. The team signed free agent second baseman

Jermaine Dye was one of the best free-agent signings the White Sox ever made and the MVP in the 2005 World Series. Dye always approaches the game as a real pro.

Tadahito Iguchi, even though no one from the White Sox front office had seen much of the Japanese player. Catcher A.J. Pierzynski was also signed as a free agent with hopes that he could handle the pitching staff and provide offensive punch from the catcher's position. And to show that the long ball wasn't completely forgotten, the void left by the departure of Magglio Ordonez to the Tigers was filled by free agent Jermaine Dye.

Guillen, who had been a coach with the Marlins when Florida beat the Cubs in the playoffs, preferred more of a National League style of play. Advancing runners with the bunt or hitting to the right side was preferred over swinging for the fences. Good teams won close games, and manufacturing runs sometimes made the defense in those tight contests.

The season opener at U.S. Cellular gave fans a good indication of how the 2005 White Sox would win games. With the game in a scoreless tie, Paul Konerko led off the seventh with a line drive into the left-field corner for a double. Jermaine Dye sent a fly to right field to advance Konerko to third. Konerko scored when Indians shortstop Jhonny Peralta muffed a grounder hit by Aaron Rowand. The Sox won, 1–0, on the strength of the two-hit, eight-inning pitching by Mark Buehrle and a one-two-three ninth-inning save by reliever Shingo Takatsu.

Some said that all the talk about small ball was hype, especially since the club still hit 200 homers that season. Yet two games against the Los Angeles Dodgers at U.S. Cellular on June 18 and 19 again demonstrated how the White Sox would scratch out wins the small ball way. Both games were come-from-behind efforts.

The White Sox looked lifeless in the June 18 game as they picked up one run and three hits in the first eight innings. Never leading in the game, the Sox went into the bottom of the ninth trailing, 3–1. They looked like losers as Iguchi (who had walked and advanced on a grounder to short) stood on second with two out and Carl Everett at the plate. Then, in a very short period of time, they looked like the first-place team that they were.

Everett could hit the long ball, but he didn't try to do too much. He singled to right, sending Iguchi home to make it a one-run game. Speedster Willie Harris was sent in to run for Everett. What was Harris supposed to do? He was sent in to steal a base and that was exactly what he did. Aaron Rowand then bounced a single through the middle, and the game was tied. A walk, a single, a stolen base and a single had netted two runs. Now the Sox were ready for some long ball.

But the team wasn't waiting for the long ball. With A. J. Pierzynski at the plate, Rowand took off for second. He would have had the base stolen, but Pierzynski fouled the pitch off. Regardless, all the momentum had shifted to the Sox. The Dodgers' body language showed they were merely waiting for something bad to happen to them, and it did.

Pierzynski sent a drive to left-center field. At first it looked like it might find its way into the gap and score Rowand from first. But it did more than that. The high fly soared into the third row of the seats for a two-run homer. The White Sox now had their first lead and the win.

The stadium erupted. Of course, the scoreboard erupted too. Pierzynski had a huge greeting party waiting for him at home plate as the cheering engulfed

U.S. Cellular. It was one the most exciting moments for the ball club since the division clinching of 2000. Since then, the fans had seen too much mediocrity, and attendance remained a problem. Now 36,067 witnessed a team that found ways to win with excellent execution. With this come-from-behind victory, the White Sox were 45–22, 6 games ahead of the second-place Minnesota Twins. The Sox had been in first place since day one.

Chicago was able to sweep the Dodgers the next night by playing small ball. Frank Thomas led off the bottom of the eighth with a walk as the Sox trailed, 3–2. Pablo Ozuna was sent in to pinch-run. Scott Podsednik laid down a bunt, but was safe at first when a hurried throw and a traffic jam of Dodger infielders resulted in the first baseman being pulled off the bag. Willie Harris also bunted and was successful in moving the runners to second and third. Aaron Rowand came through again with a line-drive single to left to drive in two, giving the Sox a 4–3 lead. The lead would hold up. This time they scored the two winning runs with the benefit of one hit, a single.

The inning ended on a double play, with Rowand caught stealing immediately after Paul Konerko struck out. Even though the third out came on the base paths, the White Sox showed they were aggressive with their running game. Defenses needed to stay alert or get beaten by this small-ball play.

Of course, small ball alone will not win championships in the long run. One reason the "Go-Go White Sox" of the fifties and sixties went to only one World Series was the team's lack of power. Yet it is also hard to argue with the success of seventeen straight winning seasons. (The Sox also won 90 or more games seven times from 1951 to 1967. Four came in 154-game seasons. In 1954, the Sox won 94 while hitting 94 homers.) It was also hard to argue with the small-ball success of the 2005 White Sox.

Choke — It Is Such an Ugly Word

The White Sox beat Baltimore on August 1 to extend a winning streak to four. At that point, they were an amazing 69–35, which was the best record in baseball. They had outscored the opposition by 100 runs. The second-place Indians were 15 games back and showing little life. The American Central Division title was in the bag, wasn't it? Didn't they say the same thing about the Cubs and their National League East aspirations in 1969?

No team, no matter how good it is, goes through a major league season without having a confidence-shaking slump. The 2005 White Sox proved they were no exception as they went on a seven-game losing streak during the middle of August. By August 20, their huge lead had been almost cut in half. Maybe the division title wasn't a sure thing after all.

The team ended the losing streak in a non-small ball way. Iguchi, Rowand,

and Konerko hit back-to-back-to-back home runs off nasty Randy Johnson during a Sunday afternoon game against the Yankees. Iguchi and Rowand hit opposite-field drives. Konerko's was high and far into the left-field seats. Johnson looked more puzzled than perturbed. Why were all his pitches being sent into orbit? He must have been really puzzled when second-string catcher Chris Wedger hit a three-run homer to cap the six-run fourth inning.

On September 7, everything appeared to be all right once again. The Sox negated most of the effects of the mid–August slump by putting together a seven-game winning streak. They gained two games on the Indians and had a comfortable lead at 9 games. Wasn't it time to start printing those playoff tickets?

But then the Sox lost seven out of their next ten. Meanwhile, for the next two weeks, the reborn Indians couldn't lose. Okay, they did lose one in 12 games from September 5 to 18 — a 2–0 defeat to Oakland. A young Dan Haren won that game, and he is now considered one of the best pitchers in baseball.

Sox fans who were around in 1969 remembered how the Mets suddenly could do no wrong. Yes, the Cubs had faltered but the Mets had gone on an incredible hot streak. Were the Indians going to repeat history and ruin another Chicago baseball season? The Sox were scheduled to play their last three games in Cleveland. Would Indian fans sing "Good-bye, Ozzie" as the Mets fans sang "Good-bye, Leo"?

Suddenly the word "choke" was being throwing around in the media. When the Sox lost a 3–2 game to Detroit, the *Tribune* ran a headline that read, "Choke hold."[7] After a 7–5 loss to last-place Kansas City, the *Tribune* had a short piece written by Bob Vanderberg that reminded Sox fans of the 1967 doubleheader loss to the then–Kansas City A's that all but destroyed the season.[8] Two days later columnist Rick Morrissey ripped the Sox, writing that they would not be held in awe like the 1969 Cubs if they blew it.

"There's too much pain," Morrissey wrote. "And there's nothing lovable about all this losing."[9]

In the end, what does all this history have to do with the 2005 Chicago White Sox? Nothing, since most of the 2005 players didn't have anything to do with past failures or disappointments. The problem is that long-time fans have experienced the accumulated emotions of these disappointments. As painful memories are evoked, it seems as if past players and teams are melded with the present. If a baseball team has the word "Chicago" going across its chests, doesn't that mean a championship is not possible? Anxiety and angst are emotions Cubs and White Sox fans share.

Does history have any effect on players? A hitter can't be thinking about some heartbreaking season decades ago as he prepares to face a major league pitcher. But have you ever seen a pitcher step on the baseline when he returns to the dugout after a completed inning? Does any player dare step on the baseline? And if outside distractions don't bother players, why did some Cub players worry so much about what Steve Stone said in the broadcast booth in 2004? Why did the Sox feel the same way about Harry Caray and Jimmy Piersall in the seventies? What about living up to fan expectations? Isn't it difficult enough to win in the present without feeling the weight of the past? How much concentration does it take to shut all of this out? Can it be shut out?

Meanwhile, the Sox couldn't afford to be distracted when Cleveland came in for a three-game series starting on September 19. The Indians were only 3½ back and suddenly looked invincible. Ozzie Guillen walked around saying he didn't think the Indians would lose another game. All the pressure seemed to be on the first-place White Sox.

Chicago lost the first game, 7–5. Paul Konerko represented the winning run at the plate with two outs in the ninth and faced a tough closer in Bob Wickman. Konerko sent a weak pop-up to short right field. Second baseman Ramon Vazquez trotted out to the outfield grass and made the catch rather easily. The Indians were now 2½ back.

Konerko had gone down to one knee in the batter's box and didn't have much of a chance to run it out. The image of the disappointed first baseman appearing to lose his balance was somewhat symbolic. It seemed like the whole team was falling on its face. Did Konerko actually stumble or was he only dejected because he knew he made the last out of the game? In contrast, the Indians looked awfully happy with the win.

Joe Crede. His offensive numbers were respectable enough in his first few years with the team, especially considering his defensive capabilities. Yet there were times early in his career that he had some strange-looking at-bats. His swings were more than defensive; he didn't appear to have any idea what he was doing. After he'd hit some limp-looking foul off to the right, fans had to wonder if he was ever to develop into a true two-dimensional player.

"What's gotten into Joe Crede?" one fan asked at a home game late in 2005. Crede had homered and singled in that game. His swing was level and hard, and the third baseman stopped having those strange looking at-bats. Crede looked like he would provide the offense expected from a corner infielder.

That is exactly the way he looked in the tenth inning of the second game against the Indians. Crede swatted a fastball on the inside part of the plate off Cleveland reliever David Riske into the seats for a game-winning homer. It was Crede's second homer of the game, and no cheapie. The ball sailed over the Sox bullpen and halfway up toward the concourse. The White Sox had won a tough game, 7–6.

"Choke is an ugly, ugly word," Rick Morrissey wrote in his column the next day. "The Sox aren't choking. They're trying to extricate themselves from the middle of a monumental collapse brought on by a relative lack of talent. There's a difference."[10]

"How can you be a choker or loser when you've won 91 games?" Morrissey

Led by Paul Konerko and Joe Crede, the White Sox celebrate during a 2004 game.

quoted Ozzie Guillen saying after Crede had won an important game for the Sox.[11]

"Get off the ledge," White Sox radio play-by-play announcer Ed Farmer yelled to near-suicidal Sox fans as Crede rounded the bases.

Well, it wasn't quite time to get off the ledge yet. The next day Cleveland flattened the Sox, 8–0, to take two out of three in the series. Actually, the game was closer than it appeared. The Indians only led 2–0 going into the eighth. But three runs in the eighth and ninth put the game away and made the Indians look like the superior team.

The White Sox then lost an extra-inning game to Minnesota while Cleveland won again, this time pounding Kansas City, 11–6. It was September 22 and the Indians were only 1½ games behind the first-place White Sox. In a little more than seven weeks, the Sox had lost 13½ games in the standings. Could 2005 end up like 1969, only without the love as Rick Morrissey had written?

They say pitching wins championships, and that was what the White Sox received in their next three games. Their bullpen threw only one inning as Chicago piled up 3–1, 8–1, and 4–1 wins over Minnesota. Even with this little streak, the White Sox picked up only one game on Cleveland. Yet games were wiped off the schedule, and the Sox now had 94 wins. At the worst it appeared that a wild card was in their future — even if they couldn't beat the Indians in Cleveland on the last weekend of the season.

Fortunately for the White Sox, the Indians proved to be human. Cleveland lost three straight one-run games — one to Kansas City when their center fielder played a routine fly ball into a game-winning double for the Royals — and two to Tampa Bay, a team that was still three years away from its first winning season. When Placido Polanco of the Tigers lined out to Paul Konerko to wrap up a Sox win on September 29, the White Sox had won the American League Central Division. After scaring themselves and their fans, the team had never spent one day out of first place.

Doug Padilla of the *Naperville Sun* wrote that the only choking done by Ozzie Guillen and Ken Williams was choking back tears of joy. Actually, it had to be tears of relief. No one would have wanted to shoulder the biggest collapse in regular-season history. The 1969 disappointment was not repeated; White Sox fans wouldn't have to experience another Chicago baseball flop that would have been remembered for decades. Yes, winning the World Series was still the main thing, but getting to the playoffs was the first and hardest step.

"I think one of the things is that a lot of people don't realize how hard it is to get to the playoffs," Ozzie Guillen said. "Playing in the playoffs is easier than to play all year long and make this thing happen. I think when you get to the playoffs, it's even up. Everybody starts over. But that is why you work so hard all year long."[12]

If some fans didn't know or realize how hard it is to gain a playoff berth, they must have realized it after the Sox near-collapse. The last two months of the '05 season seemed longer than any other complete campaign. In the end the Sox won 99, which tied them for the second-best victory total in franchise history. For all the dread and worry, Chicago still ended up with the best record in the American League and the second best in all of baseball, one win less than major league-leading St. Louis. Now it was on to the second season.

Now Admit It—Wouldn't You Like A.J. Pierzynski on Your Team?

A.J. Pierzynski didn't have the greatest of reputations when he signed as a free agent with the White Sox in early 2005. He had been accused of lacking a great work ethic. The word "cancer" was associated with him. He was sometimes described as a media hog. Some people just didn't like him. The Giants had no interest in re-signing him after one season in San Francisco.

"I know there's a lot of negative stuff about me out there, but all I can say is that I'll do my best to change that," Pierzynski said upon signing with the White Sox.[13]

Pierzynski will be remembered by White Sox fans for that dramatic home run against the Dodgers in June. He will also be remembered for hitting two home runs in the 14–2 first-game win in the Divisional Series against the Red Sox. His clouts were two of five homers hit by the White Sox as they abandoned the small ball stuff for one game and stopped an at-home post-season losing streak at nine.

But what really can be remembered about Pierzynski was his performance as a handler of pitchers, his hitting and his base running that helped Chicago eliminate Boston from the playoffs in game three in Fenway Park. Like him or not, you would want A.J. Pierzynski on your team.

In the bottom of the sixth in the third game and the White Sox leading the series, 2–0, Boston pulled to within one on a massive home run slugged by Manny Ramirez. The Red Sox then loaded the bases with the help of two walks issued by Damaso Marte. With no outs, some momentum had shifted toward Boston. Ozzie Guillen decided this was a job for Orlando "El Duque" Hernandez. If anything, the ex–Yankee knew what it was like to pitch against the Red Sox.

The Red Sox fans made all kinds of noise in anticipation of their team taking the game over. Jason Varitek was the first hitter to face El Duque. Varitek

A.J. Pierzynski — Don't you just love him?

swung at a somewhat-high 2–1 pitch and popped it up into foul territory. Paul Konerko came in and caught it in the on-deck circle. One out.

Second baseman Tony Graffanino was next. Graffanino must have wanted to make up for a second-game blunder that helped sink the Red Sox at U.S. Cellular. In the bottom of the fifth, the White Sox had scored two to cut a Boston lead to 4–2. Joe Crede stood on first and Juan Uribe tapped a slow roller to second. In trying to catch the ball and scoop it toward second in one motion, Graffanino took his eye off of it briefly and the ball trickled between his legs. "Oh, no!" moaned ESPN announcer and Red Sox fan Chris Berman. "Everyone's safe!" No, Chris, only Joe Crede and Juan Uribe were safe. One out later, Iguchi hit a three-run homer to left to give the Sox a 5–4 lead that held up for the win.

Graffanino and Hernandez battled for 11 pitches. The Red Sox second baseman fouled off three full-count offerings. One looked like ball four, but close enough that Graffanino protected the plate and fouled it off to right. After the tenth pitch, Pierzynski went out to talk to Hernandez. Maybe he wanted to get Hernandez to agree with the pitch selection. Whatever the conversation covered, Hernandez threw a breaking pitching that had Graffanino out in front. He popped the ball up and Uribe made the catch on the grass behind the mound. Two out.

The tough-to-get-out Johnny Damon was next. This was another long battle — eight pitches. Again it went to a full count and again Pierzynski went out to talk to Hernandez. Once again, Hernandez and the catcher got on the same page and once again Hernandez threw an off-speed pitch. Damon started and then tried to stop his swing. Red Sox fans began to react because it was obvious the pitch was low. They thought Hernandez had walked in the tying run. However, home plate umpire Mark Wegner pointed to Damon and raised his right hand. Strike three. Three out. The White Sox still led. Fenway went quiet. Boston was dead, and everyone knew it.

Pierzynski and Hernandez pumped their fists. It was a clutch post-season performance by both battery mates. The experience was somewhat new to Chicago baseball fans.

The Red Sox looked like they were flat-lining. The defending champions went three up, three down in the seventh and picked up a lonely single in the eighth. They trailed by only one run but gave no appearance of being able to score.

An insurance run is always good to have in Fenway and, thanks to A.J. Pierzynski and some more small ball, the White Sox picked one up in the top of the ninth.

Pierzynski began things by hitting a double high off the Green Monster in left-center. Joe Crede, not considered to be a good bunter, laid down a good one and Pierzynski stood on third. A few pitches later, Pierzynski came slowly trucking down the line and Juan Uribe laid down another nice bunt. Reliever Mike Timlin threw off-balance to home and Pierzynski scored rather easily on the suicide squeeze. The White Sox catcher called himself safe with an emphatic gesture as Timlin's back-handed throw got away. The White Sox led, 5–3.

Maybe it was more than obvious that Boston was dead. Chris Berman began calling them "valiant" when the team came up to hit in the bottom of the ninth. Valiant or not, the Red Sox never got the ball out of the infield against Jenks. Edgar Renteria's pathetic ground ball to Iguchi ended it.

Now, finally, the White Sox got to celebrate their first post-season series win in 88 years. They had lost their last four series by a cumulative record of 5–14 and hadn't pushed any series to the limit. Suddenly the word "choke" wasn't in the White Sox vocabulary.

As an objective observer, I don't think there was a dropped third strike with two out in the ninth inning of the second American League Championship Series game against the Angels. Maybe, just maybe Josh Paul made a mistake when he was unable to get his mitt under the ball. Maybe, just maybe he in effect trapped the ball by reaching down on top of it with the catch. From all appearances it was a simple strike three. Paul rolled the ball to the mound thinking the inning was over. But something told A.J. Pierzynski to run. While a stunned Angel team watched, the Sox catcher stood on first base, claiming the base was his. Home plate umpire Doug Eddings would agree, saying that Paul had trapped the ball. It had to be one of the strangest plays in a major league baseball in a long time.

Pablo Ozuna ran for Pierzynski and stole second. Then Joe Crede, that guy who used to have a horrible swing, ripped a double off the middle of the left-field fence. Ozuna scored easily and the White Sox won, 2–1. The series was tied at one.

The Angels had won game one despite having to come into Chicago with almost no sleep immediately after eliminating the Yankees in California. The shift of momentum had to be huge with the Pierzynski play. But was there any momentum at all for the Angels? Their pitching had limited the Sox to four runs in the first two games, but the Angels had scored only four themselves. Mark Buehrle had stymied them on five hits as he went the distance in game two. Anaheim had scored only one run in its last 15 innings.

Pierzynski was booed in Anaheim. Were the Angel fans and their team too pre-occupied with the strange play? Or did the White Sox pitching staff and Paul Konerko create the needed momentum in the series? Konerko homered in the first inning of games three and four. Then there was the starting staff that threw four straight complete games.

Yet this section is about A. J. Pierzynski, and he had to be involved in one more important play. In the eighth inning of a tied fifth game, Pierzynski came up to the plate with Aaron Rowand on first and two out. The most popular

Tony Graffanino is at bat here during the 2000 season with the White Sox. The second baseman made a key error in the 2005 League Division Series that helped lead to the elimination of the Boston Red Sox.

player in baseball hit a come-backer to the mound against Anaheim reliever Kelvim Escobar. Escobar knocked the ball down with his backside as he spun around after his release. The ball bounced toward the first-base line. Grabbing the ball, Escobar ran over to tag Pierzynski with his glove and then tossed a throw to first that was late. First-base umpire Randy Marsh called the most

popular player out. Pierzynski pointed
to Escobar, claiming he had not been
tagged. Marsh and home plate umpire
Ed Rapuano met to discuss the play.
The Angels left the field just as the
most popular player perched himself
on first as he had in game two. Rapuano then made the call reversal, which
was the right thing to do. Escobar had
tagged Pierzynski with an empty glove;
the ball had been in his pitching hand.
Angel manager Mike Scioscia didn't
like it and argued the call reversal.
The Anaheim fans didn't like it and
filled the stadium with boos. Yet Escobar was the one who couldn't make
up his mind whether to throw to first
or tag Pierzynski. In the end, he tagged Pierzynski with the wrong hand
and his late throw to the first baseman
who wasn't in position to take it only
made the play look worse. Joe Crede
was the now the hitter with two runners on.

Josh Paul shown here in the early part of
his career with the White Sox. He was the
victim of the A.J. Pierzynksi ploy (or
maybe just a smart move) to gain a base
on a dropped third strike in the 2005
ALCS. To say the least it was a strange
play.

Francisco Rodriguez came in to
relieve Escobar since Crede had homered off Escobar during his previous at-
bat in the seventh. The Sox third baseman bounced a single up the middle
that Adam Kennedy dived for and flagged down about 10 feet behind second
base. Rowand kept running and beat Kennedy's desperate and off-balance
from-the-knees throw to home. The White Sox now had a 4–3 lead.

In the top of the ninth the Sox scored two insurance runs mostly because
Rodriguez couldn't find the plate. With two out in the bottom of the ninth,
Casey Kotchman grounded to Paul Konerko, who made a nice grab on a short
hop. He stepped on the bag to record the final out of the game, and the White
Sox had won their first pennant in 46 years.

Pierzynski, the accused media hog, allowed a camera crew to follow him
around as he made his way to U.S. Cellular Field for the World Series. He said
this was no time to be nervous; playing in the World Series was what it was all
about. Maybe this exposure it was a bit much, but the most popular player already had had quite the postseason. From hitting two homers in one game to
scoring on a suicide squeeze, to running out a dropped third strike that was no
dropped third strike to also getting away with catcher interference, to avoiding

a phantom tag, Pierzynski was one big reason the White Sox had made it to the World Series. How can you not like the guy?

Improbable Heroes

Many times it is the unknown or average player who comes through in the postseason. No one was familiar with Gene Tenace until he hit four home runs in the 1972 World Series for the Oakland A's. Bucky Dent was an excellent shortstop, but who would have dreamed that it would be his home run that helped the Yankees beat the Red Sox in a one-game playoff for the American League Eastern Division title in 1978? Even Al Weis, who hit .155 in 187 at-bats for the White Sox in 1966, drove in the winning run in the second game of the 1969 World Series, aiding the Mets in beating the heavily favored Baltimore Orioles. In 2005, the Sox had a host of improbable heroes who helped win a World Series championship.

Improbable Hero Number One: Scott Podsednik. Podsednik was like many lead-off hitters — home runs were not his specialty. They weren't supposed to be his specialty, and that was why the White Sox traded for him in the first place. His job was to get on base and have others drive him home. In a tie contest in World Series Game 2 against the Astros, Podsednik faced Houston closer Brad Lidge with one out in the bottom of the ninth. On a 2–1 count, the left fielder sent a drive to deep right-center. To the shock of Aaron Rowand and Brian Anderson, who watched open-mouthed from the Sox dugout, and many in the U.S. Cellular crowd, Podsednik's drive landed in the second row of the seats for a game-winning homer. Podsednik was told after the game that the Baseball Hall of Fame wanted his bat. In the regular season Podsednik failed to hit a homer in 507 official at-bats. The home run was his only hit in five appearances that game.

Improbable Hero Number Two: Geoff Blum. Blum didn't even join the White Sox until the end of July. He hit .200 in 95 at-bats. Game 3 in Houston had gone into the 14th inning. Blum golfed a low inside fastball down the right-field line and over the wall. It hit against a railing and flew back onto the field. The White Sox had a one-run lead and would pick up one more run that inning. Most White Sox fans probably didn't remember that Blum was on the team.

Improbable Hero Number Three: Mark Buehrle. He is a surprise listing here for obvious reasons. Although starters make bad closers, Buehrle was called upon to get the final out in the bottom of the 14th with the Astros having the tying run on first. Buehrle, however, induced Adam Everett to pop up to Juan Uribe to end the game. The White Sox were one win from a World Series championship.

Buehrle has done it all. Two no-hitters, one a perfect game. When White Sox fans look back at the first decade of this century, they will think of Buehrle.

Improbable Hero Number Four: Willie Harris. Harris led off the eighth inning of Game 4 pinch-hitting for Freddie Garcia. His main job was to get on base, which Harris did with a nicely placed single to left field. He was sacrificed to second by Podsednik and advanced to third on a ground out by Carl Everett. Then Jermaine Dye brought Harris home with a ground single to center. Harris scored the only run of the clinching game.

Improbable Hero Number Five: Juan Uribe. With one out and a man on second in the bottom of the ninth, pinch-hitter Chris Burke hit a foul pop down the left-field line. Crede chased it but never really had a good angle on it. Running past Crede was Uribe, who took a flying leap into the stands. He came out with the ball on a catch that most Sox fans will not forget. Two out.

Orlando Palmeiro was next. He bounced one over the mound and right behind Bobby Jenks. Uribe charged in, scooped up the ball, and, in one motion, fired to Konerko. Palmeiro was out on an eye-lash close play. The White Sox were world champions.

Improbable Heroes Number Six: The Breaks. Chicago baseball teams usually don't get them, or fail to take advantage of them. Of course, there was the dropped third strike that never was, Tony Graffanino's defensive blunder, and a catcher's interference call that was not made. Also, in the seventh inning of Game 2, Jermaine Dye was sent to first base when home plate umpire Jeff Nelson ruled that Dye had been hit by a pitch. TV replays showed the ball actually hit the bottom of Dye's bat. Dye showed no reaction of being in pain because he probably wasn't hit.

Then there was the response to these breaks. Crede knocked in the winning run with a double after the Pierzynski ploy, Tadahito Iguchi hit a three-run homer after the Graffanino gaffe, and Konerko clubbed a grand slam after Dye happily took first. It was so unlike Chicago baseball teams of the past century or so.

The 2005 season was an important year for the White Sox. The team needed that World Series. The 2005 campaign marked the first year the franchise topped the two million mark in attendance since 1993, the year before the strike. Fan alienation remained a problem. The club had gambled on taking a different direction and it worked. Even with the World Series win, there was no way the team was going to begin out-drawing the Cubs. They had lost so much ground to the North Side with the effects of the strike, the White Flag Trade, and Sammy Sosa's march toward 60 home runs. The team needed to bring disgruntled fans back and start widening their base that had been eroded by decades of losing, bad public relations, and the Cubs phenomenon. The year 2005 was a huge step in the right direction.

21

The Cross-Town Classic

"The White Sox could win five straight World Series and their
fans would still be jealous of what the Cubs have."

— *Bitter-sounding Cubs fan at the Cubs fan convention in 2009.*

"Being a Cubs fan is like having a mental illness."

— *Cubs fan Greg Redlarczyk. Redlarczyk claims that he no longer
cares about what Cubs do after decades of disappointment. Other
than that, even he doesn't fully understand his past loyalty.*[1]

"It is still an exciting event. It doesn't matter what the
standings are. You're in the dumps when your team loses."

— *Cubs fan Larry Hunt describing the atmosphere at a Cubs-Sox game.*[2]

"It has the playoff pressure without the reward of a playoff."

— *White Sox fan Elizabeth Harvey regarding the White Sox–Cubs
confrontations. Harvey attended the June 18, 2009, Cubs-Sox game at
Wrigley with her niece. She said she got out of there as fast as she could
once the game was over. The Cubs had overcome a late-inning 5–1
White Sox lead to take the game, 6–5.*[3]

"Why do we have to have these fucking faggot Cubs
fans sitting by us?"

— *Cubs fan and author Kasey Ignarski said this was a greeting
he and his family received when they took a seat at U.S. Cellular
Field for a Cubs-Sox game. Ignarski and his family were easily
identified by wearing their Cubs logo stuff.*[4]

"Why are you wearing that White Sox jacket?"

—*Two Cubs fans approaching a Sox fan at the Cubs-Sox exhibition
game in the late '80s at Comiskey Park. The Sox fan claimed he
thought he would have to defend himself. He told the Cubs fans that
he wore his Cubs jacket when he went to Wrigley Field and felt
that helped stave off a further confrontation.*

"Sox Suck!"

—T-shirts worn by Cubs fans at Cubs-Sox games and at the Cubs fan convention.

"Cubs Suck!"

—T-Shirts worn by Sox fans at Cubs-Sox games and at SoxFest.

I attended the second game of the American League Division Series between the White Sox and the Rays in St. Petersburg on October 3, 2008, at Tropicana Field. In their decade-long existence, the Rays had not posted a winning record until they made the playoffs in 2008. Since Tropicana Field is a domed stadium, when Rays fans cheered or were prompted to cheer that night, the ballpark became extremely loud. Yet volume shouldn't be confused with emotion. Or electricity. "Electricity" was the most common word used by Cubs and Sox fans and players when describing the atmosphere at Cubs-Sox inter-league games. Despite the fact that the Rays were in a playoff game that day, the atmosphere didn't come close to matching the feeling generated by Wrigley Field or U.S. Cellular Cubs-Sox crowds.

Of course, the Rays have no longstanding baseball history and are still in the infant stages of building a fan base. In the team's premier year in 1998, Tampa drew a little more than 2.5 million. However, as the expansion team continued to lose season after season, attendance didn't approach the 2 million mark. Even in their World Series year, the team only exceeded 1.7 million at the gate. In their first home series of 2008, Tampa drew slightly more than 36,000 for their home opener but could top the 20,000 level only once during the next seven home dates. Fans didn't need a ticket broker to get a decent seat for a Rays game.

At the White Sox–Rays playoff game, the center-field scoreboard entertained fans between innings with a video of a comedian talking about his loyalty to the Rays. "I've been a Rays fan since June," the comedian said. "No, not June. July."

In talking to Cubs and Sox fans about their allegiance, they speak of traditional family support of their team that at times spans generations. In essence, it isn't fair to compare Chicago and Tampa baseball. Longevity is one reason Chicago is unique and the Cubs-Sox fan rivalry so intense. This was illustrated in the seventh inning of a Cubs-Sox game on July 7, 2000.

Paul Konerko stepped up to the plate with one out and two men on. The Cubs led, 2–1. Konerko tore into a Kerry Wood pitch and sent a high-soaring drive toward the left-field foul pole. The ball zoomed onto Waveland Avenue but had hooked to the foul side of the pole. One could feel the mixture of emotions. With the crack of the bat, Cubs fans gasped. Sox fans were on their feet. As the ball went foul, Cubs fans let out their feelings of relief. Sox fans sat back down with disappointment.

Sox fans were cheering when Konerko singled home the tying run. But Wrigley Field balled up into a state of mass tension one out later when Frank Thomas stepped up to the plate.

The game was still tied. The bases were loaded with two out, and Thomas had worked Wood to a full count. The crowd went silent as Wood went into his wind-up. Thomas no doubt was looking for a fastball, thinking that was still Wood's best pitch, and that Wood would not want to risk walking in a run if he missed with a breaking pitch. But a breaking pitch was what Wood threw. The surprised Thomas took strike three.

Cubs fans went nuts as Kid K struck out the Big Hurt. No matter that the Sox were on their way to the division title that year while the Cubs remained non-contenders. For the moment, the immediate game with the Sox was what really mattered. This well-pitched and evenly played game reflected the intensity of each fan base. Tension and suspense were everywhere. Taunts were thrown out during the entire contest. And it was great baseball.

During the 1960s, the Cubs and White Sox played each other once a season in an exhibition contest called the "Boys Benefit Game." While the meaningless game provided some bragging rights, it certainly wasn't hyped like the current Cubs-Sox series. After all, the game meant nothing in the standings, and minor leaguers were frequently called up to gain some major league experience. Neither set of fans liked to see its team lose, but usually the game was forgotten after a few days.

I attended the 1968 game, which was played in the middle of the All-Star break. Cubs manager Leo Durocher didn't want to play his regulars. Both teams were in ninth place at the break during the last season of one-divisional play. Just under 24,000 fans showed for the contest, although there was no "electricity" in the air. Knowledgeable White Sox fans knew their team was old, tired and almost void of talent. The Cubs, however, played much better in the second half and actually moved their way up to third. But only Cubs fans with absolutely no sense of reality (and there probably were plenty) ever entertained the idea of the Cubs having a chance to challenge the first-place St. Louis Cardinals.

The game was a boring 1–0 affair won by the White Sox, with the only run resulting from a pop-up dropped by Lee Elia. Nothing hit to the outfield got anywhere close to the warning track. When the game ended, very few fans reacted. Were White Sox fans going to brag about scoring one run? At that point of the season, the club only averaged three runs a game, anyway. (That figure represented total runs, earned and unearned.) The 1968 season would be their first losing season since 1950. Beating an uninterested Cubs team in a game hardly anyone else cared about wasn't going to make that dreadful 1968 season better.

By the late seventies, the Sox and Cubs no longer played each other. C.U.B.S. (Chicagoans United for a Baseball Series) petitioned the Cubs to start the games again, and claimed that Bill Veeck was for the idea.[5] The Cubs showed no interest, and maybe that was for the best. The late seventies was a baseball wasteland in Chicago. Neither team posted a winning season from 1978 through 1980.

The game was revived in the mid–1980s. Television commercials promoting the game showed managers Tony La Russa and Jim Frey jousting with each other. One ad had La Russa convincing Frey to come out for a beer. How many Cubs and Sox fans get together after today's over-hyped games?

Baseball was not doing well in the late 1960s, mostly due to the fact that pitchers dominated the game. In '68, Carl Yastrzemski won the American League batting title with a .301 average. He was the only American Leaguer to hit .300 who had enough plate appearances to qualify for the batting title that year. The National League had only a handful of such .300 hitters. Interest in baseball had slipped and inter-league play was suggested to spice things up. The baseball establishment instead chose to lower the mound five inches and went through with another round of expansion, adding two teams to each league. The mound flattened out some curves and expansion diluted the pitching somewhat. Offensive numbers went up in 1969. Instituting a divisional set-up that created another "pennant race" in each league also helped kindle further interest. Something had to be done. Baseball had come under fire for being too boring, too slow and too offensively impaired. It also hadn't helped that the St. Louis Cardinals and Detroit Tigers had little competition for their pennants in 1968.

In the mid–1990s major league baseball realized that fan anger regarding the strike was deep and profound. Luckily for the sport, the 1998 home run chase won back many fans. But that happened in 1998, one year after the advent of inter-league play. The hope in 1997 was that inter-league play would help fans get over 1994. White Sox fans were among the angriest after the strike; beating the Cubs could soothe that anger.

Relatively speaking, White Sox fan cared little about the first Sox inter-league game against the Cincinnati Reds just prior to the Cubs series. The Cubs had traveled to Milwaukee to play the Brewers for their first taste of playing an American League team in the regular season, but their fans had to be looking past the Brewers to the White Sox on June 16. The 1997 campaign was the last year the Brewers were an American League team. The club was founded as the Seattle Pilots in 1969.

The last time the Sox and the Cubs played in a game that meant anything was in the 1906 World Series. The White Sox won that Series in six games. The clincher came on October 14 at South Side Park, then the home stadium of the White Sox. It is the only time a Chicago baseball team has clinched a post-season series in its home park in history. It was ironic that another Chicago baseball team was the loser. Cubs owner Charles W. Murphy actually toasted the victorious White Sox in an impromptu speech to Sox fans on the field immediately after the game.

"The best team won because they played better ball and deserved to win," Murphy said. "The contests have been well-contested and Chicago people should be proud of both clubs. If we had to lose, I would rather lose to Comiskey's club than any other club in the world."[6]

Murphy actually held a White Sox banner as he made his little speech. No one would say it wasn't gracious or classy. But could anyone imagine Jerry Reinsdorf or a key Cubs front office man holding the other team's pennant and congratulating their conquerors nowadays? Would either group of fans have accepted this or would they have started throwing things? Actually, both Cubs and White Sox fans have told the author they fear a outbreak of real violence at the end of a present-day all–Chicago World Series, should that ever occur.

In 1989, the Cubs won their second division title while the White Sox finished in last place, their third cellar-dwelling campaign in 20 seasons. *Sun Times* columnist Richard Roeper said he hated the Cubs and just about everything they stood for.[7]

"Oh, it's not the sort of hatred I reserved for American Nazis or crack dealers or James Earl Ray," Roeper wrote. "It's more of a 'hate lite' I feel about Roseanne Barr, golf and Levi's Dockers TV commercials."[8]

Roeper felt about 25 percent of Cubs fans were "knowledgeable, loyal, and well-mannered."[9] He hoped those Cubs fans would have a great time at the playoffs. For the rest he had nothing but disdain.

"My problem is with the pseudo-fan, the bandwagon rider, the Corona drinking fraternity/sorority creature, the fake, the fraud, and the bogus," Roeper wrote.

Fellow *Sun-Times* columnist Dennis Byrne, also a White Sox fan, found himself writing about how Sox fans should act during the Cubs playoff run. Byrne's main problem was with Cubs fans who "wanted the Sox booted out because Chicago is a Cubs town."[10] Byrne then conceded that Chicago baseball teams rarely had a chance to win a World Series, so he was breaking his past vows about never rooting for the Cubs. "Go cubs" were the last two words in his column written in a font so small anyone with the slightest visual impairment would never have seen them.[11]

In a letter to the editor published in the October 6 edition of the *Sun-Times*, Moline, Illinois, White Sox fan Jim Bigham wrote in response to Byrne, "Wimping out under pressure is something I would have expected from a Cubs fan."[12]

A day earlier the *Sun-Times* published a letter written by Joseph Stachowski of West Town. Stachowski had not been impressed by the Roeper column.

"It is sad to see someone with a constricted soul such as Richard Roeper's," Stachowski wrote. "I'm a Chicago fan, and have attended Wrigley, Comiskey, the Stadium, and Soldier Field. Why does being a Sox or Cubs fan preclude from rooting for both?"[13]

The rooting for both teams is a minority view. Roeper had irked Stachowski when he predicted and/or hoped the San Francisco Giants would defeat the Cubs in five games. His hope and/or prediction turned out to be right on the money. The Giants and Cubs split the first two games at Wrigley while the Giants took three in a row in San Francisco. Cubs fans were driven to distraction as they watched their team lose those three West Coast games by a total of four runs.

Between 1990 and 1997, the 1993 White Sox were the only Chicago baseball team to reach the playoffs. With no World Series appearance or championship, neither team had any significant claim to the city's bragging rights. The opportunity to grab that claim came on June 16, 1997, when the Cubs invaded new Comiskey Park for the first of three all–Chicago inter-league games.

A little luster was removed from the series with the Cubs sitting in last place in the National League Central and the White Sox residing a game out of last in the American League Central. Or maybe that was more fitting considering the ineptitude of the two Chicago franchises during the last few decades. Regardless, the Cubs won the first encounter by running out to a 6–0 lead and then coasting to an 8–3 win. They pounded out 14 hits and had beat up ex-Cubs starter Jamie Navarro in a game the White Sox had little chance of winning.

Yet the real story was the non-sellout to a game that many considered historic. The White Sox had had a hard time drawing during the immediate post-strike years, yet Cubs-Sox exhibition games held at Comiskey had drawn well. So why were there 7,000 empty seats for a grudge match that counted in the standings?

Sun-Times columnist Dave Van Dyke thought the hangover from the strike was still affecting attendance overall.[14] For this game in particular, Van Dyke speculated that a White Sox policy forcing fans buying tickets for the Cubs series to purchase tickets for three other games didn't help. He wrote that the White Sox organization had hoped to drive Cubs fans away from Comiskey with the ticket-selling strategy. The policy probably did that, but apparently White Sox fans stayed away as well.

"Jerry Reinsdorf really made people angry with that ticket ploy for this series," Sox fan Mike Keniley was quoted in a Carol Slezak column the next day. "And then he keeps saying in the newspapers that it's the fans' fault. Everything is our fault. The best public relations for the Sox would be for Reinsdorf to keep his mouth shut."[15]

Bob Shoop, the next White Sox fan Slezak quoted, said, "Reinsdorf never went to his fan base, the season-ticket holder to give them first shot at the Cubs/Sox tickets. He really made people very angry."[16]

But what about the Cubs-Sox rivalry? Slezak wanted to know. Didn't White Sox fans want to out do their Cub counterparts in cheering their team on?

"The bottom line is, Cubs fans are a non-entity to us," Jim Miller told Slezak.[17]

Did this mean that the inter-city, inter-league rivalry was not going to be what everyone hoped it would be? Especially when the games were played on the South Side?

The Chicago press coverage was a bit of an overreaction. The next two games drew more than 44,000. No Sox-Cubs game since then at Comiskey/U.S. Cellular have drawn less than 38,000, and those crowds under 40,000 have only occurred because of the current decreased capacity of the upper deck. The Cubs-Sox inter-league series does more than draw crowds. Even though some Cubs and Sox fans feel the series has lost some of its novelty, it hasn't lost its emotional edge and continues to symbolize the rivalry between the fan bases. Les Grobstein told the author that he was sure White Sox fans were greatly relieved when their team swept the Cubs at in 2008.[18] After all, the Cubs had pulled the trick earlier at Wrigley. Neither set of fans wanted to see its squad lose all six games. It is hard enough facing each other after even one loss. The novelty of the series may have eroded some, but the fear of being bested by the other is still there.

"I have no real home team."
—*Andrew Shaffer, Iowa City Cubs fan.*

Much has been written about the Iowa Cubs fan. Iowa baseball fans are assumed to be Cubs fans. Like Shaffer, these fans have built allegiance largely from watching WGN-TV and following the AAA affiliate in Iowa City. There is the image of bus loads of Iowans that migrate to the North Side to catch a Cubs game. Wowed by the site of Wrigley, they then go back to their home state and return the next season to be wowed by Wrigley again. But do they have the same feelings of animosity toward Sox fans as their North Side counterparts do? Iowa Cubs fan Schaffer doesn't think so.

"I don't hate the White Sox," Shaffer maintained. He even disapproves of some of the "rudeness" Sox and Cubs fans show each other.[19]

What Shaffer meant in his quote is that he, as a fan, does not have a home major league baseball team. Not being from Chicago, he doesn't have the same sense of rivalry that the home-grown Chicago baseball fans experience. These rivalries have local origins, he believes. Iowans have their own rivalries, he said, and those rivalries have histories of their own.

"Iowa-Iowa State is pretty intense," according to Shaffer.[20]

Kevin Gillogly is a White Sox fan who now lives just outside of Washington, D.C. He is amazed and frustrated by reactions from local residents when they learn he is originally from Chicago and are shocked he is a White Sox fan. The tentacles of WGN reach to the East Coast as well.

"They automatically assume I'm a Cubs fan even if I am wearing a White Sox hat," Gillogly said. "They have a blank look on their faces when I say there is another team in Chicago. They know there is another team but they don't know who it is."[21]

Gaurav Garg is a twenty-something Cubs fan who lives in Chicago and has experienced the rivalry in a different manner. He has attended games at Wrigley when White Sox rivals from the American League Central were playing the Cubs.

"They (White Sox fans) were cheering when the Cubs lost to the Indians," Garg said. "They should have been cheering for the Indians to lose." Garg also said White Sox fans cheered for the Tigers to beat the Cubs.

"I hate White Sox fans," said Garg, who added he hated the "Sox Pride" White Sox advertisement. "All they are concerned about is how they hate Cubs fans."[22]

Then Garg retracted the "hate" sentiment and said, "White Sox fans are not bad people. They just hate the Cubs."[23]

"White Sox fans seem to have a chip on their shoulder," said Kasey Ignarski, a Cubs fan with South Side origins. "I don't understand that. I don't hate the White Sox."[24]

"Ok, let us know when the White Sox get a tradition,
I will be sure to knock it."
"Their fans' tradition for the last 27 years has been to obsess about the Cubs."
"What a punk bitch."
"I'm sorry to hear that."
"What are you trying to help Stine do?"

These quotes are responses I received when I posted a request on www.northsidebaseball.com. After introducing myself as a writer working on this project who had written about the White Sox in the past, I asked that Cub fans contact me so I could talk to them about their team's history. Although I had memories of many Cub games, I told them I hadn't experienced things as a Cub fan would, and hoped they would add some insight that I couldn't. I said they could knock White Sox tradition, but they had to be intelligent about it. Saying the "White Sox suck" wasn't acceptable. I left my e-mail address and stated that I could be contacted if anyone wanted to contribute anything to the book.

As can be seen above, the first two responses discussed White Sox tradition. Somewhat intelligent, but they were just one-liners. Those fans didn't have much else to say.

To be honest, I don't know what a "punk bitch" is. I've never heard that expression and only assumed the person wasn't interested in talking with me.

The fourth reply was in response to the fact that I had written other books about the White Sox. Apparently my publishing history didn't impress that Cubs fan.

The last response came as a result of a couple Cubs fans sharing some memories with me. The fan, using the last part of my last name, seemed offended that these Cubs fans would assist me in any way. Those fans did write some insightful things about the effects of WGN had on their childhood memories. Otherwise, no Cubs fan from this website attempted to contact me to talk about their memories or Cubs history. It is often said that Cubs fans are not concerned about the White Sox or their fans. Any jealousy or bitterness came from the South Side. These responses indicate otherwise.

On the lighter side there was this hilarious response to my request:

> From what I remember as a kid getting free tickets to Comiskey for straight "A's" and perfect attendance, White Sox tradition was getting Howry faced and beating each other bloody in the stands because the game was so boring. But the shorts that team wore were real purty.

The Howry reference was Bob Howry, who had been a part the White Flag Trade in 1997. Of course, Howry had not been around when the shorts were worn in 1976. This Cubs fan also made a parting shot to St. Louis Cardinal fans and their apparent affection for the late '60s variety show *Hee Haw*.

Hero-worship is part of sports. Although many fans recognize athletes are not heroes or role models, there is still that element in fandom. That is why fans react so strongly to things like strikes and drug scandals. They still want to believe love of the game transcends money and fame or cheating to help achieve that money and fame.

An intense hero-worship bent has helped build the Chicago Cubs fan base. There is a Norman Rockwell picture on the cover Jim Langford's book, *The Game Is Never Over*. Two Cubs coaches, one probably the manager, sit on the end of the bench with their heads resting in their hands. They are not happy with the way things are going on the field. A bat boy stands on the top of dugout steps, his cap slightly askew. Fans in the seats right behind the dugout are smiling even as they scream out taunts out at the hapless Cubbies. Cubs frustration is linked right there with Americana. Langford's book was published in 1980. On the book jacket, it is written that the 42-year-old author hopes to live long enough to see a World Series at Wrigley Field. Hopefully Langford is alive and well, and for his sake, a Series happens at Wrigley.

Langford, however, was disillusioned with the new breed of Cubs fan in the immediate post–1969 era. He wrote of the charged atmosphere at Wrigley in early 1970 that changed things for the worst. "Wrigley Field witnessed a new phenomenon," he wrote. "Gangs of rowdies were roaming through the stands, starting fights and throwing debris on the field, and jumping over walls, interrupting play."

Aramis Ramirez was instrumental in helping the Cubs win the National League Central in 2003. His shoulder injury helped contribute to the Cubs' under-achieving season in 2009.

In a biography published for the benefit of his family, Raymond Ennes lamented how things had changed in Wrigley Field.

"No longer can a father, mother, brother or sister, etc., keep and treasure a homerun ball hit into the bleachers at Wrigley Field by the opposition," Ennes wrote. "The loyal fan must throw the ball back to the playing field to show his hatred of the opposition."[25]

While past generations (Ennes was born in 1927) didn't appreciate the new fan ethic at Wrigley, and responsible Cubs fans don't condone over-the-top behavior, the roots of Wrigley Field fanaticism is what drives attendance over the three-million mark every year. It really began with the hysteria of 1969, stopped and started during the seventies, and continued on after the 1984 division title. The absence of a world championship has not dampened the Cubs fans' spirit, at least not yet.

"Passion and hope." This is what drives Cubs fans, according to North Side loyalist Jim Pagani. "Wait until next year." Pagani believes that old saying also is an important leap of faith.[26]

"It has been over 101 years since the Cubs have won the World Series," Pagani said, "but we still have faith each year, that this year will be the year.

Heartbreak after heartbreak, we are still madly in love with the Chicago Cubs."[27]

White Sox fan Elizabeth Harvey lives about a half-mile from Wrigley Field. She can live with the situation as it is now and hopes the Cubs night schedule doesn't expand. Yet she feels there is a " buzz" in her neighborhood during Cubs night games, although in 2003 she said things got a little "intense."

"There is a traffic that makes the neighborhood exciting," Harvey said. "Even as a Sox fan, I think it is cool."[28]

The home page of White Sox fan website www.whitesoxinteracive.com proudly displays a quote it generally credits to the *RedEye edition of the Chicago Tribune*. "Meet the smartest and most bitter White Sox fans around. Be careful. Some of them bite."

Bitter and smart. These two adjectives have been used in describing White Sox fans. In interviewing White Sox fans for this book and interacting with them during the years, I can attest to that fact. A White Sox fan will not likely use the words "hope springs eternal."

"I want a dynasty," White Sox fan Hal Vickery told the author. "Losing is not lovable."[29]

Vickery, thrilled with the World Series win he never thought he would see, didn't want it to stop there. The 2005 season wasn't supposed to live on like 1969 had for the Cubs and 1977 had for the White Sox. More success was supposed to follow. That is why White Sox general manager Kenny Williams bristled at the idea that the team was rebuilding in 2009. He didn't want the ghost of the 1997 White Flag Trade haunting him or to come across as someone who was looking to the future at the expense of the present. And his late-season trades were indications he wanted to win in '09, not some season far off in the distance. For some White Sox fans, rebuilding was for wimps.

And for many White Sox fans, the constant talk about the great Wrigley experience is sickening.

"It is horrible at Wrigley," Elizabeth Harvey said. "The seats are uncomfortable. I don't think it is a shrine; it's a dump. The overall experience at U.S. Cellular is much better, especially for the kids."[30]

"The Sox crowd is more into the game," according to White Sox loyalist Matt Cassidy. "The Cubs attract tourists who are out to be seen, out to drink. And the Cubs are convinced they are jinxed."[31]

Cassidy also said the Cubs organization will eventually have to do more to put a quality team on the field on a consistent basis and finally win a World Series.

"Their fans will get a little angrier, will get a little more picky," Cassidy said regarding the perpetual sellouts at Wrigley.[32]

So, other than different tastes, what are the origins of the divide of the Chicago baseball city? The divide can be traced to the beginning of the twentieth century. White Sox historian Rich Lindberg wrote in his *White Sox Ency-*

clopedia that the 1906 World Series "well could have been called the rich man-poor man games."[33] According to Lindberg, "The Cubs were the darlings of the Michigan Avenue carriage set; the Sox, who were located in the dingy stockyard area of old Bridgeport, were the workingmen's heroes."[34]

The economic demographics are probably very different today with the de-industrialization of our society and the ability of fans to travel further distances to see a game. Additionally, major league baseball as a whole has catered more to the corporate fan and the season-ticket holder. When it comes right down to it, how different are the fans that go to five or six games a year? And then again, do fans identify themselves in a certain economic way no matter what the demographics are?

Economics may have changed, but one thing has not: Chicago is still seen as a city of neighborhoods. Each has its own identity, and with that, its own sports allegiance.

"You cannot be both," Cubs fan Jim Pagani told the author. "Growing up living at 3427 North Hamilton, all of my friends and neighbors were loyal Cubs fans. If you were raised in Chicago, there is no such thing as a Chicago baseball fan. You are either a Cubs or Sox fan."[35]

Pagani, who cheered for the Astros during the 2005 World Series, thought that suburbanites were the only ones who followed and cheered for both teams. Yet fellow Cubs fan Greg Redlarczyk said his childhood memories included being harassed as the only North Side loyalist on his block. Redlarczyk grew up in the author's hometown of Hammond, Indiana. In Hammond, fan devotions were many times divided according to location. Sometimes a mere block separated groups of White Sox and Cubs fans.

There seem to be other lasting differences. When Chicagoans United for a Baseball Series (C.U.B.S.) pushed Cubs management to improve the team, the organization got flak from fellow Cubs fans. When White Sox fans boycotted their team after the White Flag Trade, it didn't matter what other Sox fans thought. White Sox fans were angered when their team sold tickets to Cubs games as part of a package; Cubs fans don't seem to mind *Tribune* ticket brokering. Cubs fans love their Wrigley experience; White Sox fans say the winning is the experience.

Yet, as this book illustrates, these two sets of fans are more alike than they think. They each reacted strongly when they thought their traditions were threatened by new ownership in the early '80s. Both groups obsess about talented teams blowing rare chances to go to the World Series. Some Cubs fans think they are jinxed; some Sox fans believe the world, starting with the Chicago media, is against them. Both are in denial. Each strongly asserts that they don't care about the other, but the emotion around Cubs-Sox games says otherwise. And each strongly identifies with his teams and the images that accompany these franchises.

As White Sox fans do, Cub fans love their scoreboard. You can't blame them.

What has this done for the baseball city of Chicago? In the 2008 season, the teams drew a combined 5,801,303 fans. While the Cubs again outdrew the White Sox, this is still an astonishing number. The constant growth of the Cubs is hard to fathom. The White Sox have rebounded from a disastrous late 1990s when their franchise barely existed. Some still lament about fans not supporting both teams. However, with an attendance figure hovering close to 6 million for a season, why are they still concerned?

Appendix: Two Opinions on Chicago Sports Journalism

In the addendum to this book are two opinions written by now former Chicago media people defending the integrity of Chicago sports journalism. For decades now, the Chicago sports media, specifically the *Chicago Tribune*, has been accused of bias in favor of the Cubs. This accusation only intensified after the Tribune Company purchased the Cubs in 1981. The author will provide no comment on either of the viewpoints. However, the media manipulation has been an important tool in fan base building for each team. It is also important to see how media players view their participation and how they defend themselves against fan attacks primarily coming from the South Side.

In researching another book in the late '90s, I went to bookstores to see what had been written on each ball club. The number of new or recent books on the Cubs outnumbered work on the White Sox by a three to one margin. It appeared that the Cubs thought that all essential media should be utilized to market their product. Writers of these books at least had to have some cooperation of the Cubs organization. The message of the Wrigley experience was constantly published even though other media reach the masses on a wider scale.

On the other side, White Sox fans, at least until 2005, had less of a chance to read about their team's history. Jerry Reinsdorf, who felt cultivating the media was important during his early days running the organization, was rarely accessible to reporters and writers without stiff conditions. For example, a *Chicago Sun-Times* interview of Reinsdorf ran the day after the 1997 White Flag Trade. The format consisted only of questions and answers. That amounts to a transcription of a conversation and no more. This mistrust of the media, at least to a degree, was reflected in the lack of White Sox reading material.

Publishing is, of course, a money-making venture. If publishers didn't think a White Sox book was going to sell, it wouldn't be published no matter how well-written. This has no direct relation to the organization's view of the media in general. The proliferation of Cubs books could have only have meant the team was more popular and publishers were more than willing to take a risk on another Cub tome even in a saturated market.

Regardless of any media bias, the White Sox were getting slaughtered by Cub propaganda in the late 1990s. A Cubs home game, with its grand singing of "Take Me Out to the Ball Game" during the seventh inning stretch, was a true television event. The neighborhood, the vines, the sunshine, and Sammy Sosa saving baseball were constantly fed into the fans' psyche. The deluge of hype was overpowering. Meanwhile on the South Side, there always seemed to be an aura of bitterness. Anger over the 1994 strike and 1997 White Flag Trade hung in the air. Many still didn't like what they thought was a drab stadium. Even in the 2000 title-winning year, opposing players were amazed by relative low attendance on the South Side. Stories about White Sox fan apathy with news photographs of empty seats were common. (Leo Bauby, the collector who provided the pictures for this book, told me that past baseball photographers told him they were instructed to keep empty seats out of photos. Talk about media manipulation.) The net result? It is often said that if you tell a person something many times over, he will believe it whether it is true or not. During the late nineties, it was hard for even White Sox fans to argue that all the fun was not being had on the North Side. One can only imagine the fan reaction and hype if the Cubs had broken through and won a World Series.

Tribune baseball writers have and continue to deny any pro–Cub bias. However, the Cubs organization was not only owned by a mega-media outlet, it used that outlet and other media to promote itself to the maximum. As this book has already shown, this was just one method the Cubs used to build an enormously popular product.

One aspect of sports journalism that hasn't been examined in this book is the impact of sports talk radio. Long time columnist Bill Gleason, who spent most of his career with the *Chicago Sun-Times*, died in January 2010. Gleason had been instrumental in putting together a radio sports program called *The Sportswriters* that aired on WGN-AM on Sunday afternoons at 4:00 P.M. The show experienced some personnel changes with time but anchored that slot during the 1970s and 1980s. Eventually it evolved into the *Sportswriters on TV*. Run on cable networks, the show made the sportswriters even more well known.

Gleason symbolized the image of the gruff, working class White Sox fan. In addition to Gleason, the show had three other panelists: Soft-spoken Ben Bentley, the moderator, was supposed to keep order on the show. Bentley had long been connected with boxing and worked for the Chicago Bulls in the team's infancy; George Langford, then sports editor of the *Tribune*, was also soft spoken and usually added a rational viewpoint. To offset these two, *Tribune* sportswriter Bill Jauss was loudly passionate about his beliefs and was often looked upon as the Cub fan/working class advocate. These counter-balancing personalities made the show work for years.

The relevancy of this show to the book is that it provided a keen prospective the dynamics of Chicago baseball fandom. *The Sportwriters* often talked about the power of WGN-TV, the appeal of Wrigley Field, what Chicago baseball fans wanted from their teams, and the struggle of new ownerships to expand their fan bases in a new era of baseball during the early 1980's. In many ways, they gave the author insights that lead to writing this book.

Sox Media Coverage Isn't What It Used to Be. It's Better.
by Tom Shaer

Do you know people (perhaps even yourself) who grew up middle class, later reached a much higher income level, but still think of themselves as less well off than they really are? White Sox fans who complain about media coverage of their team remind me of those people.

Some media outlets do give more coverage to whichever team is home, so it's possible to make a flawed comparison when the Cubs are at Wrigley Field. But with each team playing 81 games in Chicago, that balances out. More often, what remains is an old argument no longer based in reality: The mighty Cubs get more attention from the even mightier media because that team has more fans — some of whom are biased members of the press, radio and TV. Oops, I mean press, radio, TV and *Internet*. Anyway, such protestations are nonsense.

It may be dreadfully inconvenient and surely disloyal for those Sox followers who feel the Cubs receive privileged treatment, but they should get some new material. Sox officials from top to bottom tell me they don't feel more coverage goes to the other guys and I never hear fans under 40 claim their team is shortchanged. It's the older, battle-scarred, Nellie-Fox-jersey-wearing, Dick-Allen-loving (or hating), Ron-Kittle-identifying fans who did not notice when the Sox finally arrived.

The main reason for the White Sox having equal time with the Cubs has been the truly remarkable rebuilding of the franchise by Jerry Reinsdorf and his team-behind-the-team. Well before the wonderful 2005 World Series Championship, the Sox became a far healthier business than they ever were under the Comiskeys, Allyns and Bill Veeck. The onetime poor relative has

Sportscaster Tom Shaer, now also a media consultant, arrived in Chicago in 1983. He has covered both the White Sox and Cubs and takes pride in not showing bias on the air. When directly asked, he tells fans that he likes the Cubs more than any other team. Except the White Sox, whom he loves.

long enjoyed prosperity and prestige once only dreamed of by the extended family.

Sox broadcast revenue is high; attendance is healthy (averaging more than 2.5 million fans over the past five years in a two-team town); they have legions of new fans in formerly unlikely places such as the North suburbs; merchandise and sponsorship sales are among the best in baseball and their community relations department has left a legacy for future generations. This success is built on many pillars.

Despite the Sportsvision misstep, the Reinsdorfians elevated the Sox to an equal television footing with the Cubs, so it's easy to find the boys. For 21 years, they've been on WGN-TV and expanded basic cable, as are the Cubs. Such outstanding exposure is in stark contrast to the boneheaded decision by John Allyn to leave Channel 9 in 1967 for UHF — a frequency then quite inconvenient for many in Chicagoland. Veeck kept them in television Siberia on Channel 44.

The Sox are also well marketed. This ownership has never seen the team as a "South Side" entity, but rather as Chicago's American League team. It is aggressive, innovative and quicker to react to changes in the marketplace. It is no surprise that Reinsdorf serves on the board of Major League Baseball Advanced Media and was at the forefront of MLB's hugely profitable commitment to the Internet and all things digital.

Sure, the Cubs have more fans than the White Sox but the gap has been dramatically cut. Marketing surveys showed, even before the World Series title, that the two teams are equally popular in vast, highly populated Cook County. The Cubs advantage comes in downstate Illinois, Southern Wisconsin and Iowa. What do these many business elements have to do with all the media outside a ball club's control? Everything.

A media outlet cannot ignore what its customers want to see and what they want to hear about. Even if the media wished to give the Chicago Cubs a better shake than the Chicago White Sox (and I don't believe it does), millions of fans would not stand for it. That would be bad for business. Truthfully, the traditional media actually work harder to cover the Sox than the Cubs. It's a matter of logistics.

Exclusive day baseball provides fresh material for the 5 and 6 P.M. news. More importantly, afternoon games leave much more time before deadline to send in video, write newspaper copy, transmit and lay out photographs and fill time on talk shows. What is often a mad dash to meet deadlines after night games once resulted in less space in print or on the air for such late-finishing events. It was a simple reality that the paper or sportscast had to be substantially ready to go before 10 P.M.

As the Sox's popularity grew, media staffs had to hustle more and find ways to get that coverage to the customer. Advances in video, print and cellular technology also improved the speed of delivery. Significantly, the Cubs kept adding night games and the Sox got fewer West Coast starting times after being freed from their miscast role as members of the American League Western Division. Ah, equality.

Intangibles remain that benefit the Cubs. They are the more romanticized team and have a very strong national and international brand identity. However, recent disappointing postseasons have clearly lowered the appeal of that sappy media creation, "lovable losers." Further, the Cubs' bigger global image may become much smaller with superstations less unique, fewer games broadcast on WGN-TV and more to choose from with every contest of every team on satellite and MLB.com.

Another not-to-be-discounted factor is sports talk radio. It has leveled the playing field because Sox fans are clearly more vocal and edgy than are Cubs followers and more partisans of the Sox than Cubs currently host talk shows in Chicago. As for radio game broadcasts, both teams are on 50,000-watt clear channel flagship stations.

The only time there is a clear disparity between coverage of these teams is when one has a better season than the other. I suspect that a survey of Cub fans from 1957 to 1965 would have shown they felt there was much more buzz about the White Sox, who averaged more than 90 wins a year, went to a World Series and finished second five times. You do the job, you get the attention. The Sox receive their fair share of coverage, and have for a long time. And that's the way it should be.

Stop the Presses! Cubune Years Finally Are Over. Perception of Bias Toward North Siders Will Not Be Missed
by Dan McGrath

Speaking for, among others, George Langford, Gene Quinn, Tom Patterson, Dick Leslie, Bob Condor, Margaret Holt, Tim Franklin, John Cherwa, Kerry Luft, Bill Dee, and Ken Paxson, I salute you, Tom Ricketts.

Also on their behalf, I thank you.

Along with myself, the above-mentioned lady and gentlemen all held rank of *Tribune* sports editor, or some variation thereof, during Tribune Co.'s ownership of the Cubs, and the Ricketts family's purchase of the ball club relieves successor Mike Kellams of an obstinate problem: how to provide fair, balanced and objective coverage of a team your parent company happens to own, a team that shares the market with a frisky rival whose vocal backers are more than suspicious of your every move.

Let's back up a bit: Covering the team objectively hasn't been difficult; Paul Sullivan, Dave van Dyck, Phil Rogers, Rick Morrissey and their colleagues past and present have followed the Cubs with a highly critical eye for the entire 28-year run of common ownership. If you doubt that you haven't been paying attention.

It's the *perception* that we're soft on the Cubs or that we favor them over the White Sox — that's what has given us all frequent heartburn.

"The top editors of the paper made it very clear to me when I took the job: We should cover every other team in town," says Franklin, *Tribune* sports editor from 1995 to 1997 and now director of the National Sports Journalism Center at Indiana University. "And that's exactly what we did.

"The larger issue was dealing with the public perception that the *Tribune* gave the Cubs favorable treatment. I heard complaints from senior people with the other pro teams in the city. More than that, though, I heard it from the readers."

Franklin also heard from a reader who demanded he "do something" about the Cubs' problem at third base.

Langford was in the chair when the deal went down in the summer of 1981. He insisted at the time that fair, balanced and objective coverage would never be compromised. He meant it, too — George was as honest and scrupulously fair a newsman you can find, subsequently demonstrating that as the paper's Public Editor, which entailed looking out for the reader's interest and taking positions that weren't always popular in the newsroom.

But newsroom leadership never interfered with him, just as it never tried to influence the baseball decisions.

In fact, in the 12 years I supervised the paper's baseball coverage, there was not a single instance of a top editor or a suit from the Tower suggesting we to easy on the Cubs or play down the White Sox. Not one.

That's not to say Ed Lynch didn't growl at me a few times and Jim Hendry has not been grumpy on occasion, but that comes with the territory. If you've spent any time covering baseball and you haven't been snarled at, you probably never have gone into the clubhouse.

A few years back Sully and I were summoned to the principal's office for a full, frank and open exchange of ideas with then-President Andy MacPhail, but that involved interpretation of a story — we didn't view it as attempted intimidation. And it dealt with Jacque Jones, so I still think we were right.

No, flak rarely came from the Cubs. And to their credit, they were straight shooters — they respected our competitors and never fed us anything that would give us an edge.

On the South Side, though, a different story ... at least among the fan base.

We change our name to the Daily Podsednik, paint black and white pinstripes on the delivery trucks and run Ozzie Guillen's column on our front page and we still would perceived as pro–Cub, anti–White Sox. The "Cubune" as former radio mouthpiece Dave Wills so cleverly described us.

In certain south-of-Madison precincts it's simply stated the Cubs are the "moneyed" team favored by the suits and the swells from downtown — home to Tribune Tower — and northward, while the White Sox have embodied South Side working-men's grit.

I know. I grew up in it. I'm the South Side son of a Chicago policeman and if I'm "moneyed," I wish it would hurry up and get here.

Driving home from Milwaukee one night I heard nothing but anti–"Cubune" rants from Wills for nearly two hours. It hurt. I wanted to pull over, call the night desk and order up a White Sox display worthy of a playoff game. If only they had played that day. "Chris Snopek, the Prairie Years" would have seemed a little forced, especially to those sharp, ethical people on our copy desk, some of them Sox fans, who make sure we kept things balanced.

The issue predates Tribune Co.'s Cub ownership. Bill Veeck, in his second go-round with the White Sox, once howled so loud about perceived coverage inequities that Langford was moved to measure column inches. Lo and behold, slight edge to the White Sox.

I've measured it myself, and most years it's a push, though it runs in cycles, much like the news. In 1998, the Cubs made the playoffs and Sammy Sosa hit all those home runs; advantage Cubs. In 2000, the Sox won their division and went to the playoffs; in 2003 the Cubs did, and the coverage was tailored accordingly. Last year they were both playoff teams ... and can we talk 2005 for a minute?

Elaborate "Soxtober" special sections detailing the White Sox's run through the World Series. We held the presses for two hours to get Geoff Blum's 14th-inning Game 3 heroics in the paper. Wall-to-wall coverage of the victory parade. Not one but two Tribune books on a truly wondrous season. I barely recognized my Cub-une.

But the next year, the first time we played the Cubs over the White Sox on a day they both were busy, it was like it never happened. The Cub-une rides again.

Now it's in Kellams' capable hands.

And with the heartburn having subsided, I almost can laugh about it. The passion was strong and impressive, indicative of how much people care ... one reason it is so great to be a newspaperman in Chicago.

Chapter Notes

Introduction

1. Bernard Weisberger, *When Chicago Ruled Baseball—The Cubs–White Sox World Series of 1906* (New York: HarperCollins, 2006), 25.
2. Richard Lindberg, *The White Sox Encyclopedia* (Philadelphia: Temple University Press, 1997), 60.
3. Joel Zoss and John Bowman, *The American League—A History* (New York: Gallery Books, 1986), 9.
4. *Ibid.*, 13.
5. Glenn Stout, *The Cubs* (Boston: Houghton Mifflin, 2007), 52.
6. John Snyder, *Cubs Journal* (Cincinnati, OH: Emis Books, 2005), 136.
7. Stout, *The Cubs*, 53.
8. *Ibid.*
9. Sam Coombs and Bob West, eds., *Baseball: America's National Game 1993–1915* (San Francisco, Halo Books, 1991), 309.
10. Lindberg, *The White Sox Encyclopedia*, 461.
11. *Ibid.*, 477.
12. Mark Liptak, telephone interview by author, November 2008.

Chapter 1

1. Peter Claerbaut, *Durocher's Cubs: The Greatest Team That Didn't Win* (Dallas, TX: Taylor, 2000), 7.
2. Doug Feldmann, *Miracle Collapse: 1969 Cubs* (Lincoln: University of Nebraska Press, 2006), 210.
3. Les Grobstein, telephone interview by author, December 2008.
4. Jerome Holtzman, "Cubs Win, Hit the Top!" *Chicago Sun-Times*, July 3, 1967, 64.
5. Ray Brennan, "1st Place USA!" *Chicago Sun-Times*, July 3, 1967, 18.
6. Feldmann, *Miracle Collapse*, 68.
7. *Ibid.*, 23.
8. WGN-TV broadcast, April 8, 1969.
9. Feldmann, *Miracle Collapse*, 196.
10. *Ibid.*, 213.
11. *Ibid.*

12. *Ibid.*, p. 214.
13. Gerry Bilek, telephone interview by author, December 2008.

Chapter 2

1. Dan Helpingstine, *Through Hope and Despair: A Fan's Memories of the Chicago White Sox, 1967–1997* (Highland, IN: 2001), 75.
2. Joe Horlen, telephone interview by author, March 2000; Gary Peters, telephone interview by author, December 2004.
3. WGN-TV broadcast, 1963.
4. Helpingstine, *Through Hope and Despair*, 74.
5. Dick Allen and Tim Whitaker, *Crash: The Life and Times of Dick Allen* (New York: Ticknor and Fields, 1989), photo insert.
6. Leo Bauby, interview by author.
7. En.wikipedia.org/wiki/Dick-Allen, accessed by author October 2008.
8. Allen and Whitaker, *Crash,* 147.
9. www.baseball.page.com, accessed by author October 2008.

Chapter 3

1. Jack Griffin, "Love Children, Bums, Execs, Blithe Spirits Welcome Cubs," *Chicago Sun-Times*, April 15, 1970, 104.
2. Lonnie Wheeler, *Bleachers: A Summer in Wrigley Field* (Chicago: Contemporary Books, 1988), book cover.
3. Saul Wisnia, *Chicago Cubs—Yesterday and Today* (Lincolnwood, IL: Publications International, 2008), 109.
4. Mike Murphy, e-mail statement to author, November 2008.
5. *Ibid.*
6. *Ibid.*
7. *Ibid.*
8. *Ibid.*
9. Rick Talley, *The Cubs of '69: The Recollections of a Team That Should Have Been* (Chicago: Contemporary Books), 11.
10. Murphy e-mail statement.

11. Jim Weir, telephone interview with author, March 2009.
12. Feldmann, *Miracle Collapse*, 144.
13. *Ibid.*
14. *Ibid.*, 73.
15. Bill Gleason, "33,333 Give Lesson to Sox Management," *Chicago Sun-Times*, August 21, 2009, 128.
16. *Ibid.*
17. *Ibid.*
18. Jim Langford, *The Game Is Never Over: An Appreciative History of the Chicago Cubs, 1948–1980* (South Bend, IN: Icarus Press, 1980), 149.
19. Tom Fitzpatrick, "Fans in Ugly Confrontation with Ushers," *Chicago Sun Times*, April 15, 1970, 106.
20. Greg Redlarczyk, interview with author, March 2009.
21. Banks, telephone interview.
22. *Ibid.*
23. Bill Gleason, "Getting Out of Town Could Be Cubs Tonic," *Chicago Sun-Times*, September 18, 1970, 110.
24. Wisnia, *Chicago Cubs*, 109.

Chapter 4

1. Helpingstine, *Through Hope and Despair*, 62.
2. Helpingstine, *Through Hope and Despair*, 47.
3. *Ibid.*, 74.
4. En.wikipedia.org/wiki/Curse_of_Muldoon, "Curse of Muldoon."

Chapter 5

1. Chet Coppock, telephone interview by author, January 2009.
2. Banks, telephone interview.
3. Helpingstine, *Through Hope and Despair*, 10.
4. Katherine Jacobs, telephone interview by author, January 2009.
5. Mark Liptak, telephone interview by author, November 2008.
6. Coppock, telephone interview.
7. *Ibid.*
8. Janice Petterchak, *Jack Brickhouse: A Voice for All Seasons* (Chicago: Contemporary Books, 1994), 103–104.
9. Liptak, telephone interview.
10. *Ibid.*
11. Coppock, telephone interview.
12. Liptak, telephone interview.
13. Coppock, telephone interview.
14. *Ibid.*
15. Ken Boyer, WGN-TV interview with Jack Brickhouse, July 29, 1967.
16. Elizabeth Harvey, telephone interview by author, November 2008.
17. Hal Vickery, telephone interview by author, November 2008.
18. Greg Redlarczyk, interview by author, March 2009.
19. Liptak, telephone interview.

20. Lorn Brown, telephone interview by author, December 2008.
21. James Walker and Robert Bellamy, Jr., *Center Field Shot: A History of Baseball On Television* (Lincoln, NE: Bison Books, 2008), 52.
22. Tom Shaer, telephone interview with author, February 2009.
23. Teddy Greenstein, "Hawks Popularity Spikes, but a Long Way to Go," *Chicago Tribune*, February 3, 2009, sect. 2, pp. 1, 3.

Chapter 6

1. Internet quote confirmed by Brooks Boyer in e-mail to author.
2. www.chicagoist.com.
3. Chicago White Sox television commercial, "Sox Pride," June 2004.
4. Jerry Reinsdorf, February 2003.
5. "Proud Sox Take Aim at Cross-town Rivals," *Chicago Tribune*, McClatchy-Tribune Information Services, HighBeam Research, September 7, 2009, www.highbeam.com.
6. Dan Helpingstine, *Chicago White Sox: 1959 and Beyond* (Charleston, SC: Arcadia, 2004), 105–106.
7. Teddy Greenstein, telephone interview by author, June 2009.
8. Chicago.whitesox.mlb.com. Chicago White Sox: Front Office.
9. Greenstein telephone interview.
10. WSCR-AM morning show with Mike Mulligan and Brian Hanley, September 30, 2008.
11. Joe Maddon post-game press conference, October 5, 2008.
12. Mitch Rosen, telephone interview by author, March 2009.
13. *Ibid.*
14. *Ibid.*
15. *Ibid.*
16. *Ibid.*
17. Tom Shaer, telephone interview by author, February 2009.
18. *Ibid.*

Chapter 7

1. Mike Veeck, telephone interview by author, January 2009.
2. *Ibid.*
3. *Ibid.*
4. Fan discussion with author, April 1976.
5. Richard Dozer, "Kingman Blasts Cubs," *Chicago Tribune*, April 6, 1976, sect. 4, p.1.
6. *Ibid.*
7. Bob Elson 1969 radio broadcasts.
8. Veeck, telephone interview.
9. Helpingstine, *Through Hope and Despair*, 39.
10. Dan Helpingstine, *South Side Hitmen: The Story of the South Side Hitmen* (Charleston, SC: Arcadia, 2005), 25.
11. Helpingstine, *Chicago White Sox*, 75.
12. Veeck, telephone interview.

Chapter 8

1. Veeck, telephone interview.
2. Bill Gleason, "Who Is to Blame for Sox Stupidity?" *Chicago Sun-Times*, July 10, 1979, p. 86.
3. Shaer, telephone interview.
4. *Ibid.*
5. Joel Bierg, "Veeck Almost Sold to Denver," *Chicago Sun-Times*, HighBeam Research, June 5, 1988, www.highbeam.com.
6. Mike Leiderman, telephone interview with author, February 2009.
7. Jacobs, telephone interview.
8. Mike Veeck and Pete Williams, *Fun Is Good: How to Create Joy & Passion in Your Workplace and Career* (Emmaus, PA: Rodale, 2005), xxi.

Chapter 9

1. Eddie Einhorn with Ron Rapoport, *How March Became Madness: How the NCAA Tournament Became the Greatest Sporting Event in America* (Chicago: Triumph Books, 2006), 8.
2. Leiderman, telephone interview.
3. Bob Logan, *Miracle on 35th Street: Winnin' Ugly with the 1983 White Sox* (South Bend, IN: Icarus Press, 1983), 142.
4. Helpingstine, *Through Hope and Despair*, 75.
5. Logan, *Miracle*, 142.
6. Einhorn, *How March Became*, p. x.
7. William Taafe, "Tooting His Own Einhorn," *Sports Illustrated Vault*, online article.
8. Leiderman, telephone interview.
9. Taffe, "Tooting His Own Einhorn," online article.
10. Liptak, telephone interview.
11. *Ibid.*
12. Einhorn, *How March Became*, p. 58.
13. Taffe, "Tooting His Own Einhorn," online article.
14. *Ibid.*

Chapter 10

1. C.U.B.S. Newsletter, Spring 1979, p. 1.
2. Dave Nightengale, "Cub Advisors Get Their Chance," *Chicago Tribune*, January 7, 1979, p. E2.
3. *C.U.B.S. Newsletter*, December 1978, p. 1.
4. Nightingale, "Cub Advisors," E2.
5. *C.U.B.S. Newsletter*, Spring 1979, p. 2.
6. *Ibid.*
7. *C.U.B.S. Newsletter*, 1980.
8. *Ibid.*
9. Paul Sullivan, "Cubs Lead the League in Feisty Fan Groups," *Chicago Tribune*, August 10, 1982, p. B2.
10. *Ibid.*

Chapter 11

1. Helpingstine, *Through Hope and Despair*, 87.
2. Helpingstine, *South Side Hitmen*, 41.
3. Helpingstine, *Through Hope and Despair*, 89.
4. *Ibid.*
5. Loren Brown, telephone interview by author, December 2008.
6. Richard Roeper, "They Were the South Side Hitmen," *Chicago Sun-Times*, July 4, 2006, p. 11.
7. Helpingstine, *South Side Hitmen*, 41.
8. Roeper, "The South Side Hitmen," 11.
9. Helpingstine, *Through Hope and Despair*, 92.
10. Roeper, "The South Side Hitmen," 11.
11. *Ibid.*
12. E-mail interview with Doug Feldmann, July 2009.
13. Claerbaut, p. 123
14. E-mail interview with Doug Feldmann
15. Claerbaut, *Durocher's Cubs*, 95.
16. *Ibid.*, 127.
17. Roeper, "The South Side Hitmen," 11.
18. *Ibid.*
19. Rick Talley, "Two Miracles Incite Sox Fans," *Chicago Tribune*, July 5, 1978, sect. 5, p. 1.
20. *Ibid.*, 2.
21. E-mail interview with Doug Feldmann.
22. *Ibid.*

Chapter 12

1. Andrew Shaffer, telephone interview by author, February 2008.
2. Ron Rapoport, telephone interview by author, March 2009.
3. Dave Abrams, telephone interview by author, May 2009.
4. www.joeposnanski.com.
5. *Ibid.*
6. Rapoport, telephone interview.
7. Abrams, telephone interview.
8. *Ibid.*
9. *Ibid.*
10. *Ibid.*
11. *Ibid.*
12. *Ibid.*
13. *Ibid.*

Chapter 13

1. www.cubsbythenumbers.com.
2. *Ibid.*
3. Bob Verdi, "Green Says, 'Wrigley Field Lights an Eventuality,'" *Chicago Tribune*, March 11, 1982, sect. 5, p. 1.
4. Bob Verdi, "Bottom Drops Out on Cubs Image," May 1, 1983, *Chicago Tribune*, sect. 2, p. 1.
5. James Mullen, "P.K. Wrigley Has Last Laugh at Critics" *Chicago Sun-Times*, July 5, 1967, p. 82.
6. *Ibid.*
7. *Ibid.*
8. Jerome Holtzman, "Bad Blood Bubbles as

Reds Beat Cubs," *Chicago Tribune*, April 7, 1982, sect. 4, p. 1.

9. Elia.

10. John Mutka, *Gary Post-Tribune*.

11. Robert Markus, "Elia Swings for the Fences," *Chicago Tribune*, April 30, 1983, sect. 2, p. 1.

12. YouTube video.

13. Markus, "Elia Swings," p. 1.

14. Verdi, "Bottom Drops," p. 1.

15. *Ibid.*

16. www.cubsbythenumbers.com.

17. Bob Logan, "Dallas Green Vows to Make Cubs Rebuilding Plan Work," *Chicago Tribune*, October 16, 1981, sect. 6, p. 5.

18. Verdi, "Green Says," p. 1.

19. *Ibid.*

20. *Ibid.*

21. John Husar, "Cavemen Prevail in Wrigley Field," *Chicago Tribune*, October 5, 1982, sect. 4, p. 3.

22. Robert Markus and Peter Fuller, "Cubs Ax Chops Up Office Staff," *Chicago Tribune*, October 5, 1982, sect. 4, p. 1.

23. Husar, "Cavemen," p. 3.

24. Phone message per Philadelphia public relations staff member.

Chapter 14

1. Fred Mitchell, "Green Explodes; Cubs Bombed," *Chicago Tribune*, March 26, 1984, sect. 4, p. 18.

2. *Ibid.*

3. *Ibid.*

4. Steve Daley, "Ink Gets Spilled All Over Cubs," *Chicago Tribune*, March 4, 1984, sect. 4, p. 2.

5. Bill James, "Cubs Appear Ripe for Miracle Season," *Chicago Tribune*, April 1, 1984, sect. 4, p. 4.

6. Fred Mitchell, "Cubs Punch Out the Giants," *Chicago Tribune*, April 4, 1984, sect. 4, p. 1.

7. Fred Mitchell, "Cubs Blow Them Away," *Chicago Tribune*, October 3, 1984, sect. 4, p. 4.

8. *Ibid.*

9. *Ibid.*

10. Fred Mitchell, "Cubs Speed Kills Padres," *Chicago Tribune*, October 4, 1984, sect. 4, p. 1.

11. Mitchell, "Cubs Speed," p. 1.

12. Les Grobstein, telephone interview by author, December 2008.

13. John Kuenster, "A Crushing Defeat: The 1984 Game Between the Chicago Cubs and San Diego Padres," *Baseball Digest*, May 2001, online.

14. Grobstein, telephone interview.

15. *Ibid.*

16. Kuenster, "A Crushing Defeat."

17. *Ibid.*

18. *Ibid.*

19. Fred Mitchell, "Cubs Fan the Cards," *Chicago Tribune*, October 1, 2004, sect. 4, p. 3.

20. Kasey Ignarski, telephone interview by author.

21. *Ibid.*

Chapter 15

1. Leiderman, telephone interview.

2. Shaer, telephone interview.

3. *Ibid.*

4. "Letters to the Editor," *Chicago Tribune*, February 11, 1981.

5. "Letters to the Editor," *Chicago Tribune*, November 25, 1981, sect. 1, p. 12.

6. Grobstein interview.

7. *Ibid.*

8. Phil Hersh, "Sox Owner a Liar: Caray," *Chicago Sun-Times*, February 17, 1981, p. 84.

9. *Ibid.*

10. *Ibid.*

11. *Ibid.*

12. Jerome Holtzman, "Happy Hour: White Sox Sign Caray," *Chicago Sun-Times*, March 4, 1982, p. 112.

13. *Ibid.*

14. Harry Caray and Bob Verdi, *Holy Cow* (New York: Villard, 1989), 228.

15. *Ibid.*, 228–229.

16. Bob Verdi, "Piersall Ump Fun No Comedy," *Chicago Tribune*, June 1, 1981, sect. 4, p. 1.

17. *Ibid.*, 4.

18. Ron Rapoport, "Piersall on the Outs with Umps," *Chicago Sun-Times*, June 1, 1981, p. 80.

19. Caray and Verdi, *Holy Cow*, 224.

20. Richard Dozer, "Sox Suspend Piersall After Insult to Players' Wives," *Chicago Tribune*, September 10, 1981, sect. 4, p. 1.

21. *Ibid.*

22. Caray and Verdi, *Holy Cow*, 229.

23. Ron Alridge, "Sox Make Error in Piersall Case," *Chicago Tribune*, September 11, 1981, sect. 6, p. 5.

24. Phil Hersh, *Chicago Sun-Times*, "Sox Make Waves, Er, Air Waves," *Chicago Sun-Times*, November 25, 1981, pp. 84, 92.

25. *Ibid.*

26. *Ibid.*

27. David Israel, "Einhorn's Wheeling Dealing Adds to Sox Credibility," *Chicago Tribune*, March 15, 1981, sect. 4, p. 3.

28. Kevin Lamb, "Fisk Is Sox Big Catch," March 10, 1981, p. 88.

29. Jerome Holtzman, "Hill's Sight Is Hanging with Sox," *Chicago Sun-Times*, March 26, 1981, p. 126.

30. Jerome Holtzman, "Sox Get Luzinski — For Cash," *Chicago Sun-Times*, March 31, 1981, p. 86.

31. *Ibid.*

32. David Condon, *Chicago Tribune*, 81 opener.

Chapter 16

1. Bob Logan, *Miracle on 35th Street: Winnin' Ugly with the 1983 White Sox* (South Bend, IN: Icarus Press, 1983), 140.

2. *Ibid.*, 141.

3. Tom Paciorek, telephone interview by author, July 2009.

4. *Chicago Sun-Times*, "Letters to the Editor," September 18, 1983, p. 137.

5. *Chicago Sun-Times*, "Letters to the Editor," September 18, 1983, p. 137.

6. *Ibid.*

7. Bob Verdi, *Chicago Tribune*, "Owning Up to the Sox," *Chicago Tribune*, July 11, 1982, sect. 4, p. 1.

8. *Ibid.*

9. Jimmy Piersall with Richard Whittingham, *The Truth Hurts* (Chicago: Contemporary Books, 1984), 173–175.

10. Rob Rains, *Tony La Russa: Man on a Mission* (Chicago: Triumph, 2009), 65.

11. Skip Myslenski, "Old Ghosts Haunt Piersall," *Chicago Tribune*, August 8, 1982, sect. 4, p. 4.

12. Rains, *Tony La Russa*, 82.

13. Logan, *Miracle on 35th Street*, 116.

14. *Ibid.*, 62.

15. *Chicago Tribune*, "Text of Management's Dismissal Telegram to Piersall," April 7, 1983, sect. 4, p. 3.

16. Steve Daley, "Truth No Defense in Jimmy's Case," *Chicago Tribune*, April 6, 1983, sect 4, p. 1.

17. Logan, *Miracle on 35th Street*, 116.

18. Paciorek, telephone interview.

19. *Ibid.*

20. Logan, *Miracle on 35th Street*, 1.

21. Helpingstine, *Through Hope and Despair*, 126.

22. Paciorek telephone interview.

23. Logan, *Miracle on 35th Street*, 17.

Chapter 17

1. Mike Kiley, "Orie on Astros' Lone Hit: Call It an Error," *Chicago Sun-Times*, May 7, 1998, p. 111.

2. *Ibid.*

3. *Ibid.*

4. Melissa Isaccson and Bonnie DeSimmone, "Wood: I Choked, Let the City Down," *Chicago Tribune*, October 16, 1983, sect. 7, p. 3.

5. Kerry Wood advertisement, network.na tionalpost.com.np/blog/postedsports/archive/200 9/o1/01/18/kerry-wood-goes...

Chapter 18

1. *Chicago Tribune,* October 13, 2003, 28.

2. www.jaypinkerton.com, "Did Steve Bartman Cost the Cubs the Series?" accessed by author, June 2009.

3. Sports.espn.go.com.mlb/recap?gameId= 231014116, October 14, 2003.

4. *Ibid.*

5. YouTube video.

6. Jon Yates and Brent McNeil, "Loss Leaves Faith Shaken Many," *Chicago Tribune*, October 15, 2003, sect. 1, p. 28.

7. *Ibid.*

8. *Ibid.*

9. *Ibid.*

10. Jeff Carroll, "Wood: I Choked," *The Times*, October 13, 2003, p. C-3.

11. En.wikipedia.org/wiki/Steve_Stone.

12. *Ibid.*

13. Jay Mariotti, *Chicago Sun-Times*, October 15, 2003.

14. Sports.espn.go.com/mlb/news/sorty?=342 3732, accessed by author, July 2009.

15. *Ibid.*

16. *Ibid.*

17. Bonnie DeSimone and Teddy Greenstein, *Chicago Tribune*, "Cubs Too Easy on Fan," October 15, 2003, sect. 10, p. 5.

18. *Ibid.*

Chapter 19

1. Joanna Cagan and Neil deMause, *Field of Schemes: How the Great Stadium Swindle Turns Public Money into Private Profit* (Monroe, ME: Common Courage Press, 1998), 131.

2. *Ibid.*, 134.

3. *Ibid.*, 135.

4. *Ibid.*, 136.

5. Dan Dorfman, interview by author, February 2009.

6. Gerry Bilek, telephone interview by author, December 2008.

7. Helpingstine, *Through Hope and Despair*, 196.

8. Phil Rosenthal, "Sox' Poll Can't Solve Riddle of Missing Fans," *Chicago Sun-Times*, September 9, 1996, p. 86.

9. *Chicago Sun-Times*, "Dear Sun Times," August 10, 1997, p. 10A.

10. *Ibid.*

11. *Ibid.*

12. *Ibid.*

13. Richard Roeper, *Sox and the City: A Fan's Love Affair with the White Sox from the Heartbreak of '67 to the Wizards of Oz* (Chicago: Chicago Review Press, 2005), 168.

14. Jay Mariotti, "Are Reinsdorf's Sox on a Slow Road to Ruin?" *Chicago Sun-Times*, August 7, 1997, p. 97.

15. Dorfman, interview.

16. Helpingstine, *Through Hope and Despair*, 216.

17. *Ibid.*

18. www.baseball-alamanac.com/index.

19. *Ibid.*

20. Skip Bayless, "Fans Who Stayed Away Were Sox's Best Friends," *Chicago Tribune*, September 27, 2000, sect. 4, p. 1.

21. *Ibid.*

22. *Ibid.*

23. Helpingstine, *Through Hope and Despair*, 219.

24. Norman Macht, Richard Crepeau and Lee Lowenfish, "Landis and Baseball Before Jackie

Robinson: Does Baseball Deserve This Black Eye?" *The Baseball Research Journal*, Summer 2009.

25. Tom Shaer, e-mail statement to author, August 2009.

Chapter 20

1. George Bova, editor, *"Dedicated to... What Winning the World Series Means to Chicago White Sox Fans"* (Bloomington, IN: AuthorHouse, 2006), 21.

2. *Ibid.*, 133.

3. *Ibid.*, 115.

4. *Ibid.*, 150.

5. *Ibid.*, 106.

6. *"Sox Pride: The Story of the 2005 World Champion Chicago White Sox,"* DVD, Comcast SportsNet.

7. *Chicago Tribune*, "Choke Hold," September 28, 2005, sect. 4, p. 1.

8. Bob Vanderberg, "Playoff hopes went poof once before in K.C.," *Chicago Tribune*, September 16, 2005, sect. 4, p. 2.

9. Rick Morrissey, "Sox's Great Season Turns Quite Grating," *Chicago Tribune*, September 18, 2005, sect. 3, p. 6.

10. Rick Morrissey, *Chicago Tribune*, September 21, 2005.

11. *Ibid.*

12. Doug Padilla, "Put It on the Board, Yes! Sox Clinch AL Central Division," *Naperville Sun*, HighBeam Research, www.highbeam.com.

13. Rick Morrissey, "Cancer? Pierzynski May Cure What Ails Sox," *Chicago Tribune*, January 9, 2009, sect. 3, p. 10.

Chapter 21

1. Greg Redlarczyk interview.

2. Larry Hunt, telephone interview by author, March 2009.

3. Harvey, telephone interview.

4. Ignarski, telephone interview.

5. C.U.B.S. Newsletter, Spring 1980.

6. Bruce Rubenstein, *Chicago in the World Series 1903–2005: The Cubs and White Sox in Championship Play* (Jefferson, NC: McFarland, 2006).

7. Richard Roeper, "We're All Cub Fans: Don't You Believe It," *Chicago Sun-Times*, September 2, 1989, 11.

8. *Ibid.*

9. *Ibid.*

10. Dennis Byrne, "Sox Moment of Truth," *Chicago Sun-Times*, September 28, 1989, p. 43.

11. *Ibid.*

12. Letters to the Editor, *Chicago Sun-Times*, "No True Sox Fan Ever Sells out Under Pressure," October 6, 1979, p. 37.

13. Letters to the Editor, *Chicago Sun-Times*, "We're Not Cubs Fans," October 5, 1989, p. 38.

14. Dave Van Dyke, *Chicago Sun-Times*, June 19, 1997, p. 98.

15. Carol Slezak, *Chicago Sun-Times*, June 18, 1997, p. 132.

16. *Ibid.*

17. *Ibid.*

18. Les Grobstein, telephone interview by author.

19. Andrew Shaffer, telephone interview by author, March 2009.

20. *Ibid.*

21. Kevin Gillogly, telephone interview by author, February 2009.

22. Gaurav Garg, telephone interview by author, March 2009.

23. *Ibid.*

24. Ignarski, telephone interview.

25. Raymond Ennes, *Letters to My Children* (New York: Vantage, 1990), 27.

26. Jim Pagani, interview with author, June, 2009.

27. *Ibid.*

28. Harvey, telephone interview.

29. Hal Vickery, telephone interview with author, December 2008.

30. Harvey, telephone interview.

31. Matt Cassiday, telephone interview with author, December 2008.

32. *Ibid.*

33. Lindberg, *The White Sox Encyclopedia*, 478.

34. *Ibid.*

35. Pagani interview.

Bibliography

Books

Allen, Dick, and Tim Whittaker. *The Life and Times of Dick Allen.* New York: Ticknor and Fields, 1989.

Borsvold, David. *Cleveland Indians: The Cleveland Press Years 1920–1982.* Charleston, SC: Arcadia, 2003.

Bova, George, ed. *Dedicated to... What Winning the World Series Means to Chicago White Sox Fans.* Bloomington, IN: AuthorHouse, 2006.

Cagan, Joanna, and Neil deMause. *Field of Schemes: How the Great Stadium Swindle Turns Public Money into Private Profit.* Monroe, ME: Common Courage Press, 2008.

Caray, Harry, and Bob Verdi. *Holy Cow!* New York: Villard, 1989.

Claerbaut, Peter. *Durocher's Cubs: The Greatest Team That Didn't Win.* Dallas, TX: Taylor, 2000.

Crepeau, Richard. "Landis, Baseball, and Racism: A Brief Comment." *The Baseball Research Journal* 38, No. 1 (Summer 2009): 31–32.

Einhorn, Eddie, and Ron Rapoport. *How March Became Madness.* Chicago: Triumph Books, 2006.

Ennes, Raymond, P. *Letters to My Children.* New York, Vantage Press, 1990.

Faulk, David, and Dan Riley, eds. *The Cubs Reader.* New York: Houghton Mifflin, 1991.

Feldmann, Doug. *Miracle Collapse: The 1969 Chicago Cubs.* Lincoln: University of Nebraska Press, 2006.

Golenbock, Peter. *Wrigleyville: A Magical History Tour of the Chicago Cubs.* New York: St. Martin's, 1996.

Helpingstine, Dan. *Chicago White Sox: 1959 and Beyond.* Charleston, SC: Arcadia, 2004.

_____. *Through Hope and Despair: A Fan's Memories of the Chicago White Sox, 1967–1997.* Highland, IN, 2001.

_____. *South Side Hitmen: The Story of the 1977 Chicago White Sox.* Charleston, SC: Arcadia, 2005.

Langford, Jim. *The Game Is Never Over: An Appreciative History of the Chicago Cubs, 1948–1980.* South Bend, IN: Icarus Press, 1980.

Lindberg, Richard. *The White Sox Encyclopedia.* Philadelphia: Temple University Press, 1997.

Logan, Bob. *Miracle on 35th Street: Winnin' Ugly with the 1983 White Sox.* South Bend, IN: Icarus Press, 1983.

Lowenfish, Lee. "The Gentleman's Agreement and the Ferocious Gentleman Who Broke It." *The Baseball Research Journal,* 38 No. 1 (Summer 2009): 33–34.

Macht, Norman, L. "Does Baseball Deserve This Black Eye?" *The Baseball Research Journal,* 38 No. 1 (Summer 2009): 26–30.

Petterchak, Janice. *Jack Brickhouse: A Voice for All Seasons*. Chicago: Contemporary, 1994.

Piersall, Jimmy, with Richard Whittingham. *The Truth Hurts*. Chicago: Contemporary, 1984.

Rains, Rob. *Tony La Russa: A Man on a Mission*. Chicago: Triumph Books, 2009.

Roeper, Richard. *Sox and the City: A Fan's Love Affair with the White Sox from the Heartbreak of '67 to the Wizards of Oz*. Chicago: Chicago Review Press, 2006.

Rubenstein, Bruce. *Chicago in the World Series 1903–2005: The Cubs and White Sox in Championship Play*. Jefferson, NC: McFarland, 2006.

Taafe, William. "Tooting His Own Einhorn." *Sports Illustrated Vault*, www.sportsillustrated.cnn.com/vault, September 2001.

Talley, Rick. *The Cubs of '69: Recollections of the Team That Should Have Been*. Chicago: Contemporary Books, 1989.

Veeck, Mike, and Pete Williams. *Fun Is Good: How to Create Joy & Passion in Your Workplace and Career*. Emmaus, PA: Rodale Press, 2005.

Walker, James, and Louis Bellamy Jr. *Center Field Shot: A History of Baseball on Television*. Lincoln: University of Nebraska Press, 2008.

Wheeler, Lonnie. *Bleachers: A Summer in Wrigley Field*. Chicago: Contemporary Books, 1988.

Wisnia, Saul. *Chicago Cubs: Yesterday and Today*. Lincolnwood, IL: Publications International, 2008.

Newsletters

Published by C.U.B.S. (Chicagoans United for a Baseball Series): December 1978, January 1979, February 1979, January 1980

Websites

baseballalmanac.com
chicagobythenumbers.com
chicagoist.com
espngo.com
jaypinkerton.com
network.nationalpost.com
northsidebaseball.com
retrosheet.org
sportsillustrated.cnn.com
whitesox.com
whitesoxinteractive.com
wikipedia.org

Index